Measures of Socioeconomic Status

Current Issues

AAAS Selected Symposia Series

 Published by Westview Press, Inc.
5500 Central Avenue, Boulder, Colorado

for the

 American Association for the Advancement of Science
1776 Massachusetts Avenue, N.W., Washington, D.C.

Measures of Socioeconomic Status

Current Issues

Edited by Mary G. Powers

AAAS Selected Symposium **81**

AAAS Selected Symposia Series

This book is based on a symposium which was held at the 1981 AAAS National
Annual Meeting in Toronto, Ontario, January 3-8. The symposium was spon-
sored by the Population Association of America and by AAAS Section U
(Statistics).

Published in 1982 in the United States of America by
      Westview Press, Inc.
      5500 Central Avenue
      Boulder, Colorado 80301
      Frederick A. Praeger, President and Publisher

Library of Congress Catalog Card Number 82-50647
ISBN 0-86531-395-4

Printed and bound in the United States of America

About the Book

Any study of social stratification, social mobility, occupation change, or public welfare uses some index to measure socioeconomic status or occupational prestige. This book presents for the first time a collection of papers by the major contributors to the development of such indexes. A state-of-the-art review, the book provides a basis for comparing the various approaches to understanding social stratification and social mobility and to evaluating some of the current controversies surrounding these approaches. The authors discuss and assess measures of socioeconomic status developed in the United States and Canada over the last three decades, covering occupational status scores and multivariate indexes of socioeconomic status derived from census data as well as measures of occupational prestige derived from survey responses. They pay particular attention to the implications of the increased labor-force participation of women for current measures of occupational status and prestige.

About the Series

The *AAAS Selected Symposia Series* was begun in 1977 to provide a means for more permanently recording and more widely disseminating some of the valuable material which is discussed at the AAAS Annual National Meetings. The volumes in this *Series* are based on symposia held at the Meetings which address topics of current and continuing significance, both within and among the sciences, and in the areas in which science and technology impact on public policy. The *Series* format is designed to provide for rapid dissemination of information, so the papers are not typeset but are reproduced directly from the camera-copy submitted by the authors. The papers are organized and edited by the symposium arrangers who then become the editors of the various volumes. Most papers published in this *Series* are original contributions which have not been previously published, although in some cases additional papers from other sources have been added by an editor to provide a more comprehensive view of a particular topic. Symposia may be reports of new research or reviews of established work, particularly work of an interdisciplinary nature, since the AAAS Annual Meetings typically embrace the full range of the sciences and their societal implications.

WILLIAM D. CAREY
Executive Officer
American Association for
the Advancement of Science

Contents

About the Editor and Authors. viii

1 Measures of Socioeconomic Status:
   An Introduction--*Mary G. Powers*. 1

2 Measurement of Socioeconomic Status from
   United States Census Data--*Charles B. Nam,
   E. Walter Terrie* 29

3 Socioeconomic Measures from Canadian
   Census Data-- *Bernard R. Blishen,
   William K. Carroll* 43

4 Occupational Status Scores: Changes
   Introduced by the Inclusion of Women--
   Mary G. Powers, Joan J. Holmberg 55

5 A Revised Socioeconomic Index of
   Occupational Status: Application in
   Analysis of Sex Differences in Attainment--
   David Lee Featherman, Gillian Stevens 83

6 Women, Men, and Socioeconomic Indices:
   An Assessment--*Monica Boyd, Hugh A. McRoberts*. . 129

7 Status Attainment of Young White Men and
   Women: Two Socioeconomic Measures--
   *Rosemary Santana Cooney, Alice Sokolove Clague,
   Joseph J. Salvo* 161

Index 201

About the Editor and Authors

Mary G. Powers, *a professor in the departments of sociology and anthropology at Fordham University, has specialized in the study of social stratification, social demography, and urban ecology.* She has done extensive *research on socioeconomic and occupational status measurement, including stability and change of scores, variations in status level among ethnic groups, the relationship of socioeconomic status to fertility, and changes in occupational status scores which result when women are included in the data base.* She is currently chair of the Census *Advisory Committee on Population Statistics, and she is a former member of the board of directors of the Population Association of America.*

Bernard R. Blishen *is a professor of sociology at York University in Toronto.* His research has been concerned with *social class and opportunity in Canada, Canadian immigrants and occupational status, and socioeconomic indices based on the 1951-71 Canadian census.*

Monica Boyd, *a demographer, is associate professor of sociology and anthropology at Carleton University in Ottawa. She has done research on sex differences in occupational attainment, income, and labor markets, and on the socioeconomic status of separated, divorced, and immigrant women, and she is the author of a forthcoming book,* Ascription and Achievement: Studies in Mobility and Status Attainment *(with J. Goyder et al.). A former member of the Canadian Advisory Council on the Status of Women, she is presently on the board of directors of the Population Association of America and a councilor of the Canadian Population Society.*

William K. Carroll *is assistant professor of sociology at the University of Victoria.* His primary research interests

*are the relationships between ethnicity, gender, and socio-
economic status in Canada.*

Alice Sokolove Clague *is a statistician in the United
Nations Statistical Office. Her specialty is demography,
and her current research deals with the earnings attainment
process and the multiple dimensions of sexual inequality in
the labor force.*

Rosemary Santana Cooney *is associate professor of
sociology and research associate at the Hispanic Research
Center at Fordham University. Her specialty is the study of
the labor force and minority groups, and she has published
on earnings attainment, female participation in the labor
force and the multiple dimensions of sexual inequality.*

David Lee Featherman, *professor of sociology at the
University of Wisconsin at Madison, is also affiliated with
the Center for Demography and Ecology, the Institute for
Research on Poverty, and the Faye McBeath Institute for
Gerontology and Adult Development. He has published widely
in his field, and his books include* Socioeconomic Background
and Achievement *(with O. B. Duncan and B. Duncan; Seminar,
1971) and* The Process of Stratification *and* Opportunity and
Change *(both with R. M. Hauser; Academic, 1977 and 1978, respectively).*

Joan J. Holmberg *is chairperson and assistant professor
of the Department of Sociology and Anthropology at Wagner
College in New York City. A specialist in urban sociology
and demography, she has done research on occupational status
scores and women.*

Hugh A. McRoberts *is associate professor of sociology at
Carleton University in Ottawa. He has published on inequality
and stratification in Canadian society and on a revised socioeconomic index for occupations in Canada.*

Charles B. Nam *is professor and former director of the
Center for the Study of Population, Institute for Social
Research, Florida State University at Tallahassee. He has
studied socioeconomic structure and change, the demography
of education, mortality among the elderly, and youth and
population change. His books include* Nationality Groups
and Social Stratification *(Arno, 1981), and* Population:
The Dynamics of Demographic Change *(with S. O. Gustavus) and*
Population and Society *(Houghton-Mifflin, 1976 and 1968,
respectively). He is a past president of the Population
Association of America and of the Southern Sociological
Society.*

Joseph J. Salvo *is a demographer at the U.S. Bureau of the Census. He has done research on the earnings attainment process and on the multiple dimensions of sexual inequality in the labor force.*

Gillian Stevens *is assistant professor of sociology at the University of Illinois at Urbana-Champaign. A specialist in demography, she has been concerned with women's fertility, social mobility, and socioeconomic status.*

E. Walter Terrie *is a computer research specialist at the Institute for Social Research, Florida State University at Tallahassee. His research has focused on the dimensions of occupational status change in the United States from 1960 to 1970.*

1. Measures of Socioeconomic Status: An Introduction

This volume reviews the major approaches to the conceptualization and measurement of socioeconomic status which have developed in North America over the past thirty-five years, and evaluates these measures in the light of current theoretical and methodological issues.

The parallel development of socioeconomic measures in Canada and the United States reflects the dominant influence of Max Weber in social stratification theory and research. Weber's articulation of the distinct but interrelated class, status and power dimensions of stratification forms the theoretical basis for most measures of socioeconomic status and prestige which have been developed in North America. Neither the precise nature of the interrelationship among the three dimensions nor the variables underlying each dimension have been specified. There is general consensus, however, that class, or the social and economic life chances individuals experience, is closely related to their status, or the regard with which they are held by others. The logic underlying this consensus is that class or economic position generates income which results in similar life styles among individuals in the same class. Those life styles contribute to the evaluations made of individuals and to the prestige assigned to them by others. Recently, it has been argued also" . . . that prestige ultimately is rooted in power relations . . . " (Treiman, 1977:1).

This general theoretical framework strongly influenced the development of measures of socioeconomic status. Research seeking to locate

1

individual positions in a stratification system
required a summary measure or index which would
accurately and simply assign individuals to such
positions. Socioeconomic indices were designed to
provide such summary information about the social
standing of all individuals in a society in the
absence of detailed information about the entire
complex of variables involved in overall socioeconomic standing. Such summary measures describe
an individual's location along a single hierarchy
and omit many of the complexities of group inequalities.

Two recent reviews and evaluations agree that
empirical research as well as existing theory demonstrate that occupation is the most adequate
single indicator of position in a complex stratification system (Haug, 1977; Treiman, 1977).
Because of the overriding importance of occupation
as an indicator of socioeconomic status, considerable effort has been devoted to refining the
conceptualization and measurement of occupation and
to developing indices of occupational status. The
focus here is on the latter, the development of
measures of occupational status and prestige
(North and Hatt, 1947; Blishen, 1958, 1967;
Duncan, 1961; Nam and Powers, 1965, 1968; Siegel,
1971; and Treiman, 1977). These status and prestige scores rank large numbers of occupations
along a single hierarchy. All of them have been
widely used in social science research. Duncan's
Socioeconomic Index (1961; Featherman and Hauser,
1975) has been particularly influential in studies
of the status attainment process in the United
States.

Once occupation became accepted as an indicator of socioeconomic status, sociologists began
to inquire as to the meaning of occupational
status. Although there was general consensus that
occupation is the best indicator of socioeconomic
position, there has not been agreement as to the
characteristics of occupations to be used in
ranking them. As a result, and as noted above, a
considerable number of scales and indices of socioeconomic and occupational status have been developed. They tend to be highly intercorrelated,
but vary in concept and calculation procedures.
Historically, one can categorize two major
approaches. On the one hand occupational status

has been interpreted as being synonymous with
prestige, or position based on a subjective evaluation that individuals make of one another. On the
other hand, it has been defined in terms of more
objective criteria such as the educational level
required for the occupation and the income associated with it. One approach measures occupational
status in terms of the prestige accorded a sample
of occupations by a sample of individual raters.
The second assigns a status score based on some
form of objective measure such as ranking the
average educational and/or income levels of occupations. A review of the development of the major
North American socioeconomic and prestige indices
follows along with a discussion of the conceptual
and methodological issues treated in the papers
included in the book.

Measures of Occupational Prestige

Prior to 1950 most studies of occupational
status assumed 1) that the source of prestige of
an occupation lay in the opinions of people rather
than in the characteristics of the occupation,
and 2) that people could estimate and articulate
the prestige levels. (Counts, 1925; Anderson,
1927; Hartman, 1934; Nietz, 1935). Most of them
also included only a small number of occupations
and raters. The raters tended to be college
students, school teachers, and school children,
among whom there was basic agreement in the ranking
produced. The occupations at the extreme ends of
the scale were ranked with a very high degree of
consistency. There was somewhat less agreement
about those in the middle. In effect, most of
the early studies showed that people could produce
some sort of rank order of occupations when forced
to do so with a relatively small number of occupations.

Perhaps the first sophisticated scale of
occupational prestige is the one developed by the
National Opinion Research Center (NORC). In the
Spring of 1947 the National Opinion Research
Center sampled a cross section of the American
population to determine basic public attitudes
towards occupations. In the Fall of that year
Cecil North and Paul Hatt wrote a preliminary
analysis of the data (North & Hatt, 1947). Hence
the scale is sometimes referred to as the North-

Hatt scale. Because that seminal study provided a starting point for most other research for the next three decades, it is examined in some detail.

A list of 100 occupations was constructed which was presumed to be representative of the entire range of legitimate occupations in the United States. In an attempt to keep the number within practical limits, the list was reduced to 78 occupations eliminating "women's occupations" such as private secretary, dressmaker, trained nurse, etc. Before going into the field however, twelve occupations were added and the final list included 90 occupations.

A sample of 2930 people was asked to evaluate each of the 90 occupations according to their "own personal opinion of the general standing" of a person engaged in that occupation. A five point scale was provided with ratings of 1) excellent standing, 2) good standing, 3) average standing, 4) somewhat below average standing, 5) poor standing. An "x-rating" which meant "I don't know where to place that one" also was shown to the respondents. On the basis of the overall replies, the responses were scored 100, 80, 60, 40 and 20 respectively. The "don't know" responses were counted but were not assigned any particular value and were not entered into the basic computation of the score. The prestige rating for each of the 90 occupations was calculated by taking the mean score assigned to the occupation by the sample. The result was a scale ranging from 96 for Supreme Court Justice to 33 for shoe shiner. The occupations were then rearranged and ranked from 1 through 90 (Reiss, Duncan, Hatt and North, 1961).

The NORC study is a landmark study for a number of reasons. It included a sizeable number of occupations, but more important, it included a large enough sample of respondents so that some attention could be paid to the effect of age, educational level, etc. on ranking. Indeed, although there was a fairly high consistency of response, there were some significant differences. For example, professional occupations, particularly scientific jobs, were ranked higher by the college educated than by all others. Those who completed no more than eighth grade tended to rank skilled jobs such as carpenter, and operative work such as railroad conductor higher than others.

Another innovation in this study was the fact that respondents were asked <u>why</u> they rated some occupations as they did. They were asked to name the "one main thing" about the jobs they rated as "excellent" that gave them that standing. There was no predominant answer and, in fact, no majority response. About 60 percent of the responses were equally divided among answers such as "the job pays well," "it has social prestige," "it requires a lot of education or hard work," "it performs a service to humanity" and/or "it's essential". Responses related to the income and education associated with the job were most frequently mentioned. It has been suggested that the apparent lack of agreement on what constitutes an occupation's standing implies either that people have a single image of occupations to which they respond intuitively, or that various criteria for judgment are highly interrelated (Svalastoga, 1965).

The study contained some clear biases, however. About one-third of all the occupations listed were professional jobs, a high proportion compared to the number in the total labor force. Another point to be noted about this study is that the scientific jobs which were ranked so high were unfamiliar to many people. "Nuclear Physicists" were singled out to be defined by respondents in an attempt to infer how many people might have evaluated an occupation without being able to define it. Only three percent of the respondents were able to give a completely correct definition of nuclear physicists and 18 percent a partially correct one. (Svalastoga, 1965; 419)

Other shortcomings of the NORC scale were also noted (Hatt, 1950; Davies, 1952). One difficulty with occupational prestige measures discussed by Hatt as early as 1950 concerns the fact that when asked to rank occupations relative to one another, people are forced to place in a hierarchy occupations which would appear on the same group level if a point score rating system were used. Hatt developed the idea of parallel status ladders which he called situses. He identified at least eight separate situses: the political, professional, business, recreation and aesthetics, agricultural, manual work, military and service occupations. This concept of situs was an important addition to the literature and used in the 1963 re-test of the NORC occupational prestige scores to analyze changes in prestige for homogeneous groups of occupations. (Hodge, Siegel, and Rossi, 1964) Beyond that, however, it has not been widely used. The NORC scores were a major contribution to the study of occupational prestige, particularly after the 1963 replication demonstrated the stability of the ratings over time.

Twenty years after the original NORC study a prestige score for occupations was developed in Canada by Pineo and Porter (1967) based on the average evaluation given a sample of occupation titles by a national sample of the Canadian population. That score has been used in Canada both independently and in conjunction with the development of other objective measures (Blishen and Carroll, this volume).

In spite of conceptual and methodological difficulties of the prestige scales, they continue to be widely used. The most recent adaptation of the NORC prestige scores in the U.S. appeared in a doctoral dissertation by Siegel in 1971. He derived a new set of occupational prestige scores by combining the occupational prestige ratings collected in three separate studies, the NORC 1963 replication and two other studies conducted in 1964 and 1965 by Siegel and his colleagues. The occupational prestige ratings collected in the surveys were based on different samples, different lists of occupations and on somewhat different methodologies but all were combined into a single list. All the studies combined included over 600 occupational titles, only 412 of which were distinct, the others having been rated more than once. This overlap of identically worded titles permitted the transformations to occur. The overlapping titles were used to predict their prestige scores in the Hodge, Siegel & Rossi metric. Regression equations were used to provide what Siegel called "prestige scores in uniform metric" for all of the titles not rated in the Hodge, Siegel & Rossi study. Prestige scores were then assigned to each of the detailed occupational titles shown in the 1960 census of population.

Perhaps because of the recency of its development and the complicated nature of the
statistical procedures, the Siegel prestige scores
in uniform metric have not been as widely used as
the original NORC scores or the 1963 replication.
The set of scores provided by Siegel has an advantage over the earlier NORC work insofar as
it provides a score for each of the detailed
occupational categories listed in the census. Many
of the difficulties inherent in the earlier studies
remain, however. Indeed the errors may be com-
pounded because so many of the scores were derived
from mathematic estimates rather than from direct
ratings by respondents.

Measures of Socioeconomic Status

Dissatisfaction with the limitations of the
original NORC study of occupational prestige contributed to efforts to develop a socioeconomic index of occupations based on more objective criteria.
The results include some strictly objective indicators (Nam and Powers, 1965), some which combined
prestige and socioeconomic dimensions (Duncan,
1961), and some which did first one and then the
other (Blishen, 1958 and 1967).

In Canada Bernard Blishen developed the first
sophisticated strictly objective measure of occupational status when he ranked the 343 occupations
listed in the 1951 Canadian Census on the basis of
the mean income and education levels of incumbents
in each occupation (Blishen, 1958). In the United
States Otis Dudley Duncan devised a socioeconomic
index for all occupations which integrated prestige
scores with objective data on education and income
for a wide range of occupations (Duncan, 1961), and
Nam and his associates at the Census Bureau constructed both an occupational status score based
on strictly objective criteria of income and education and a multiple-item index of socioeconomic
status (U.S. Bureau of the Census, 1963; Nam,
Powers, and Glick, 1964; Nam and Powers, 1965).
These measures and others in the considerable body
of literature which exists on this subject have
been thoroughly reviewed and evaluated (Haug,
1977). A brief review of the origin and development of the three noted above is presented here in
order to provide a context for the issues raised

and the modifications in measurement proposed
in the papers in this volume.

In the Duncan SEI, education and income were
used to classify occupations according to socioeconomic levels. The underlying logic was
essentially that suggested by Hatt much earlier.
If education is a prerequisite for an occupation
and income is a measure of the reward bestowed on
it, then occupation may be viewed as an intervening
activity between these two variables and hence
a good single indicator of status (Duncan, 1961).
The income and educational levels of each occupation in the 1950 Census were calculated according
to the proportion of incumbents found toward the
"upper end" of the income and education distribution for the total male labor force. These
were defined as 1) the percent in each occupation
with a high school education and 2) the percent reporting incomes of $3500 or more. Age-specific
education and income patterns for each occupation
were incorporated as weights with indirect stan-
dardization used to obtain age adjusted indicators
for income and education. As in the earlier
studies, the analysis was limited to the male
labor force.

The prestige dimension of occupational status
was incorporated into the SEI by using multiple
regression analysis to arrive at estimates of
prestige based on the 45 occupations in the original NORC study which precisely matched census
categories. An estimate of the prestige of
occupations was based on the linear multiple regression of the percent "excellent" or "good"
prestige ratings on the average income and education of the 45 occupational categories which
were comparable in the 1947 NORC study and the
1950 census titles. Using the regression weights
resulting from the calculation, all the 1950 census occupations were assigned a score ranging
from 0 to 96 based on their education and income
distribution.

Duncan's SEI has become a widely used
measure. Nonetheless, it has been the subject of
considerable criticism, much of which centers
around use of the 1947 NORC prestige scores
(Haug, 1972; Siegel, 1971; Haug, 1977). The
following is typical of such criticism:

"Regression and correlation techniques
are peculiarly sensitive to the
characteristics of the sample upon
which they are based, and given the well
known bias in the titles represented
in the NORC atudy, one must question
the reliability of any results derived
from a sub-sample of them. If we
regard Duncan's 45 titles as a sample
of the 452 distinct census detailed
occupational categories, we find the
major occupational groups "professional,
technical and kindred workers" and
"service workers, except private
household" are grossly over-represented
while "operative and kindred workers"
and laborers "are grossly under represented" (Siegel, 1971: 14).

In essence, the Duncan SEI scores are an
approximation of the ratings occupations would
have received in the NORC study of 1947 if the
raters had been asked to rate them and they knew
the amount of education an occupation required and
the income accruing to it. The basis for this
rationale is the high correlation between income
and education and the NORC subjective ratings
for the 45 occupations used to predict the other
scores. In fact, Duncan noted that the index
does not predict the prestige ratings that would
have occurred if the NORC study were replicated
to include additional occupations because this
larger number of occupations would be much less
known to the public than the original set (Duncan,
1961: 129). More important, however, is the
question to what extent does an understanding of
the objective characteristics of an occupation,
notably education and income, provide the only or
even major basis for a prestige rating. Certainly
knowledge about the education levels and income of
occupations would enter into judgment of its
prestige value but there is considerable evidence
to suggest that factors other than such knowledge
also enter into the ranking (Svalastoga, 1965).

Although the use of occupations to measure
social standing has been viewed positively in
terms of bringing objectivity to the study of
stratification, it has also been suggested that
some of the objectivity is cancelled out by

ranking occupational standing according to the
subjective evaluation represented by the NORC
prestige scores. In spite of the criticism and
the shortcomings, however, the Duncan SEI scores
continue to enjoy widespread use. An updated
version has been constructed (Stevens and
Featherman, this volume) which attempts to deal
with some of the shortcomings of the original
scores.

Another major attempt to develop objective
measures of occupational status came with the development of the occupational status scores for
the 1960 census population.

Census Measures of Socioeconomic Status

Although we are primarily concerned with
measures of socioeconomic status and occupational
status developed since 1960, it is important to
note that just as there is a long history of
measures of occupational prestige, there is also
a long history of describing American society
with objective status indicators from the U.S.
Census.

One of the earliest analyses of Census
occupation data which explicitly discussed the
socioeconomic character of occupations was made
by William C. Hunt in 1897. Hunt described
occupational trends between 1870 and 1890 by age
and sex and, in the process, regrouped specific
occupations into four major groups of proprietors
and professional people, clerical workers, skilled
workers and a laboring class (Hunt, 1897).

This was the first major attempt to trans-
late census statistics into broad social strata
and to use occupation as an index of status. It
has not received the attention and acknowledgement
of the next major effort at such analysis, that by
Alba Edwards (1917). Edwards improved and ex-
panded Hunt's classification to nine major categories explicitly though roughly grouped
according to skill level and indicative of social
strata or "social-economic groups". The 428 occupations in the 1910 Census were assigned to the
nine categories solely on the basis of Edwards'
opinion as to where they belonged. Edwards continued work on the scheme and published a revised

version in 1933(Edwards, 1933) as well as an
official Census publication (1943) in which he
noted the hierarchical character of the scheme as
well as his belief that the groups comprised distinct social-economic strata. The scheme developed by Edwards in 1933 was the basis both for
contemporary Census occupational groups and for a
wide array of social science analyses of patterns
and trends of socio-economic status.

Edwards social economic groups and his
arguments for using occupation as a socioeconomic
scale have been widely used and cited in social
science research. His analysis of 1940 Census data
included a rationale for the homogeneity of the
groupings and a specific statement that the basis
for including workers in each group was partly
economic and partly social (Edwards, 1943). He
included in his rationale an analysis of data on
education and income levels of each of his six
major groups and demonstrated a generally descending order of status even though each group included a wide range of occupations.

The Edwards scheme has permitted analysts
to examine the socioeconomic structure of the U.S.
population at several points in time and to study
change over time. It has also provided a simple,
index for social scientists to use in other surveys and studies. This permitted comparisons of
the socioeconomic status of respondents in
various special purpose studies with national and
regional profiles.

The work by Nam and his colleagues in
connection with the 1960 Census built on and extended Edwards earlier work to develop the most
recent multiple-item socioeconomic status score
as well as a more refined occupational status
score. A detailed review of the development of
these latter measures appears in the paper by Nam
and Terrie in this volume.

Although Edwards scale was widely used,
it was recognized as being a rather crude measure
of status. During the 1950's in connection with
planning activities for the 1960 Census, Bureau
staff reviewed the use of the occupation classification for the analysis of social status and
agreed that a more refined measure of status

was needed. It was also agreed that occupation
alone was not the best index for understanding
social stratification in the United States and that
some sort of multi-dimensional measure should be
constructed for use in the analysis of the 1960
Census results. Because it was expected that data
users would continue to use occupation as a single
indicator, it was also decided to update and re-
vise the occupational status measure. As a result,
the Census Bureau initiated a comprehensive effort
to develop both a new measure of occupational
status and a multivariable measure of socioeconomic
status (U.S. Bureau of the Census, 1963). The
occupational status indicator continues to be more
widely used than the multi-variable index as indicated in the readings in this volume.

     The work on new measures of socioeconomic
status incorporated findings from the vast literature on stratification which had accumulated
during the forties and fifties and also took note
of the fact that Census information on education
and income meant that it was no longer necessary
to rely on individual judgment to estimate the
status of occupations as Edwards had done. Before
describing the specific scores developed by Nam
and his associates, it might be useful to review
the occupational classification scheme itself, because nearly all the indicators of occupational
status incorporate the census scheme into the
measures. Describing the labor force in a complex
society like the United States is no easy task.
The division of labor is elaborate and several
classifications exist. The Dictionary of Occupational Titles (U.S. Dept. of Labor, 1977) lists
over 20,000 occupations and focuses on describing
the work performed by each, the aptitudes and
skills required, and the physical demands and working conditions. The Standard Occupational Classification (U.S. Department of Commerce, 1977)
attempts to standardize the different systems
used by various government agencies into a single
system of occupational categories. Until very
recently(Cain and Treiman, 1981; Gottfredson, 1978)
neither of these was widely used in socioeconomic
analyses. A different occupational coding and
classification scheme has been developed by the
U.S. Census Bureau based on the responses to
several items on the decennial censuses. Questions
are asked about the type of business or industry

in which one is employed as well as about occupational title and job duties. In 1960 and 1970 all
of this was combined into an occupational classification scheme of over 500 occupations which could
be reduced to twelve major groups. The detailed
list of occupations is generally used to assign
status scores to occupations because of the hetero-
geneity of the major groups. The detailed list has
been used both in studies of prestige and socioeconomic status.

Although the terms are often used synonomous-
ly, as noted earlier status and prestige are distinct and different dimensions of occupation. The
status, or the objective conditions of an occupation, clearly influences the prestige accorded it.
Nonetheless, prestige is accorded an occupation by
the public on the basis of several other dimensions
also--influence, job security, scarcity, etc. The
two most significant elements of status are education and income (Reiss, et al 1961) although
many other factors are relevant. Income and education were the variables selected to measure
occupational status by Nam and his associates. The
distinction between prestige and status was maintained, and no attempt was made to calibrate the
Nam-Powers occupational status scores with any
prestige measure. They are, thus, "pure" socioeconomic measures--and indeed the only ones that
do not combine subjective and objective dimensions.
Comparisons of socioeconomic and prestige measures
made so far (Featherman and Hauser, 1976[b]; Treas
and Tyree, 1979) have not included these scores
and hence have compared "pure" prestige scores
with those which incorporate both prestige and objective status dimensions. A more complete evaluation remains to be done.

The Nam-Powers occupational status scores
were calculated on the basis of the median education and income levels of occupations. Originally they were based on data for men in the experienced civilian labor force and more recently,
on data for all persons in the experienced
civilian labor force. The scores are determined
by the relative education and income levels of
detailed occupations. As such, they are the
properties of occupations, with values between 0
and 100. The scores also lend themselves to
simple interpretation. Any score indicates the

approximate percentage of males or all persons
in the experienced civilian labor force who are in
occupations having combined average levels of
education and income below that for the given
occupation. The methodology permits relatively
easy replication and updating for each decade and
for various population groups. They are available
for 1950, 1960 and 1970 (Nam, Powers and Glick,
1964; Nam and Powers, 1968; Nam, LaRocque, Powers
and Holmberg, 1975; Powers and Holmberg, 1978).
Some of these updated scores appear in two papers
in this volume (Powers and Holmberg and Cooney,
Clague and Salvo).

Multiple Item Indicators of Socioeconomic Status

Although most users appear to prefer the
simplicity of single-item indicators of status, a
variety of multiple-item indicators were also in
use by the 1950s (Kiser and Whelpton, 1949,
Warner, et al., 1949; Hollingshead, 1958). The
social scientists at the Census Bureau also developed a multiple-item indicator of socioeconomic
status (Nam and Terrie, this volume). The basic
argument for such a multiple-item indicator is the
fact that status, however defined, is conceived as
multi-dimensional. Even though occupation may
account for most of status, the other items in a
multiple-item index may tap other dimensions. The
multiple-item index developed by the Census social
scientists combined indicators for occupation,
education and family income for key persons in
each family and assigned the resulting score to
all family members (U.S. Bureau of the Census
1963; Nam, Powers and Glick, 1964; Nam and Terrie,
this volume). The components of the index,
occupation, education, and family income, were
selected because they operationalize different
aspects of socioeconomic status noted in stratification theory and because they are items on which
data are collected regularly in censuses and
surveys. Other items which might also have been
included, such as residence and race, were felt
to be correlates of, rather than components of,
socioeconomic status. Socioeconomic levels vary
by race, age, ethnic group, etc. It is exactly
these variations which social scientists and
policy makers wish to observe and compare to some
national standard. If they are built into the
measure as either components or controls such

variations cannot be observed. Hence what was
developed is a multiple-item index which refines
the objective occupational status score by accounting for variations in status among individuals
within an occupational category which result from
differences in education levels and family income.

Current Issues

        All of the above measures have been used in
studies of the socioeconomic level of the population and various subgroups in it, in studies of
socioeconomic change over time, research on social
mobility and, most recently, in status attainment
research as well as in research where occupational
status serves as a control variable. Several
issues have surfaced concerning the adequacy of
any of these scores to describe the status attainment process of various subgroups of the population, notably. women, and the relative worth of
prestige versus socioeconomic indicators in the
study of status attainment.

        The increased participation of North American
women in the labor force has been accompanied by
an increased awareness of status differences, income inequality, and an interest in examining and
measuring sex differences in status attainment.
Studies of sex differences in occupational status
attainment have, until very recently, used the
occupational status and prestige measures discussed above--all of which have been based on the
labor force characteristics of male incumbents.
The findings of similar distributions of occupational status by sex and similar patterns of
status attainment by sex have been questioned by
many (See Powers and Holmberg and Boyd and
McRoberts this volume for a review). Hence the
increase in the number of women in the labor force
has been an impetus to the inclusion of women in
both measures of occupational status and in status
attainment models.

        The papers in this volume focus on updating
the existing measures of socioeconomic status
and their use in models of status attainment.
Existing criticisms of the status attainment
models point to the need for reevaluation of these
models and such reevaluations are currently
appearing in the literature (Acker, 1973;
Featherman and Hauser, 1976b;Horan, 1978). The

papers in this book focus on measurement issues
rather than other aspects of the model which must
also be evaluated in light of new specifications of
Marxian theory and of multiple labor markets.

The Nam and Terrie paper reviews the origin
and development of measures of socioeconomic status
and prestige from U.S. Census data. These include
measures developed by social scientists at the
Bureau of the Census and elsewhere. They examine
the arguments of the advocates of the "pure"
prestige approach and those of the socioeconomic
determinants of prestige, and discuss the development by Nam and his associates of a measure of
occupational SES without reference to prestige.

Nam and Terrie also present a case for the
use of multiple-item indicators of socioeconomic
status with particular attention to the multiple-
item socioeconomic status score developed by Nam
and his colleagues in connection with the 1960 U.S.
Census. That measure uses indicators of occupation, education and family income for key persons
in each family to assign scores to each family
member. They note:

> "A basic assumption in the construction
> of the original measure was that the
> status level of a family is determined
> largely by the status attributes of
> the family breadwinner and that
> educational and occupational indicators
> for the chief income recipient of a
> family thus should be assigned to
> other family members."

The chief income recipient could be either male or
female. In 1960 it was most often male, and even
where there was more than one earner in the family,
the education and occupation of the chief income
recipient alone was counted, along with family
income, to indicate the family's status. The
second earner was counted only to the extent that
she/he contributed to family income. The authors
note that this is one of several areas requiring
future research, particularly in light of the updating that has already been done with 1970 Census
data which incorporates data for women into the
occupational status measure (Nam, et al, 1975;
Powers & Holmberg, 1978).

As noted previously, the development of
socioeconomic measures from Canadian Census data
originated with Bernard Blishen (1958), and in fact,
predates the Duncan and Nam/Powers work in the
United States. The Blishen-Carroll paper in this
volume reviews the origin and various revisions
of the Blishen scores, as well as the theoretical
and methodological bases for the measures. They
also describe some of the results obtained from
analyses using the measures in Canadian society
and discuss the updating and revision of the score
proposed for the 1981 Canadian Census of the population.

The theoretical basis for the Blishen scale
is Weber's distinction of the class, status and
power elements of a stratification system. The
basic assumption is that although the stratification system in contemporary industrial societies
is multi-dimensional, the "prime determinent" of
position is occupation. Although the initial
measures (1958) did not incorporate a prestige
dimension into the occupational scale, subsequent
revisions using the 1961 and 1971 Canadian Census
data did do so. (Blishen, 1967; Blishen &
McRoberts, 1976). Regression techniques were used
to weight occupations in the 1961 and 1971 male
labor-force with the prestige scores obtained in
the Pineo-Porter (1967) survey of occupational
prestige. Hence the original Blishen scales were
more similar to those developed by Nam and Powers
(discussed above) but the revisions are more
similar to the Duncan SEI scores.

The paper goes on to discuss current efforts
to incorporate sex differences in occupational
prestige. Their approach to the current issue is
to construct separate scales for male and female
occupational prestige. They argue that the
differences in male and female occupational prestige found in a "limited regional study" require
the construction of a female based occupational
scale.

The paper by Powers and Holmberg suggests
the opposite conclusion. It examines the impact
of women's labor force participation on occupational scores. In particular, the paper compares
the Nam/Powers occupational status scores based on
the characteristics of the 1970 male labor force

with a set of occupational status scores based on
the characteristics of the total 1970 labor force.

Although the two sets of scores are highly
correlated, important differences are found in the
scores for specific occupations as well as for
major occupational groups. Scores based on the
total civilian labor force tended to be higher
than scores based solely on the male civilian
labor force. Although the mean difference between
the two sets of scores was only +3, thirty occupations showed differences of two standard deviations
or more, 12 or more points, from the mean difference. Of the latter, twenty-six predominantly
female occupations registered significant negative
score differences. The occupational concentration
of women and their generally lower income level
served to depress the scores of 20 predominantly
female occupations and contributed to a small
general upgrading of the majority of detailed
occupations. It also influenced the alignment of
the major occupational groups. Using the traditional list of 12 major occupational categories,
the positions of clerical workers and craftsmen were
reversed when status scores were derived from data
on all incumbents in the labor force rather than
on male incumbents alone. The paper suggests that
with the increased participation of women in the
labor force and the concomitant change in sex
composition of the work force, the traditional
approaches to the measurement of occupational
status based solely on male incumbents may no
longer be valid for examining the occupational hierarchy of contemporary American society or the status
attainment processes within it.

The paper by Featherman and Stevens provides
a "contemporary version" of the Duncan SEI, which
seeks to take into account changes in the occupational classification scheme as well as changes
in the education and income characteristics of the
U.S. labor force which have occurred since 1950.
The updated version of the socioeconomic index
examines and incorporates several measures of income and education. One measure was equivalent to
Duncan's original version, but for the total labor
force rather than the male labor force. A second
measure increased the education and income levels
to include about the same proportion of the

education and income distribution in 1970 as
Duncan's measure did for the 1950 labor force. A
third repeated the second, but for the male labor
force only. They also experimented with the
prestige measure, using both Siegel's (1971)
prestige scores and an approximation of the NORC
prestige scores used by Duncan. They then reestimated the SEI prediction equations for the
occupation titles used in the original study by
Duncan.

Their evaluations of the various equations
led Featherman and Stevens to conclude that the
two equations which most closely paralleled
Duncan's were the best ones to generate socioeconomic scores. The main difference over time in
the prediction of prestige from socioeconomic data
was that education was a more prominent predictor
for the more recent data than for the earlier
data--especially when using an equation based on
the total labor force rather than on males alone.

Featherman and Stevens also compare the new
versions of the SEI with the original and with
Siegel's occupational prestige scores in models
of occupational attainment for men and women.
They demonstrate that sex differences in occupational attainment are dependent on the particular
index used. All the revised Duncan socioeconomic
indices increase the effect of first full-time
occupation relative to education. Featherman and
Stevens do not attach much importance to differences resulting from the various forms of SEI,
however. They note that all forms of the SEI
explain more of the variance in attainment than
the prestige index. Also, one would draw different
conclusions about the paths to attainment of men
and women based on the prestige index rather than
the SEI.

Featherman and Stevens recommend a "socioeconomic" index over a prestige index for the study
of mobility and attainment processes. Their
research suggests " . . . that mobility processes
are more clearly revealed by . . ." the various
forms of the SEI than by pure prestige measures.
It is important to remember, however, that all
forms of the SEI have a built-in prestige component. The question of prestige vs. socioeconomic

indices is of importance precisely because most
empirical examinations of the two types of indices
omit a "pure" socioeconomic index and compare a
"pure" prestige measure (NORC, Siegel) with one
which has both components (Duncan, 1961;
Featherman and Hauser, 1976). This raises the
question of what might be revealed through the use
of a strictly socioeconomic index without any
reference to prestige. Such an analysis appears
in the Cooney, Clague and Salvo paper (this volume).

A second approach to the development and use
of socioeconomic indices which incorporates data
on women is suggested in the paper by Boyd and
McRoberts. They examine sex differences in status
attainment when the index used is based on
". . . a female hierarchy of socioeconomic status."
They note that previous studies of occupational
attainment which include women " . . . show
striking similarity among men and women in how
background resources . . ." affect current occupational status (Featherman and Hauser, 1976; Sewell,
Hauser and Wolf, 1980; Treiman and Terrell, 1975;
Treas and Tyree, 1979). Most of this research
shows that the occupational status of women in the
labor force is equal to or higher than that of men
but that women experience lower career mobility.
The contradiction of these similarities in average
status levels and in the effects of family background on status attainment on the one hand and
existing income inequality by sex and occupation
segregation by sex on the other led many analysts,
including Boyd and McRoberts, to conclude that
something needed to be done to correct for the bias
resulting from using male based indices to examine
occupational status attainment by sex.

Boyd and McRoberts note that several
approaches to correcting for the possible error
of a male based index appear in the literature.
One approach brings women into the construction of
the index by using all persons in the labor force
as the reference population (Powers and Holmberg,
1978). A second develops sex-specific socioeconomic scores (Blishen and McRoberts, 1976;
Blishen and Carroll, this volume). The underlying assumption of the latter is that there are
sex specific hierarchies of occupational desire-
ability.

Given the several alternatives to recalcu-
lating socioeconomic scores to include women, Boyd
and McRoberts summarize the results of several
studies which use the various indices to measure
the occupational status of men and women and
assess the empirical consequences of using the
various indices. They found that sex differences
in socioeconomic status varied with the measure
used. They also demonstrated that women had lower
average levels of socioeconomic status than men
when the measures used were based on the total
labor force or were sex specific, a finding which
challenged earlier findings of similarity between
the sexes.

They raise the question of how the use of
various indices affects the results of the status
attainment model for men and women and report the
results of their own research using the female
based Blishen-Carroll scales in a comparison
of the status of Canadian men and women. In effect,
they reverse the error of using a male-based scale
by using one based on data for women to examine
the status attainment of men as well as women.
As expected, sex differences both in status level
and the status attainment process varied depending
on whether male and female based index was used.

Boyd and McRoberts pointed to the need for
an assessment of the status attainment model using
a socioeconomic index derived from the income and
education of the total labor force. The paper by
Cooney, Clague and Salvo provides such an assessment. Their paper examines the effect of using
different socioeconomic status scores on the processes of occupational status attainment of men and
women. They provide a detailed review of the four
major studies of status attainment by sex, all of
which use the SEI. The review points out the am-
biguities and inconsistencies as well as the similarities among the findings, and indicates that
any generalization suggesting that the status
attainment processes are the same for men and women
is premature.

Cooney, Clague and Salvo used both the Nam-
Powers scores and the Duncan SEI to examine the educational and occupational status attainment processes of young white men and women. Their findings
challenge the notion that..."the process linking
family background characteristics to educational and

occupational status is similar for men and women".
Using the SEI, their data from the National
Longitudenal Surveys show significant sex differences in the impact of education, father's occupation, mother's education and mother's occupation
on the process of occupational attainment. The
use of the Nam-Powers measure led to similar results, but showed much lower occupational status
returns to education for young men than the SEI
did.

Comparisons of men and women were significantly affected by the measure used. The Nam-
Powers scores show that the first jobs of men
and women had similar status levels, whereas, the
SEI suggested that the first jobs held by women had
higher status levels than the first jobs of men.
There were also important differences in the
effect of education on first job depending on which
measure was used. The paper clearly demonstrates
that the choice of measure influences the conclusions reached concerning the status levels of
men and women and the process of status attainment by sex.

Summary

The papers in this volume indicate that
occupation continues to be an important indicator
of socioeconomic status. Broad changes in the
occupational structure in recent decades require
continuous reexamination of existing measures.
Previous findings with respect to the socioeconomic and prestige distributions of occupations
and the relative merits of each have been challenged. The papers also suggest that previous findings with respect to sex differences in occupational status and the process of status attainment
are problematic.

The utilization of measures of occupational
status developed in the fifties and sixties to
examine currently significant sociological
questions concerning sexual inequality in the occupational structure and the process of status
attainment by sex has generated new interest in old
questions as to the adequacy and accuracy of the
measures used. It has also resulted in several
improvements in existing measures and the
clarification of implicit and often forgotten

assumptions underlying those measures. The results of the research reported in this volume are
of particular theoretical and methodological importance for future work on the comparative socioeconomic status and the process of status attainment of minorities as well as women. They also
impact on future models of the relationship between occupation and social class and on research
focusing on the socio-economic levels of families,
particularly dual career families.

Acknowledgements

The editor wishes to acknowledge the collab-
orative nature of this endeavor and to thank all
of the contributors for their cooperation as well
as for a set of uniformly high quality papers.
Also thanks go to Kathryn Wolff and Joellen
Fritsche of the Publications Office of AAAS for
their valuable technical assistance, editorial
instructions, and good-humored patience. Finally,
the support of Fordham University is gratefully
acknowledged for secretarial and other assistance
in planning the symposium on which this volume is
based, and in its final preparation.

References

Acker, Joan
   1973   "Women and Social Stratification,"
              American Journal of Sociology 78:
              936-945.

Anderson, W.A.
   1927-28   "Occupational Attitudes and Choices of
              a Group of College Men," I & II Social
              Forces, 6:278-283 & 6:467-473.

Blau, Peter and O.D. Duncan.
   1967   The American Occupational Structure,
              New York: John Wiley.

Blishen, Bernard R.
   1958   "The Construction and Use of An Occupa-
              tional Class Scale," Canadian Journal
              of Economics and Political Science,
              24:519-531.

Blishen, Bernard R.
   1967   "A Socioeconomic Index for Occupations

in Canada," <u>Canadian Review of Sociology and Anthropology</u>. 4:41-53.

Blishen, Bernard R. and William K. Carroll
1978   "Sex Differences in a Socioeconomic Index for Occupations in Canada," <u>Canadian Review of Sociology and Anthropology</u>, 15:352-371.

Blishen, Bernard R. and Hugh McRoberts
1976   "A Revised Socioeconomic Index for Occupations in Canada," <u>Canadian Review of Sociology and Anthropology</u>, 13:71-79.

Cain, Pamela S. and Treiman, Donald Jr.
1981   "The Dictionary of Occupational Titles as a Source of Occupational Data," <u>American Sociological Review</u>, 46:253-278.

Counts, George S.
1925   "The Social Status of Occupations: A Problem in Vocational Guidance," <u>School Review</u>, 33:16-27.

Davies, A.F.
1952   "Prestige of Occupations," <u>British Journal of Sociology</u>, III:134-147.

Duncan, O.D.
1961   "A Socioeconomic Index for All Occupations" in A.J. Reiss, Jr., et al, eds. <u>Occupations and Social Status</u>, 115-124.

Edwards, Alba M.
1943   <u>Comparative Occupation Statistics for the United States: 1870-1940</u>, U.S. Census of Population, 1940, Washington, D.C.: U.S. Government Printing Office.

Edwards, Alba M.
1933   "A Social Economic Grouping of the Gainful Workers of the United States," <u>Journal of the American Statistical Association</u>, XXVIII:378.

Edwards, Alba M.
1917   "Social Economic Groups of the United

States" <u>Quarterly Journal of the</u>
<u>American Statistical Association</u>,
XV: 643-646.

Featherman, David, L. and R.M. Hauser
  1975   "Design for a Replicate Study of
            Social Mobility in the United States,"
            K. Land and S. Spilerman (eds.),
            <u>Social Indicator Models</u>, New York:
            Russell Sage 219-52.

Featherman, David L. and Robert M. Hauser
  1976a   "Sexual Inequalities and Socioeconomic
            Achievement in the United States,
            1962-1973," <u>American Sociological</u>
            <u>Review</u>, 41:462-83.

Featherman, David, L. and Robert M. Hauser
  1976b   "Prestige or Socioeconomic Scales in
            the Study of Occupational Achieve-
            ment?" <u>Sociological Methods and</u>
            <u>Research</u> 4:402-422.

Gottfredson, Linda S.
  1978   <u>The Construct Validity of Holland's</u>
            <u>Occupational Classification in Terms</u>
            <u>of Prestige, Census, Department of</u>
            <u>Labor and Other Classification</u>
            <u>Systems</u>, Baltimore, Md.: The Johns
            Hopkins University, Center for Social
            Organization of Schools, Report
            No. 260.

Hartman, G.W.
  1934   "The Prestige of Occupations,"
            <u>Personnel Journal</u> 13:144-152.

Hatt, Paul K.
  1950   "Occupations and Social Stratifica-
            tion," <u>American Journal of Sociology</u>,
            55:533-543.

Haug, Marie E.
  1972   "Social Class Measurement: A Methodo-
            logical Critique," G.W. Thielbar,
            S.D. Feldman (eds.) <u>Social Inequality</u>,
            Boston: Little, Brown & Co. 429-451.

Haug, Marie E.
  1977   "Measurement in Social Stratifica-

tion," Annual Review of Sociology,
3:51-79. Palo Alto: Annual Reviews,
Inc.

Hodge, Robert W., Paul Siegel and Peter H. Rossi
    1964   "Occupational Prestige in the United
                States, 1925-63," American Journal of
                Sociology 70:286-302.

Hollingshead, August B. and Frederick C. Redlich
    1958   Social Class and Mental Illness,
                New York: John Wiley, 387-397.

Horan, Patrick
    1978   "Is Status Attainment Research Atheo-
                retical?" American Sociological
                Review, 43:534-541

Hunt, William C.
    1897   "Workers at Gainful Occupations at the
                Federal Censuses of 1870, 1880, and
                1890," Bulletin of the Department of
                Labor, No. II.

Kiser, Clyde V. and P.K. Whelpton
    1949   "Social and Psychological Factors
                Affecting Fertility: IV, Fertility
                Planning and Fertility Rates by
                Socioeconomic Status," Milbank Mem-
                orial Fund Quarterly 27:188-244.

McClendon, Mekee J.
    1976   "The Occupational Attainment Process
                of Males and Females," American
                Sociological Review 41:52-64.

Nam, Charles B., Mary G. Powers and Paul C. Glick
    1964   "Socioeconomic Characteristics of the
                Population: 1960. Current Population
                Reports Series, p. 23 No. 12, Wash-
                ington, D.C., United States Government
                Printing Office.

Nam, Charles B. and Mary G. Powers
    1965   "Variations in Socioeconomic Structure
                by Race, Residence and the Life-cycle."
                American Sociological Review, 30:97-103.

Nam, Charles B. and Mary G. Powers
    1968   "Changes in the Relative Status of

Workers in the United States, 1950-1960," Social Forces, 47:158-170.

Nam, Charles B., John LaRocque, Mary G. Powers and
    Joan J. Holmberg
  1975   "Occupational Status Scores: Stability
            and Change," Proceedings of the
            American Statistical Association,
            Social Statistics Section.

Nietz, J.A.
  1935   "The Depression and the Social Status
            of Occupations," Elementary School
            Journal, XXV: 454-461.

North, C.C. and P.K. Hatt
  1947   "Jobs and Occupations: A Popular
            Evaluation," Opinion News 9:3-13.

Pineo, Peter C. and John Porter
  1967   "Occupational Prestige in Canada,"
            Canadian Review of Sociology and An-
            thropology, 4:24-40.

Powers, Mary G. and Joan J. Holmberg
  1978   "Occupational Status Scores: Changes
            Introduced by the Inclusion of
            Women." Demography, 15: 183-204.

Reiss, A.J., O.D. Duncan, P.K. Hatt and C.C. North
  1961   Occupations and Social Status, New
            York: The Free Press of Glencoe, Inc.

Sewell, William, Robert M. Hauser and Wendy C. Wolf
  1980   "Sex, Schooling and Occupational
            Status," American Journal of Sociology
            86:551-583.

Siegel, Paul M.
  1971   "Prestige in the American Occupational
            Structure" Unpublished Ph.D. disser-
            tation. University of Chicago.

Svalastoga, Kaare
  1965   Social Differentiation, New York:
            David McKay Co.

Treas, Judith and Andrea Tyree
  1979   "Prestige versus Socioeconomic Status
            in the Attainment Process of American

Men and Women," <u>Social Research</u>,
8:201-221.

Treiman, Donald J.
    1974   <u>Occupational Prestige in Comparative
                Perspective</u>, New York: Academic Press.

Treiman, Donald J. and Kermit Terrell
    1975   "Sex and the Process of Status
                Attainment: A Comparison of Working
                Men and Women," <u>American Sociological
                Review</u>, 40:174-200.

U.S. Bureau of the Census
    1963   "Methodology and Scores of Socio-
                economic Status," Working Paper
                No. 15, Washington, D.C. U.S. Govern-
                ment Printing Office.

U.S. Department of Commerce
    1977   Office of Federal Statistical Policy
                and Standards, <u>Standard Occupational
                Classification</u>, U.S. Government
                Printing Office.

U.S. Department of Labor
    1977   <u>Dictionary of Occupational Titles</u>,
                Fourth Edition. Washington, D.C.: U.S.
                Government Printing Office.

Warner, W. Lloyd, Marcia Meeker and Kenneth Eells
    1959   <u>Social Class in America</u>, Chicago:
                Science Research Associates, 121-159.

Charles B. Nam, E. Walter Terrie

2. Measurement of Socioeconomic Status from United States Census Data

Introduction

The origin of the term "socioeconomic status" (SES) is difficult to determine, but social scientists have long used the phrase to denote the relative location of an individual or group within a socially desirable hierarchy. Max Weber identified three distinct but interrelated aspects of the social hierarchy--namely, class, status, and party (Gerth and Mills, 1958). He regarded "party" as the power to influence one's own affairs and that of others, "status" as the regard with which individuals are held by others, and "class" as the social and economic life chances which people experienced. It is in this latter sense that researchers have looked for measures of socioeconomic status as a basis for indicating social class, and it is this common understanding of the term that led to the definition of "socioeconomic" in Webster's Third New International Dictionary (1976) as "of, relating to, or involving a combination of social and economic factors; specifically, of or relating to income and social position considered as a single factor."

The inability of social researchers to develop consensus on the real distinctions between class, status, and party, and further difficulty in specifying the nature of the interrelationships and the variables which are determinants of each aspect, has placed measurement of socioeconomic status in an uncertain position. The numbers and types of indexes and scales of SES are considerable and, while most of them are highly intercorrelated empirically, they each offer variations in concept and in procedures for their calculation.

The dominant approaches among the variations are customarily classified as being either "subjectively" or "objectively" determined--recognition that the two major paths to identifying relative social position have been, on the one hand, judgments by persons as to the standing of a position and, on the other hand, the value of the position as inferred from the qualifications for its attainment and the monetary reward bestowed upon it.

In community studies of the 1930's and 1940's, assignment of status to individuals and families could be reasonably well based on the judgmental or reputational approach because the relationships and activities of people in the small and middlesized places which were studied was a matter of record or common knowledge and there was general agreement among residents about almost everyone's social standing.

In more densely populated areas, the reputational approach was not effective. High residential mobility, the greater differentiation of social roles, and the increasing secretiveness which accompanied many relationships and activities made it impossible for people to be aware of, and correctly perceive, the social standings of others. Researchers subsequently turned to measurement of status which did not require personal knowledge of the circumstances of other individuals. Recorded information (for individuals or aggregates) became the source of socioeconomic indicators.

Given the limitations imposed on researchers of relying on record data for socioeconomic studies of anonymous populations, it became desirable to look for economical ways to extract SES information. Following years of analysis, occupation became accepted as the best single item to characterize a person's status. The issue then became one of how to arrange occupations in a hierarchical fashion. Concerns about statistical reliability and validity were established. One school of thought argued for retaining the judgmental approach and restricting it to rating the prestige of occupational categories, with validity implicit in the popular perceptions of occupations. A second school argued for the face validity of socioeconomic factors (namely education and income) as estimators of the occupation's standing. A third school accepted the validity of the popular perceptions as well as the meaningfulness of the socioeconomic determinants and used the latter to gauge the former.

Involved in these alternative approaches are several issues in the formation of a hierarchical scale for occupations. Among these are 1) selecting an appropriate underlying criterion for differentiating occupations, 2) developing a suitable operational definition of this criterion and 3) applying this operational definition to an acceptable occupational taxonomy.

The subject of an appropriate dimension along which to order occupations has received considerable attention. The two main contenders have been prestige (subjectively-perceived instrinsic worth or value) and status (objectively-determined position). Although often confused and used interchangeably, status and prestige are two separate and distinct concepts. Occupational status usually refers to the educational requirements and economic rewards associated with an occupation, while occupational prestige refers to an evaluation people generally have of the occupation's desirability. Early attempts to order occupations were mostly prestige-based. Counts (1925) ordered 45 occupations selected by some unspecified process that he claimed represented the entire range of vocations. This ordering was accomplished by six different groups of respondents who were instructed to first place the occupations into nine categories from most looked up to to least looked up to, and then to arrange them into a single list from highest to lowest. Counts was able to show a high level of agreement among his six groups of raters, thus establishing empirically for the first time a high degree of congruity in the perceptions of occupational prestige by different groups of respondents.

This tradition of prestige-based occupational scales was advanced considerably by North and Hatt's (1947) study of a national probability sample of 2,920 respondents who were asked their opinions of the desirability of 90 different occupations. This study was notable in several respects. First, it used a statistically defensible sample of raters, rather than a sample of convenience; second, it attempted to order the occupations along an interval metric; and third, it served as the focal point for all subsequent prestige-based occupational scoring. North and Hatt's study was replicated by Hodge, Siegel and Rossi (1964), and a very high agreement between the two sets of ranking was found for the occupations covered.

One difficulty with prestige-based studies to this

point in time was that they were conducted using relatively small and, as many have argued, unrepresentative groups
of occupations. This characteristic severely restricted
their usefulness for other research endeavors. Two
approaches to extending the number of occupations for
which a prestige-based score could be assigned have been
used.

One of these approaches was developed by Siegel
(1971) who used data from three separate occupational
prestige studies. Siegel combined the job titles into a
single list and translated their scale scores onto a
single metric. The result was a prestige scale based
directly on social valuations from ·national probability
samples for about 350 detailed occupational titles.

The second and most popular of these approaches was
that of Duncan (1961), who calculated the regression
equation relating age-standardized income and education of
the incumbents to occupational prestige. The specific
measures used were 1) the proportion of males who were at
least high school graduates, 2) the proportion of males
earning $3500 or more in 1949 and 3) the proportion of
respondents rating each occupation as excellent or good.
The income and education data were determined for 45
occupations from the 1950 Census whose titles could be
matched to North-Hatt occupational titles. Eighty-three
percent of the variance in prestige, as operationally
defined by Duncan, was accounted for by these income and
education measures. Thus, Duncan was able to show that
occupational prestige could be indexed by the socioeconomic variables income and education. It was then
possible to estimate a prestige score for any occupation
for which one could collect data on the income and
education of the incumbents. Duncan did, in fact, do this
for those detailed occupations identified in the 1950
U.S. census occupational taxonomy. This well known
Socioeconomic Index of Occupations has been widely used,
studied and critiqued (Haug, 1977). A similar measure was
developed by Blishen (1958) based on Canadian data.

Not surprisingly, a debate between "prestige purists"
and socioeconomically-indexed prestige advocates has
arisen. Interestingly, this argument seems to turn on the
question of whether prestige is an estimator of socioeconomic status. Siegel (1971:238) argues "we are left to
conclude that if the socioeconomic status of occupations--
as opposed to their prestige--is of interest, any reason-

able combination of the education and income of occupational incumbents is as good as any other. . . . Thus, its usefulness as a surrogate for prestige is devalued by the availability of prestige scores for occupation. . ." In contrast, Duncan, Featherman and Duncan (1972) argue that it makes more sense to assume that prestige is an unbiased, though errored, indicator of socioeconomic status than to assume the converse. Featherman and Hauser (1976) make a stronger statement saying, "Our provisional conclusion is that prestige scores are 'error-prone' estimates of the socioeconomic attributes of occupations."

There appears to be a clear understanding on both sides of this debate that prestige and socioeconomic status are not the same thing. Featherman and Hauser argue, "Whatever it is that prestige scores scale--and this does not appear to be prestige in the classical sense of deference/derogation (see Goldthorpe and Hope, 1972)-- it is substantively different from socioeconomic status."

Treas and Tyree (1979) extend the argument and seek to show that the choice between prestige and socioeconomic status is crucial in the study of intergenerational status mobility. They conclude that ". . . the judicious selection of a socioeconomic scale to study social mobility can . . . substantially reduce random measurement error" and that their paper, ". . . has demonstrated that the socioeconomic index is superior to prestige scaling for the purpose of status attainment research." Treas and Tyree also make the point that, "The choice of a scale must be guided as much by theoretical considerations as by methodological concerns."

The existing controversy between advocates of the pure prestige approach and those of SES determination of prestige of occupations seems to ignore the third possibility of direct measurement of occupational SES without reference to prestige. This approach was used in the work of Hollingshead and Redlich (1958), by Blau and Duncan (1967) in research not widely acknowledged today, and by Nam, Powers and Glick (1964) in connection with the 1960 Census. This orientation begins with the notion that often one wants a measure of class or life chances or objective status conditions, and this criterion for valuing occupations leads one to pure socioeconomic indicators of occupational rankings. This third, purely socioeconomic, approach has been evident in work produced by the U.S. Bureau of the Census for the past century.

Historical Perspective of SES Data from U.S. Census

In the United States, recorded census information has been used for socioeconomic analysis as far back as the first census. In 1790, occupational data for some areas of Pennsylvania permitted description of the social stratification of the areas. Combined occupational and industrial information became part of the complete national census inquiry beginning in 1820. A question on literacy was entered on the schedule in 1840 and one on school attendance in 1850. Occupations and industries in which persons worked were distinguished in 1850 as well. Class of worker, or source of employment, was introduced in 1910, and educational attainment, income, and extended accounts of housing characteristics first became regular census features in 1940.

Some have argued that these items of basic information, in and of themselves, do not constitute measures of socioeconomic status, that it is necessary to place them in some framework and assign values to the categories. Even accepting that argument, one can point to historical uses of the data by Census Bureau employees to more adequately represent socioeconomic conditions. Before the turn of this century, Hunt (1897) analyzed 1870, 1880, and 1890 census returns on occupation, grouped them into broad occupational classes, and concluded that "the great body of workers has, as a whole, progressed and has perceptibly risen in the social scale of life." About the time of World War I, Edwards (1917) attempted to refine Hunt's work and, adding 1900 and 1910 data, grouped detailed occupational categories into a six-fold "social-economic" grouping with subcategories within several of the groupings. Subsequently, he argued that these represented not only distinct social-economic strata but also "are arranged approximately in descending order of the social-economic status of the workers comprising them." In the late 1950's, a new generation of census social scientists set about to further modify and refine the earlier Census Bureau efforts by relating occupation, education, and income data, resulting in what are generally referred to as the Nam-Powers SES measures (1965).

One segment of this work was a purely socioeconomic occupational status scale which was created initially in conjunction with the 1960 U. S. Census, using 1950-based data. The technique scores occupations on the combined average level of income and education for each occupation. The actual operational definition involves the following: (U. S. Bureau of the Census, 1963; Nam Powers, 1968).

". . . (a) arraying occupations (actually occupation-industry combinations) according to the median educational level of males 14 years old and over in the experienced civilian labor force, (b) arraying occupations separately according to the median income level of the same population, (c) using the number of persons engaged in each occupation, determining the cumulative interval of persons in each occupation for each of the two arrays, and (d) averaging the mid-points of the two cumulative distributions of occupants and dividing by the total experienced labor force to get a status score for the occupation."

This method was subsequently applied to 1960 and 1970 census data, and to males and females both separately and combined. Scores produced by this method permit one to specify the percentage of persons in occupations with lower average income and education than in the occupation being scored. As should be apparent from the operational definition, these scores are solely status-based and are devoid of any prestige component.

The scores have been widely used as explanatory and control variables in many areas of social science and health research. They have not been as widely used as the Duncan scores in analytical studies of status attainment and mobility. Yet, a scale of this type would seem to be ideal for much of that type of research. First, it has a purely socioeconomic basis and would be advantageous where the analyst wants to treat status in terms of objective socioeconomic conditions. Second, it has a straight-forward interpretation in terms of the percentage of persons in the population considered who have higher or lower socioeconomic rank. Third, it is based solely on census data and does not rely on independent survey or record data. Consequently, it may be readily updated after each succeeding census.

Multiple-Item SES Measures

Although single-item indicators of socioeconomic

status, such as scales of occupation, are frequently preferred for reasons of ease in estimating class and for simplicity of interpretation, a variety of multiple-item indicators of socioeconomic status can be found in the research literature. At least three arguments can be advanced for a multiple-item approach, each of which assumes an underlying general class dimension. First, if interest is in accounting for the socioeconomic status levels of individuals or groups, we should try to explain as much of the general class variable as possible and additional items will usually add to the explanation of variance in class. Second, even though one item (e.g., occupation) may account for more of the phenomenon we call class than other items, it is likely that different items tap somewhat different dimensions of general socioeconomic status and together will more fully represent overall socioeconomic class. Third, if class can be measured in terms of a combination of dimensions, the extent to which these various indicators describe class in the same way or differently can be examined. That is, their consistency or inconsistency in this respect will provide additional information about socioeconomic status patterns.

Elaborating the first two arguments, however much an improvement over earlier ones is the occupational index outlined, the fact remains that it is concerned with only a single item which does not capture all of the variation in socioeconomic status. This is mainly because the score relates to the occupational aggregate, or the average person in an occupation, and there still remains variation around that average. Within any occupation, there are persons who have more or less education and income which may be associated with different levels of responsibility and performance in that occupation.

As a result, a multiple-item approach was devised by Nam and colleagues (U. S. Bureau of the Census, 1963) which used indicators of occupation, education, and family income for key persons in each family and assigned resulting scores to each family member. This multiple-item SES approach has been used in a number of studies (e.g., Myrianthopoulous and French, 1968; Broman, Nichols, and Kennedy, 1975; Chiricos and Waldo, 1975).

Several considerations had to be made in the choice of items to be included, how they were to be rated and combined, and various other statistical procedures to be followed. A basic assumption in the construction of the multiple-item socioeconomic index was that the status level of a family is determined largely by the status attributes of the family breadwinner and that the educational and occupational indictors for the chief income recipient of a family thus should be assigned to other family members. This principal person may be male or female and there may be more than one earner in the family, but the chief income recipient's educational and occupational characteristics plus family income will be indicative of the family's status.

The component items of the measure (occupation, education, and family income) were selected because they represent somewhat different aspects of socioeconomic status and, in addition, because they are items on which information is collected through the Census Bureau's censuses and surveys. A housing item (e.g., rent or value of home) was not included because relevant housing information is not obtained regularly in Census Bureau inquiries. An ethnic characteristic (e.g., race or nationality) was not included because it was felt that such an item can be more properly treated as a correlate of, rather than as a component of, socioeconomic status.

The choice of a particular index of each component item was based, in part, on the kinds of data available in census reports and, in part, on the expected uses to which the socioeconomic data would be put. Family income, rather than the income of the chief income recipient, was chosen because it was felt that the socioeconomic status of a family was related more closely to the family income of the chief earner. Multiple earners, for example, permit the purchase of more consumption goods. In the process of developing the family income scores, the effect of measuring family income in different ways (simple family income, per capita family income, and family income adjusted for differences in the composition of the family) was studied. The available data showed that the effect of the adjustments on a person's socioeconomic score was generally minor, and this fact argued for maintaining the simple measure of family income.

The scores assigned to the categories of the component items were derived by calculating midpoints of cumulative percentage intervals for the chief income recipient's education and occupation, and family income, as outlined for occupation earlier, and then averaging the three component scores.

It would have been possible to "build in" to the scores for items, or the summary socioeconomic measure, adjustments for differences among socioeconomic groups in age, residence, and other demographic characteristics. This was not done because it was felt that often these items would be the subjects of socioeconomic analysis and, where it was deemed important for other types of analysis, the desired adjustments could be made in the tabulation process.

It was pointed out that combination of the three component items into the summary measure was on the basis of simple averaging of the three scores. Consideration was given to differential weighting of the component items; however, at the time this measure was developed, there was no adequate basis for establishing internal weights. Moreover, there is no independent criterion of socioeconomic status against which these scores can be regressed.

Another way of viewing the multiple-item approach being used is to say that the education and family income scores help in refining the occupational score by accounting for some of the variation in status among individuals within an occupational category.

It should be noted that the scores for each of the component items are distributed so that about 10 percent of the persons in the population fall in each tenth of the distribution of the item. In the case of the summary socioeconomic scores, however, larger percentages of persons are generally found in the central part of the distribution and smaller percentages are at the extremes (Nam and Powers, 1965).

An objection, sometimes raised with regard to the derivation of multiple-item socioeconomic indexes, is that the components of such indexes not only are frequently of a different sort but also each may place the subject being studied at different status levels. One response to such an objection is that (a) socioeconomic status is basically an attribute of individuals which is broader in concept than any one measurable characteristic and a multiple-item approach can, therefore, more closely approximate the attribute, and (b) the extent of similarity or dissimilarity of two or more indicators of status in itself is a meaningful aspect of one's socioeconomic profile and analytically separate from the overall status level.

The notion of status inconsistency is well established in the social science literature. It is used to refer to disparities among statuses in varying situations (e.g., characteristics of different groups or aggregates, characteristics of different individuals, or different characteristics of the same individual). It seems appropriate to have such a measure that can be used with census data.

The fundamental approach that was developed at the Bureau in generating the status consistency type was to compare the percentile scores for the three component items of the overall status measure. Determination of consistency or inconsistency, and the nature of inconsistency, was based on a discrepancy of 20 or fewer percentile points between pairs of items. This level of discrepancy was chosen, after inspection of sample data showing variations in distributions, as representing a critical dividing line.

Thirteen status consistency types were derived which identified different specific patterns of inconsistency (such as occupation and income consistent, education high).

Issues for the Future

There are several key issues concerning the measurement of SES from U. S. Census data which should be treated in the coming decade. Three of them require particular attention.

First is the issue of occupational classification. From a socioeconomic perspective, many of the detailed occupational categories reported by the Census Bureau are too heterogeneous to permit the appropriate scale values to be assigned. This is especially true of managerial, proprietor, and farming occupations, for which the size of establishment is quite critical in defining the socioeconomic level of the occupation. The Census of Great Britain, among others, provides a model for meaningful classification in this regard. The new occupational classification system of the 1980 U.S. Census relies even less than previously on socioeconomic criteria for distinctions. Moreover, the new coding and categorization schemes differ so much from those of earlier years that historical comparisons will be seriously impaired.

Second, where variables such as education and income

are used to gauge the status level of occupations or where multiple-item measures of class are developed, it will be necessary to produce a defensible scheme for weighting the component items. In the absence of a suitable criterion for validating SES, weighting schemes should be based on the internal relationships among component items and the contribution which each makes to the overall SES measure. With regard to estimating occupational status from U. S. Census data, the relative contributions of education and income have been changing over time (Terrie, 1979). The variance in years of school completed has been narrowing as compared to that of income. Yet, it may be that other indicators of education or credentials, such as the type and quality of training for occupations, continue to be quite variable. If so, we need to obtain census information on these other dimensions.

Third, more attention should be given to the population categories for whom status is determined. It has been traditional to base the measurement of SES on the characteristics of males or the principal earner in the family. Starting with the 1970 Census data, the Nam-Powers occupational status scores were derived independently for men, women, and both sexes combined (Nam, et al., 1975; Powers and Holmberg, 1978). As sex differences in occupational structure diminish, occupational scales common to both sexes will be more common. However, because of multiple earners and various status determiners in family units, there is a growing need for family or household SES measures which consider the contributions of all members.

Above all, continuing examination of the way we measure socioeconomic status and its relationship to the real world of social stratification is an absolute necessity if we are to capture what has been and will likely continue to be, one of the pervasive features of all societies.

REFERENCES

Blau, Peter M., and Otis Dudley Duncan
  1967 The American Occupational Structure. New York:
        John Wiley.
Blishen, Bernard R.
  1958 The construction and use of occupational class
        scale.   Canadian   Journal   of   Economics   and
        Political Science. 24: 519-531.

Broman, Sarah H., Paul L. Nichols, and Wallace A.
    Kennedy
  1975 Preschool IQ: Prenatal and Early Developmental
        Correlates. New York: John Wiley.
Chiricos, Theodore G., and Gordon P. Waldo
  1975 Socioeconomic status and criminal sentencing: an
        empirical assessment of a conflict proposition.
        American Sociological Review 40: 753-772.
Counts, G. S.
  1925 The social status of occupations: a problem in
        vocational guidance. School Review 33: 16-27.
Duncan, Otis Dudley
  1961 A socioeconomic index for all occupations. In
        Albert J. Reiss, Jr.   Occupations and Social
        Status. New York: The Free Press of Glencoe.
Duncan, Otis Dudley, David L. Featherman, and Beverly
    Duncan
  1972 Socioeconomic Background and Achievement.   New
        York: Seminar Press.
Edwards, Alba M.
  1917 Social-economic groups of the United States.
        Quarterly Journal of the American Statistical
        Association. 15: 643-644.
Featherman, David L., and Robert M. Hauser
  1976 Prestige or socioeconomic scales in the study of
        occupational achievement?   Sociological Methods
        and Research. 4: 402-422.
Gerth, H. H., and C. Wright Mills
  1958 From Max Weber: Essays in Sociology. New York:
        Oxford University Press.
Goldthorpe, John, and Keith Hope
  1972 Occupational grading and occupational prestige.
        In John Goldthorpe and Keith Hope, eds.   The
        Analysis of Social Mobility: Methods and
        Approaches. Oxford: Clarendon Press.
Haug, Marie R.
  1977 Measurement in social stratification.   Annual
        Review of Sociology. 3: 51-77.
Hodge, Robert W., Paul M. Siegel, and Peter H. Rossi
  1964 Occupational prestige in the United States, 1925-
        63. American Journal of Sociology. 70: 286-302.
Hollingshead, August B., and Frederick C. Redlich
  1958 Social Class and Mental Illness: A Community
        Study. New York: John Wiley.
Hunt, William C.
  1897 Workers at gainful occupations at the federal
        censuses of 1870, 1880, and 1890. Bulletin of the
        Department of Labor, No. 11.

Myrianthopoulos, N. C., and K. S. French
  1968   An application of the U. S. Bureau of the Census
         socioeconomic index to a large diversified patient
         population. Social Science and Medicine. Vol. 2.
Nam, Charles B., and Mary G. Powers
  1965   Variations in socioeconomic structure by race,
         residence, and the life cycle. American
         Sociological Review. 30: 97-103.
Nam, Charles B., and Mary G. Powers
  1968   Changes in the relative status level of workers in
         the United States, 1950-1960. Social Forces. 47:
         158-170.
Nam, Charles B., Mary G. Powers, and Paul C. Glick
  1964   Socioeconomic characteristics of the population:
         1960. Current Population Reports, Series P-23,
         No. 12.
Nam, Charles B., John LaRocque, Mary G. Powers, and Joan
      Holmberg
  1975   Occupational status scores: stability and
         change. Proceedings of the American Statistical
         Association, Social Statistics Section.
North, C. C., and P. K. Hatt
  1947   Jobs and occupations: a popular evaluation.
         Opinion News. 9: 3-13.
Powers, Mary G., and Joan J. Holmberg
  1978   Occupational status scores: changes introduced
         by the inclusion of women. Demography 15: 183-
         204.
Siegel, Paul M.
  1971   Prestige in the American Occupational Structure.
         Unpublished Ph.D. dissertation. University of
         Chicago.
Terrie, E. Walter
  1979   Dimensions of Occupational Status Change in the U.
         S., 1960 to 1970. Unpublished Ph.D. disserta-
         tion. Florida State University.
Treas, Judith, and Andrea Tyree
  1979   Prestige versus socioeconomic status in the
         attainment processes of American men and women.
         Social Science Research 8: 201-221.
U. S. Bureau of the Census
  1963   Methodology and Scores of Socioeconomic Status.
         Working Paper No. 15. Washington: Bureau of the
         Census.
Webster's Third New International Dictionary
  1976   Springfield: G & C Merriam Co.

Bernard R. Blishen, William K. Carroll

3. Socioeconomic Measures from Canadian Census Data

The purpose of this paper is three-fold: 1) to briefly review the work completed so far on the socioeconomic ranking of occupations in Canada; 2) to describe the results obtained when these measures are used to analyse certain features of Canadian society; and 3) to outline the plans for the construction of a socioeconomic scale based on the forth-coming 1981 census of the Canadian labour force.

Existing Theory and Research

In the construction of these socioeconomic measures in Canada the influence of Weber's conception of class is clear. Both Marx and Weber sought to link stratification to the socioeconomic system. For Marx class categories are based

> on a group's relationship to the means of produc-
> tion, resulting in a structural division, at the
> broadest level, between capital and labour
> (Haug, 1977:52).

Haug (1977) suggests that Weber's conception is the one more widely used and accepted as the basis for studies of strati-fication.

Weber sought to distinguish between economic position, which he called class, and two other types of stratification, status and party, which share a reciprocal relationship with class position. The class order creates the status order by providing income which is spent on goods and services accord-ing to a certain style of life which is shared by others in the same class position. The similarity in lifestyle gener-ates various forms of interaction between individuals, who develop a degree of consensus and social solidarity which can be used to protect their distinctive style of life and their economic position. Thus, the status order reacts upon the

43

class system. Besides the class and status orders there
exist parties which seek power to influence and direct community action regardless of whether this action has an
economic or social basis. This power order could affect the
rules governing economic action even when such power has a
social rather than an economic base.

From Weber it is possible to derive a number of stratification variables besides these three. Haug (1977) has
suggested that both theory and current practice argue that
occupation be selected as the most feasible single indicator
of relative position in a multiple social stratification
system. Treiman (1977) has reviewed past attempts in different countries and agrees that occupation is the most adequate
as well as the most comparable indicator in all but heavily
agricultural societies. The Canadian scales constructed so
far are based upon the assumption that the stratification
system in modern industrial societies is determined by all
the elements mentioned, but the prime determinant is occupation. Nonetheless, as Haug (1977) points out, the selection of occupations as the prime indicator of socioeconomic
position does not address the question of how and by what
criteria occupations are to be evaluated in order to rank
them. Following Weber's idea that class has an economic
base, occupations can be ranked in terms of the education and
income of their incumbents. But occupations are also strati-
fied on the basis of their social standing. Thus, prestige--
the public's estimate of the social standing of occupations--
can also be used as a ranking criterion. Reiss (1961) suggests that prestige may be related to income and education.
As he says,

> . . . a man qualifies himself for occupational life
> by obtaining an education; as a consequence of pur-
> suing his occupation he obtains income. Occupation
> therefore, is the intervening activity linking
> income to education. If we categorize an occupation
> according to the prevailing levels of education and
> income of its incumbents, we are not only estimating
> its "social status" and its "economic status," we
> are also describing one of its major "causes" and
> one of its major "effects." It would not be sur-
> prising if an occupation's "prestige" turned out
> to be closely related to one or both of these
> factors (1961:116-117).

Achieved status on an occupational hierarchy is affected
by ascribed statuses, such as ethnic status. Such statuses
are those roles to which an individual is assigned on the
basis of characteristics over which he has no control. All

such statuses are assigned to individuals without reference
to their innate abilities. Some result from being born into
a family, as in the case of ethnicity. Many are correlated;
in other words, they are not randomly assorted. For example,
white, anglo-saxon and protestant are a set of correlated
statuses. In certain situations, however, a particular
ascribed status may be salient in terms of the individual's
actions in that situation.

In Canadian society ethnic differences are supported by
a tradition of ethnic pluralism, particularly with respect
to the two dominant groups, the French and the English. As
well, ethnic differences of immigrants to Canada increasingly
add to ethnic diversity. Ethnic status thus becomes salient
in social interaction. People who share the same ethnic
status tend to interact with each other more than with others
of a different ethnic status. Particularly in the case of
more recent immigrants to Canada, the enduring effect of
ethnic status and interaction on socioeconomic position
requires investigation.

A great deal of work has been done on the measurement of
social stratification. Haug (1977) has thoroughly reviewed
the development of scales in the United States, Canada, and
Great Britain. The construction of the Canadian scales will
be briefly reviewed here in order to provide a perspective
on their current application and their future development.

In Canada, Jacob Tuckman constructed the first socioeconomic scale (1947). This work was based on only twenty-
five occupations ranked on prestige by a selected group of
college students and job applicants. In 1958, Blishen (1958)
constructed a socioeconomic measure in which 343 occupations
listed in the 1951 census were ranked on the basis of the
standard scores derived from mean income and mean education
of the incumbents of each occupation in the census listing.
A later attempt to develop a prestige scale of occupations
in Canada was made by Peter C. Pineo and John Porter (1967)
who ranked a list of occupational titles on the basis of the
average evaluation of each title made by a national sample of
the population. At the same time that Porter and Pineo
(1967) published the results of their study, Blishen (1967)
published a revised version of his earlier scale based on
1961 census data for the male labour force. In the later
version of his scale, Blishen (1967) used the Pineo-Porter
prestige scores of occupations which corresponded to those
used in the 1961 census, along with their income and education characteristics to construct a regression equation. The
regression weights were then applied to 320 occupations in
the male labour force listed in the census thereby producing

a socioeconomic score for each. Blishen and McRoberts
(1976), following the same method used to construct the 1961
scale, published a revised scale for 480 occupations based on
1971 census data for the male labour force.

In his unpublished analysis of the dynamics of the
vertical mosaic for the period 1951-71, Carroll (1977)
revised Blishen's 1951 scale to make it comparable with the
1961 and 1971 scales. As noted earlier the 1951 scale was
constructed without using the Pineo-Porter prestige scale.
From this latter scale 64 occupations were chosen which
matched occupations in the 1951 Blishen scale, and were
treated as cases in a multiple regression which included
their prestige scores as the dependent variable, and their
average income and years of schooling as independent variables. The methodology is equivalent to that employed in
developing the 1961 and 1971 Blishen scales, except that
averages rather than proportions above a certain level are
the indicators of the prevailing levels of income and education in the occupations. Using the resulting equation,
socioeconomic scores for each of the male occupations in the
1951 census were derived and compared with the existing 1951
scores. The two scales were highly correlated with a Pearson
correlation of 0.996 which indicates that the scales are for
all pratical purposes identical.

One of the criticisms levelled at many of the socioeconomic scales is that they are based on male labour force
data only. As Haug (1977) points out, this practice ignores
the fact that a number of occupations such as nurse and
social worker are predominantly female in composition. Despite this female predominance they are scaled on the basis of
certain characteristics of the minority of the male incumbents. In the construction of his 1951 scale Blishen (1958)
attempted to meet this problem by including predominantly
female occupations. Where an occupation for either sex had a
proportion of incumbents of less than one-tenth of the incumbents of the occupation for the opposite sex it was omitted.
The final scale included a number of occupations that were
repeated, once for females and once for males. In his 1961
scale Blishen included only those occupations reported in the
male labour force, regardless of the fact that some of them
were predominantly female in composition on the assumption
"that the family's social status is dependent upon the occupation of the husband rather than the wife when both are
working" (1958:42). However, in her review of the literature
on measurement in social stratification Haug (1977) casts

some doubt on the cross-sex validity of measure-
ments of stratification based on male prestige,

education and income data, particularly in countries
with high proportions of women in the work force as
is currently the case in the United States   (1977:72).

An associated problem that has emerged in the development of socioeconomic measures is the prestige differences
between male dominated and female dominated occupations.   In
the United States, Bose (1973) reports that the evaluation of
prestige does vary by sex, but Treiman and Terrell (1975)
argue for the invariance of occupational prestige by sex,
stating that the sex of the rater has no effect on the evaluation of occupational prestige; that occupations with both
male and female titles tend to receive similar evaluations
when included in the same prestige scale; and that occupations identified as female got much the same ranking as those
not so identified.

Recently, in Canada, Guppy and Siltanen (1977), in a
limited regional study, compared the "Allocation of Male and
Female Occupational Prestige," and suggested that

> females in female dominated occupations receive
> lower prestige in the overall occupational hierarchy,
> but receive higher esteem as members of an appro-
> priate female occupation. Males, on the other hand,
> receive lower prestige in female dominated occupa-
> tions as well as receiving lower esteem in terms of
> being in an occupation considered to be inappro-
> priate for a male   (1977:320).

It appears from this study that

> men and women in the same occupation do not share
> the same allocation of prestige or esteem. The
> effects of the sex of the worker and the sex com-
> position of the occupation on the social evaluation
> of occupations are sufficient to warrant the use of
> separate scales for male and female occupational
> prestige. Given the difference in male and female
> occupational prestige, coupled with the differences
> in male/female earnings and education, a female
> based occupational status scale is essential if
> researchers are to continue the use of occupational
> status scales in their analysis of social stratifi-
> cation   (1977:329).

Following this study, Blishen and Carroll (1978)
developed a female based occupational scale which uses the
same methodology as that used by Blishen and McRoberts (1976)
in the construction of the male based occupational scale.

They derived "female socioeconomic scores for the 465 census
occupational categories having female incumbents in 1970"
(1978:353). They show "a very strong relationship between
male and female socioeconomic scores (r=.843)". As they
point out,

> This result is not surprising since the separate
> scales consist of combinations of income and edu-
> cational levels for men and women which best predict
> the common criterion, occupational prestige (1978:
> 355).

Another socioeconomic measure based on Canadian census
data is the one constructed for use in the Canadian Mobility
Study. For this study a socioeconomic classification of
occupations was constructed. This is an alternative arrange-
ment of the unit groups which are the "fundamental particle"
of the code for tabulations emerging out of the 1971 Canadian
census. Thousands of occupations listed in the Canadian
Classification and Dictionary of Occupations (1971) are
pooled into 486 unit groups. These unit groups are combined
into sixteen groups on the basis of what Pineo, Porter and
McRoberts (1977) claim is "an informed assessment" of the
social standing (or occupational prestige) of the occupation
(1977:97). These researchers claim that this classification
appears "to cover the male labour force well," but

> the coverage for women is less adequate--collapsing
> and regrouping are required if the code is to serve
> well as a measure of the occupational distribution
> of the female labour force (1977:100).

Recently Jones (1980) has shown that skill is an important dimension of the socioeconomic classification constructed
by Pineo, Porter and McRoberts. He notes

> that the Blishen Scale, whose education component
> represents employment practices rather than an
> independent assessment of skills associated with
> occupations, can serve as a surrogate indicator
> for skill (1980:182).

He goes on to say

> that the Blishen scale captures general skills,
> that is, formal education, better than occupational-
> ly specific skills (1980:182).

The Use of Socioeconomic Scales

The scales that were constructed by Blishen using 1951, 1961, and 1971 Census data were extensively used as an explanatory variable in many areas of social, political and economic study. They have been used less frequently as a dependent variable in studies which attempt to explain the effect of social variables on socioeconomic status. Perhaps the most important of these are concerned with the view that Canada is a vertical mosaic of ethnic groups: a view most cogently expressed by the late John Porter (1965), who showed that until 1961 the socioeconomic rank order of ethnic groups in Canada had persisted over time. He showed that the British have high occupational status. The Germans, Scandinavians, and Dutch are nearest to the British in their occupational levels. The Italians, Polish, Ukrainians, and groups from Southeast Europe occupy the lower end of the occupational spectrum while the French are between the last and the groups from Northern Europe (1965).

Following Porter's (1965) analysis, Blishen (1970) sought to provide more details on the nature of the Canadian mosaic. Using six classes based on his 1961 socioeconomic scale he showed that when ethnic groups are ranked according to their mean socioeconomic score, between 1951 and 1961 the Jewish and British groups maintained their rank position of first and second respectively; the position of the French and Italian groups worsened, while the Native Indians retained the lowest rank order. He also showed that the post World War II immigrant inflows into Canada tended to bolster the existing socioeconomic distribution of immigrants. For example, post World War II immigrants from the United States and to a lesser extent immigrants from Britain locating in the Atlantic provinces or Quebec were over-represented at the highest socioeconomic levels to a greater extent than the native-born. In Ontario and the West, the Canadian-born fared better but again, immigrants from the United States and Britain fared better still.

Despite the evidence presented by Porter (1965) and Blishen (1970), Darroch (1980) reexamines the main cross-sectional evidence used by Porter and Blishen and suggests that their interpretation of a persisting ethnic mosaic in Canada

> may seriously exaggerate both the generality and the strength of the relationship between ethnic status and socioeconomic status (1980:203-204).

His reinterpretation of the evidence indicates "that occupational differences have systematically declined over time" (1980:225).

Carroll (1977) also contends that ethnicity is not as important as others have claimed in explaining differences in socioeconomic status. He found that for the thirteen largest ethnic groups, ethnicity explains 4.0 percent of the variance in socioeconomic status in 1951, 4.2 percent in 1961, and only 2.6 percent in 1971. In general, the percentage of the variance in socioeconomic status explained by ethnicity is small and decreasing. This finding appears to correspond to the interpretation provided by Darroch (1980). Carroll takes Blishen's (1970) earlier claim based on 1961 census data, that post-war immigration has contributed to a continuance of ethnic stratification in Canada, and indicates that by excluding immigrants from the analysis of the 1971 census data, the proportion of the variance in socioeconomic status attributable to ethnicity should decline below the 2.5 percent for the total population. He shows this to be the case: the variance drops to 1.6 percent indicating that immigration does contribute substantially to the observed pattern of ethnic stratification in 1971. Among immigrants a substantail percentage of the variance in socioeconomic status is explained by country of birth which explains 17.7 percent of the variance in socioeconomic status for immigrants who arrived in Canada between 1961 and 1970, 16.7 percent for immigrants who arrived between 1946 and 1960, and 3.4 percent for immigrants who came to Canada before 1946. In other words, a great deal of variation in socioeconomic status is explained by country of origin among recently arrived immigrants, but the variance decreases markedly as the length of time spent in Canada since immigration increases.

This analysis of these important features of Canadian society will be carried further when the results of the 1981 Canadian census are available. A socioeconomic scale of occupations based on the 1981 census data will be constructed in a fashion to be described later. This will allow us to compare the importance of ethnic and other social variables in the socioeconomic structure of Canada for a thirty year period from 1951 to 1981.

An important feature of this future analysis will be an examination of the significance of sex in the socioeconomic structure of this country. Using the female socioeconomic scale of occupations described earlier, Blishen and Carroll (1978) found that

women tend to be found in occupations having
high education levels, but receive generally
depressed incomes, while men are concentrated
in occupations having low education levels, but
are paid a good deal more than women   (1978:358).

As the authors point out,

Besides evidencing a general pattern of occupational differentiation that can only be described
as discriminatory to working women, our findings
caution against the exclusive use of occupationally
based socioeconomic indices--in the study of sexual
stratification   (1978:358).

We referred earlier to the Canadian Mobility Study for
which a socioeconomic classification of occupations was
developed.   The investigators analyse differences in intergenerational occupational mobility between Francophones in
Quebec and Anglophones in the rest of Canada which they find
are primarily the result of differences occurring in the distribution of the labour force of the two groups, and these
mobility differences have diminished to the extent that there
appears to be a convergence of mobility patterns between the
two populations especially for the most recent entrants into
the labour force.   In effect, the authors of this study
provide evidence of the diminishing importance of language in
socioeconomic stratification in Canada.

The Construction of a 1981 Socioeconomic Scale

As noted earlier, the Blishen scale will be revised when
1981 census data are available.

The method to be used in the construction of the 1981
scale will be the same as that used in the construction of
the 1961 and 1971 scales.   The percentage of males in each
occupation reported in the 1981 census whose real income is
the 1981 equivalent of $6,500 or over in 1971, and the per-
centage of those who have reached high school graduation or
higher will be calculated.   In addition to these income and
education variables for each occupation a prestige variable
will be used by assigning approximations of the Pineo-Porter
(1967) prestige scale scores to occupational titles.   Hodge,
Siegel and Rossi (1964) have shown that the prestige ranking
of occupations changes very little over time.   Consequently,
unless a more recent prestige ranking of occupations in
Canada is available before the development of the 1981 scale,
the regression equation will use the available Pineo-Porter

prestige scores. A regression equation will be constructed using as the dependent variable the prestige scores of as many of the Pineo-Porter (1967) occupational titles as correspond to the 1981 census occupational titles. The independent variables will be the corresponding income and educational levels of the same occupation. The resulting equation will be used to produce a socioeconomic score for each occupational title. Occupations will then be ranked on the basis of this score. A final step in the construction of the 1981 scale will be the determination of class intervals. They will be based upon the use of the tens digits of the scale value for each occupation which in 1961 and 1971 resulted in six classes.

Socioeconomic scores will be computed for occupations in the female labour force reported in the 1981 census using the same method used to construct the scale for occupations in the male labour force.

As well as national male and female occupational scales for 1981, regional scales will also be constructed using the same methodology. These regional or provincial scales are necessary because of the provincial differences in occupational distribution which are a reflection of "the unique politico-cultural process to be found in each of the ten Canadian provinces" (Mills, 1968:243). The regression equation for each provincial scale will use 1981 provincial income and education levels as the independent variables and the Pineo-Porter national prestige scale as the dependent variable.

These provincial scales will be used to determine provincial differences in the structure of the vertical mosaic.

References

Blishen, Bernard R.
>   1958   "The Construction and Use of An Occupational Class Scale." Canadian Journal of Economics and Political Science 24.

>   1967   "A Socio-economic Index for Occupations in Canada." Canadian Review of Sociology and Anthropology 4.

>   1970   "Social Class and Opportunity in Canada." Canadian Review of Sociology and Anthropology 7.

Blishen, Bernard R., and McRoberts, Hugh.
1976   "A Revised Socio-Economic Index for Occupations
in Canada." Canadian Review of Sociology and
Anthropology 13.

Blishen, Bernard R. and Carroll, William K.
1978   "Sex Differences In A Socioeconomic Index for
Occupations in Canada." Canadian Review of
Sociology and Anthropology 15.

Bose, C. E.
1973   "Jobs and Gender: Sex and Occupational Prestige." Research Report. Baltimore: Cen.
Metrop. Plann. Res., John Hopkins University.

Canada, Department of Manpower and Immigration.
1971   Canadian Classification and Dictionary of
Occupations, Vol. 1, Classification and Definitions; Vol. 2, Occupational Qualification
Requirements.

Carroll, William K.
1977   "How Vertical the Mosaic? An Empirical Analysis of Ethnic Stratification In Canada."
Mimeographed. Toronto: York University.

Darroch, A. Gordon
1980   "Another Look At Ethnicity, Stratification and
Social Mobility in Canada." In Ethnicity and
Ethnic Relations In Canada, edited by Jay E.
Goldstein and Rita M. Bienvenue. Toronto:
Butterworths.

Guppy, L. N., and Siltanen, J. L.
1977   "A Comparison of the Allocation of Male and
Female Occupational Prestige." Canadian Review
of Sociology and Anthropology 14.

Haug, Marie R.
1977   "Measurement in Social Stratification." Annual
Review of Sociology 3.

Hodge, R. W., Siegel, P. M., and Rossi, P. H.
1964   "Occupational Prestige In the United States,
1925-63." American Journal of Sociology 70.

Jones, Frank.
1980   "Skill as a Dimension of Occupational Classification." Canadian Review of Sociology and
Anthropology 17.

Mills, Donald L.
    1968   "The Occupational Composition of the Prairie
                Provinces: A Regional-National Comparison."
                Transactions of the Royal Society of Canada,
                Vol. VI.

Pineo, P. C., and Porter, John.
    1967   "Occupational Prestige In Canada." Canadian
                Review of Sociology and Anthropology 4.

Pineo, P. C., Porter, J., and McRoberts, H.
    1977   "The 1971 Census and the Socioeconomic Classi-
                fication of Occupations." Canadian Review of
                Sociology and Anthropology 14.

Porter, John.
    1965   The Vertical Mosaic. Toronto: University of
                Toronto Press.

Reiss, Albert J.
    1961   Occupations and Social Status. New York:
                The Free Press.

Treiman, D. J. and Terrell, K.
    1975   "Sex and the Process of Status Attainment: A
                Comparison of Working Women and Men." Ameri-
                can Sociological Review 40.

Treiman, D. J.
    1977   Occupational Prestige In Comparative Perspec-
                tive. New York: Academic Press.

Tuckman, Jacob.
    1947   "The Social Status of Occupations in Canada."
                Canadian Journal of Psychology, 1.

4. Occupational Status Scores: Changes Introduced by the Inclusion of Women

This paper compares occupational status scores based on the characteristics of the 1970 male experienced civilian labor force with a set of occupational status scores based on the characteristics of the 1970 total experienced civilian labor force, both men and women. The increased participation of women in the labor force and the concomitant changing sex composition of the work force suggest that the traditional approaches to the measurement of occupational status based solely on male incumbents may no longer be valid for examining the occupational hierarchy of contemporary American society.

Women in the Labor Force

The growth of the female segment of the labor force is not a new phenomenon. Increases in the proportion of the labor force who were women have been recorded each decade since 1900. By 1970, women comprised 38 percent of the total labor force or about thirty-one million workers (U.S. Bureau of the Census, 1973). By 1975, women made up 40 percent of the total experienced civilian labor force in the United States (St. Marie and Bedwerzik, 1976).

Most empirical studies of the increased participation of women in the labor force emphasize

This paper is a minor revision of one by the same title which appeared in Demography (May, 1978), pp. 183-204.

the extent and type of female labor force participation (Sweet, 1973; Waite, 1976) and the status
attainment of women (Oppenheimer, 1970 and 1973;
Tyree and Treas, 1974; Treiman and Terrell, 1975;
Featherman and Hauser, 1976). The findings of such
research, particularly findings of similarity with
respect to the process of status attainment have
been suspect because of the reliance on a male-
based measure of occupational status. The increased participation of women in labor force
activity impacts on the measurement of occupational
status. This paper examines changes in one measure
of occupational status as a result of including
women in the data base.

Occupational Status Measures

The review of previous work on the development and refinement of measures of occupational
status in the Introduction to this volume indicates
that essentially two approaches have been utilized.
One approach emphasizes the subjective dimension of
occupational status, and researchers using this
approach have secured from their respondents
"prestige" ratings of selected occupations. This
approach has characterized the work of a number of
social scientists but in recent decades has gained
recognition through various research activities
undertaken by the National Opinion Research Center
(Hodge,Siegel & Rossi, 1964;Reiss,et al 1961; Hatt,
1950). The second approach concentrates on the
objective dimension of occupational status. Investigators interested in this approach have developed occupational status scores for detailed
occupations based on the income and educational
characteristics of occupational incumbents. Otis
Dudley Duncan (1961) partially utilized this
approach to construct his socio-economic index.
Charles B. Nam and his associates at the Bureau of
the Census (1963b) employed this approach in the
measures of occupational status they developed as
part of a multivariate socio-economic status
score.

Researchers utilizing either approach have
consistently ignored the characteristics of women.
They have generally developed status measures
based on the male occupational experience and have
derived occupational status scores based on the
characteristics of the male labor force without con-

sidering the proportion of women engaged in labor
force activity or employed in a particular occupational stratum.

Changes in the composition of the labor force
are well documented, but there have been few
attempts to measure the impact of increased female
labor force participation on measures of occupational status. It is only within the past few
years that social scientists have seriously
attempted to compare the occupational hierarchies
of men and women. The empirical evidence produced
by such research indicates a high correlation between occupational status scores for men and
occupational status scores for women when either
subjective or objective criteria are used as the
basis of measurement. After reviewing such evidence, Treiman and Terrell (1975) concluded,
". . . there is a single occupational status hierarchy which holds for both male and female workers,
and hence, that the occupational attainment of men
and women legitimately can be compared by means of
a single occupational scale." The single scale
they suggest is based on male incumbents.

As McClendon (1976) noted, however, even
though occupational status structures for men and
women may be similar, that similarity results from
quite different patterns of concentration within
the occupational hierarchy. That is, women have
been concentrated in white-collar occupations,
particularly in clerical positions, and in blue-
collar service occupations (Oppenheimer, 1970;
1973). Concentration patterns have been noted also
among the male working population (Weisshoff, 1972),
but men tend to be more evenly distributed throughout the occupational structure than women (Table 1).

Although the current picture is still one of
concentration of a large segment of the female
labor force in relatively few occupations, there is
also evidence of a decline in job segregation
accompanying the increased participation of women
in the labor force (DeCesare, 1975; Garfinkel,
1975; Hedges and Bemis, 1974). It should be
possible to assign these women an occupational
status score which is derived from a data base
which recognizes their participation. Therefore,
we suggest that a single hierarchy of occupational
status scores be developed based on data for all

TABLE 1

DISTRIBUTION OF THE EXPERIENCED CIVILIAN LABOR
FORCE BY MAJOR OCCUPATIONAL CATEGORY AND
BY SEX, 1970

Occupation	Male	Female
Total	100.00	100.00
Professional,Tech. & Kind. Workers	14.12	15.31
Managers & Administrators,except Farm	10.89	3.55
Sales Workers	6.79	7.37
Clerical & Kind. Workers	7.54	34.44
Craftsmen & Kind. Workers	21.31	1.79
Operatives,except Transport	13.79	14.51
Transport Equipment Operatives	5.95	.46
Laborers, except Farm	6.93	1.01
Farmers & Farm Mgrs.	2.75	.24
Farm Laborers & Farm Foreman	1.72	.59
Service Workers,except Private Hshld.	8.10	16.58
Private Hshld Workers	.08	3.89
Unemployed Persons	.04	.28

Source: U.S. Bureau of the Census. 1970 Census of
Population: Occupational Characteristics.
Final Report PC(2)-7A. Table 1.

incumbents in the detailed occupational classification scheme. Insofar as the unit of analysis
in this research is the occupation, and the pre-
sumption is that some objective measure of status
may be attached to it, we feel that the measure is
best derived from the unweighted characteristics
of all incumbents--women, ethnic minorities, youth,
etc. The remainder of this paper will address some
of the above issues by examining one set of occupational scores based on 1970 data.

1970 Occupational Status Scores

Procedures for computing the occupational
status score utilized in this paper are those developed by Nam and his colleagues at the Census
Bureau in connection with preparatory work for the
1960 Census of Population (U.S. Bureau of the
Census, 1963b; Nam, Powers and Glick, 1964; Nam
and Powers, 1965). Later work on the occupational
component was continued by Nam and Powers (1968 and
Nam, et al., 1975).

The present paper extends the prior work of
Nam and Powers by comparing 1970 occupational
status scores for men with a set of occupational
status scores derived from the characteristics
of the 1970 total experienced civilian labor force,
both men and women. Both sets of scores range
from 0 to 99, with several occupations registering
identical status scores (Appendix A). When the
two sets of scores were compared, the resulting
Pearson r of +.98 indicated a high correlation
between the 1970 scores for men and the 1970
scores for the total population, both men and
women, in the experienced civilian labor force.
Because of the similar methodology utilized in
computing both sets of scores, such a high
correlation was to be expected, and is consistent
with the high correlation found between scores for
men and women based on other data (Treiman and
Terrell, 1975; Bose, 1973).

A further examination of the status scores
for each of the 589 detailed occupations demonstrated a tendency for the scores based on the
total civilian labor force to be higher than the
scores based solely on the male civilian labor
force. The mean difference between the two sets
of scores was +3 suggesting that the inclusion of

relatively large numbers of women who were concentrated in relatively fewer occupations than men
served to inflate the scores assigned higher status
occupations when the total labor force was the base
population. In general, the analysis of the
differences showed minor variations between scores
based on male incumbents and scores based on all
incumbents, except for thirty detailed occupations
which registered significant differences. For the
purpose of this study, a significant difference
was defined as a difference of two standard deviations or more, 12 or more points, from the mean
difference of +3. For twenty-six of the occupations showing significant differences, the scores
based on all incumbents were lower than scores
based on male incumbents. For the other four
occupations, the reverse situation occurred.

        Our examination of the twenty-six occupations
which registered significant negative score
differences indicates that most of them were
traditional female occupations, employing high
proportions of women. Because women are generally
paid less than men employed in the same occupation, it is not surprising that the median income
level of all twenty-six occupations dropped substantially when women were included in the base
population. In addition, for nineteen of the
twenty-six occupations the inclusion of women resulted in a decreased median educational level.
For seven occupations the educational level increased or remained the same when women were included in the base population. Overall, the range
of difference in the median education of men and
women in these 26 occupations was not as large
as the range of income differences. As a result
of large differences in the median income of men
and women in these 26 occupations, and the
relatively large proportion of women employed in
them, they received a significantly lower ranking
on the occupational hierarchy based on the characteristics of all incumbents than they did based on
the characteristics of male incumbents.

        Only four occupations recorded significant
positive differences. The occupation, "Teachers,
public pre-kindergarten and kindergarten," which
employed a high proportion of women in 1970 mani-
fested an increased median income and a similar
median education when they were included in the

base. The occupation, "Home Management Advisors,"
which was also a female dominated occupation in
1970, recorded a decreased median income but an
increased median education when women were added
to the data base. The occupation, "Laborers,
ordnance," which was a relatively integrated
occupation in 1970, registered both an increased
median income and increased median education when
female incumbents were added to the base population.
The male dominated occupation, "Laborers, blast
furnaces, steel works, rolling and finishing
mills," evidenced a decreased median income and a
similar median education with the inclusion of
female workers.

The analysis of the thirty occupations which
registered significant differences between the
scores based on the characteristics of the total
labor force and scores based solely on the characteristics of male incumbents points to the general
effect of including women in the calculations of
scores for the total list of detailed occupations.
The occupational concentration of women combined
with their generally lower income level served to
depress the scores of 26 predominantly "female"
occupations. This contributed to a general upgrading of the status position of the vast majority
of the detailed occupations. Essentially, the inclusion of women in the calculation of the occupational status score influenced the scores not only
by changing the scores of those occupations which
included large proportions of women, but by
changing the total alignment of the occupational
hierarchy. In doing so, the introduction of women
into the base population only slightly affected
the relative status position of most detailed
occupations, and had a relatively large impact on
a small number of occupations.

Weighted Average Occupational Status Scores

Although the detailed hierarchy of occupations is regarded as the best source for the
placement of individuals relative to one another,
many users concerned with ranking a sample or
client population by occupational status rely on
the major occupational groups. Therefore,
weighted average occupational scores for the two
population groups under consideration were also
computed for each of the major occupational groups

TABLE 2

WEIGHTED AVERAGE OCCUPATIONAL STATUS SCORES+

Occupation	Scores Based on Male CLF	Scores Based on Total CLF
Professional, Tech. & Kind. Workers	85	82
Managers, Administrators, except Farm	79	80
Sales Workers	66	55
Clerical & Kind. Workers	56	51
Craftsmen and Kind. Workers	49	55
Operatives except Transp.	33	33
Transport Equip. Operators	32	42
Laborers, except Farm	15	23
Farmers & Farm Managers	20	31
Farm Laborers & Farm Foreman	4	6
Service Workers	25	24
Private Hshld Workers	4	4

+Based on the Characteristics of the Total Experienced Civilian Labor Force and the Male Experienced Civilian Labor Force in the 1970 Census of Population

delineated by the U.S. Bureau of the Census in
1970 (Table 2). As expected from the strong
correlation observed between the two sets of
scores, a ranking of major occupational categories
based on weighted average scores for the total
experienced civilian labor force produced a
ranking similar to that obtained from weighted
scores for the male population. The category,
"Professional, Technical and Kindred Workers," received the highest ranking in each population
group. "Managers and Administrators" ranked second.
The lower status occupational groups also maintained similar positions whether based on men or
on all workers. "Service Workers" ranked immedi-
ately below "Farmers and Farm Managers," followed
by "Laborers," "Farm Laborers and Foremen" and
"Private Household Workers," respectively.

Some important difference also must be
noted. Differences in the rank accorded sales
workers, clerical workers and craftsmen occurred
when the base shifted from male workers to all
workers. Based on the weighted score for men,
sales workers ranked third, followed by clerical
workers and then craftsmen. Based on the weighted
score for the total experienced civilian labor
force, sales workers and craftsmen registered
identical status scores and hence similar ranking.
Clerical workers ranked below these two categories.
These shifts in ranking reflect the impact of including female workers in the construction of
scores. Women were over-represented among sales
and clerical workers in 1970 and their median income was several thousand dollars below that of men
employed in sales and clerical occupations. The
inclusion of women, who were concentrated in lower
level positions within each of these two major
occupational groups, served to diminish the status
positions of these occupations while at the same
time influencing the higher ranking of craftsmen,
a major occupational category made up of occupations in which women were significantly under-
represented in 1970. This is consistent with the
suggestion of some students of stratification in
the United States that the differences which remain between craftsmen and clerical workers, if
any, are relatively small.

The different ranking assigned operatives
and transport equipment operatives in each popu-

lation group also indicates the impact of including
data for women in the calculation of the scores.
Only a small proportion of women were employed in
transport equipment occupations in 1970, whereas a
much larger proportion was engaged in occupations
within the operatives category. Given the generally lower income received by women, the presence
of a large number of women in the operative category and their relative absence among transport
equipment operatives influenced the lower ranking
of operatives and the higher ranking of transport
equipment operatives when the total experienced
labor force was used as the base population.

Conclusions and Implications

As indicated earlier in this paper, the
status of an occupation traditionally has been derived from the characteristics of the male incumbents. Status scores based on the characteristics of the total experienced civilian labor force,
which were discussed in this paper, were highly
correlated with a set of scores derived from the
characteristics of the male segment of the labor
force. Such a correlation has limited value, however. A comparison of occupational status scores
based on data for men with scores based on data
for the total labor force indicated important
differences among specific detailed occupations
as well as at the level of the major occupational
groups. The scores derived from the data for all
incumbents reflect the different patterns of concentration by sex and the different income and
educational levels of men and women in the experienced civilian labor force and thus are more
valid objective measures of the status of occupations than scores based solely on the characteristics of men in the labor force.

These findings are of special theoretical and
methodological significance for research on: (1)
the relation between occupation and class, (2) the
assignment of socio-economic status to married
women and to families, and (3) the processes of
status attainment. Occupation and social class
are frequently linked in the literature on social
stratification. Occupation is the most frequent
indicator of social class. Indeed the terms are
occasionally used synonymously as in identifying
the working class with blue-collar occupations and

the middle class with white-collar occupations.
Social class continues to be a difficult and elu-
sive concept, however, and its relation to the
occupational structure is open to investigation.
Some recent research on the occupational composition of social classes is illustrative
(Vanneman, 1977; Wright, 1977).

Using data from the 1969 Institute of Social
Relations Survey of Working Conditions, Wright
approximated an operational definition of social
class as conceptualized in Marxian terms and derived five social classes. He then investigated
the relationship between those five classes and the
twelve broad occupational categories traditionally
defined. Because only twelve broad categories
were used, it is not surprising that he found
different class levels within occupational categories. The twelve categories are known to be
heterogeneous with respect to the characteristics
of incumbents, complexity of task performed, etc.
Wright's findings suggest that the ranking of broad
occupational categories based on data for all incumbents is more theoretically valid than the traditional ranking which placed all clerical and sales
workers above craftsmen. Moreover, detailed occupational categories ranked in terms of the socioeconomic characteristics of all incumbents would
permit greater specification of the relationship between class and occupation.

A second area of research for which the
findings in this paper have important implications
concerns the use of occupation as an index of
social class for women and their families. When
occupation has been used to estimate the social
class position of women or their families, the
characteristics of women generally have been
ignored and they have been assigned the status
level of male family heads. At an earlier time
when relatively few women were in the labor force,
it may have been empirically valid to assign all
family members the status of the male family head.
In view of the fact that women are now a significant part of the occupational and class hierarchies, it is time to re-examine this practice and
to evaluate their contribution to the social class
position of their families (Acker, 1973; De Jong,
et al., 1971; Haug, 1973). If occupation is used
as an index of class position and if husbands and

wives tend to be of the same occupational status
level, it might be redundant to include an index
of occupational status for both. It is, therefore,
important to investigate the extent to which the
occupational status levels of husbands' and wives'
are similar or different. Attempts to do so have
been hampered by the need to resort to broad occupational categories. As noted in one such study,
the distinctions found between husbands and wives
occupational levels might be due to the use of
broad and heterogeneous occupational categories
(Haug, 1973: 88). The occupational status hierarchy in Appendix A would contribute to a more
refined method of allocating status by making
available a single occupational status hierarchy
for detailed occupations based on data for all incumbents. The same set of scores could be used to
compare husbands' and wives' occupational status.
It is conceivable that families may be comprised
of individuals with different status levels. Indeed, this is an area worthy of investigation and
it may be time to test our assumption that all
family members have the same status.

These findings also have important implications for research on status attainment. Several
studies have reported that the average occupational status level for men and women in the
United States is approximately equal, and that the
process of status attainment is similar for both
men and women (Treiman and Terrell, 1975;
Featherman and Hauser, 1976; McClendon, 1976).
These findings appear to contradict the well-
known disparity in earnings by sex. Because of
this, there is a need to re-evaluate the measure
of socio-economic status used. The measure used
in most of the research has been Duncan's Socioeconomic Index, which is based on the characteristics of the male labor force. Although the
methodological problems of applying such scores to
women have been addressed (McClendon, 1976), they
have not been resolved. Substantively different
conclusions about the status attainment process
might be reached if an alternate measure, which
incorporates data for women, were used.

Appendix A

Table A-1.   Occupational Status Scores Based on the Character-
istics of the Male Experienced Civilian Labor Force and on the
Characteristics of the Total Experienced Labor Force: United
States, 1970.

| | Scores Based On | |
Occupation	Male Incumbents	All Incumbents
Professional, technical, and kindred workers		
Accountants	88	89
Architects	95	97
Computer specialists		
Computer programmers	84	89
Computer systems analysts	91	93
Computer specialists, n.e.c. (not elsewhere classified)	91	93
Engineers		
Aeronautical and astronautical	96	96
Chemical	96	97
Civil	93	95
Electrical and electronic	94	95
Industrial	91	93
Mechanical	94	95
Metallurgical and materials	95	96
Mining	92	94
Petroleum	95	96
Sales	93	94
Engineers, n.e.c.	93	94
Farm management advisors	90	94
Foresters and conservationists	70	78
Home management advisors	58	77
Lawyers and judges		
Judges	98	99
Lawyers	98	99
Librarians, archivists, and curators		
Librarians	72	75
Archivists and curators	72	80
Mathematical specialists		
Actuaries	97	94
Mathematicians	97	96
Statisticians	91	88
Life and physical scientists		
Agricultural	87	91
Atmospheric and space	95	95
Biological	91	91
Chemists	92	94
Geologists	97	97
Marine	95	96
Physicists and astronomers	98	99
Life and physical, n.e.c.	97	97
Operations and systems researchers and analysts	88	91
Personnel and labor relations workers	89	89
Physicians, dentists, and related practitioners		
Chiropractors	93	95
Dentists	98	99
Optometrists	98	99
Pharmacists	93	94
Physicians, medical and osteopathic	99	99
Podiatrists	98	99
Veterinarians	98	99
Health practitioners, n.e.c.	87	94
Registered nurses, dietitians, and therapists		
Dietitians	51	56
Registered nurses	62	66
Therapists	72	73

Table A-1, continued

Occupation	Scores Based On	
	Male Incumbents	All Incumbents
Health technologists and technicians		
Clinical laboratory technologists and technicians	68	70
Dental hygienists	85	70
Health record technologists and technicians	55	68
Radiologic technologists and technicians	70	64
Therapy assistants	61	54
Health technologists and technicians, n.e.c.	64	63
Religious workers		
Clergymen	68	77
Religious workers, n.e.c.	61	59
Social scientists		
Economists	95	96
Political scientists	97	98
Psychologists	96	96
Sociologists	93	94
Urban and regional planners	91	95
Social scientists, n.e.c.	91	91
Social and recreation workers		
Social workers	80	82
Recreation workers	57	58
Teachers, college and university		
Agriculture	95	97
Atmospheric and Space	94	96
Biology	95	96
Chemistry	95	97
Physics	94	97
Engineering	97	98
Mathematics	92	95
Health specialties	98	96
Psychology	97	96
Business and commerce	95	95
Economics	97	98
History	93	95
Sociology	93	94
Social science teachers, n.e.c.	95	96
Art, Drama, and Music	91	92
Coaches and physical education	91	94
Education	98	98
English	91	91
Foreign language	91	89
Home economics	96	87
Law	98	99
Theology	88	91
Trade, industrial and technical	89	90
Miscellaneous teachers, college and university	92	94
Teachers, college and university, subject not specified	89	87
Teachers, except college and university		
Adult education	84	81
Elementary school		
Public	79	80
Private	67	66
Prekindergarten and kindergarten		
Public	52	72
Private	55	47
Secondary school		
Public	85	86
Private	75	77
Teachers, except college and university, n.e.c.	64	52
Engineering and science technicians		
Agriculture and biological technicians, except health	60	65
Chemical technicians	72	79
Draftsmen	73	80

Table A-1, continued

| | Scores Based On | |
| | Male | All |
Occupation	Incumbents	Incumbents
Electrical and electronic engineering	76	82
Industrial engineering	74	79
Mechanical engineering	80	86
Mathematical	81	86
Surveyors	61	72
Engineering and science technicians, n.e.c.	67	77
Technicians, except health, engineering, and science		
Airplane pilots	93	94
Air traffic controllers	84	85
Embalmers	65	75
Flight engineers	89	91
Radio operators	57	60
Tool programmers, numerical control	83	87
Technicians, n.e.c.	67	79
Vocational and educational counselors	91	92
Writers, artists, and entertainers		
Actors	64	71
Athletes and kindred workers	54	56
Authors	89	90
Dancers	47	40
Designers	87	89
Editors and reporters	89	86
Musicians and composers	45	49
Painters and sculptors	81	77
Photographers	69	75
Public relations men and publicity writers	90	91
Radio and television announcers	59	71
Writers, artists, and entertainers, n.e.c.	80	80
Research workers, not specified	88	86
Professional, technical, and kindred workers, n.e.c.-- allocated	76	72
Managers and administrators, except farm		
Assessors, controllers, and treasurers; local public administration	71	67
Bank officers and financial managers	89	90
Buyers and shippers, farm products	60	65
Buyers, wholesale and retail trade	79	78
Credit men	81	80
Funeral directors	75	85
Health administrators	91	90
Construction inspectors, public administration	72	77
Inspectors, except construction; public administration		
Federal public administration and postal service	79	84
State public administration	69	77
Local public administration	68	74
Managers and superintendents, building	61	55
Office managers, n.e.c.	83	81
Officers, pilots and pursers, ship	62	63
Officials and administrators; public administration, n.e.c.		
Federal public administration and postal service	92	92
State public administration	84	88
Local public administration	77	79
Officials of lodges, societies, and unions	82	86
Postmasters and mail superintendents	78	78
Purchasing agents and buyers, n.e.c.	82	87
Railroad conductors	68	69
Restaurant, cafeteria, and bar managers	63	56
Sales managers and department heads, retail trade	76	74
Sales managers, except retail trade	92	94
School administrators, college	97	97
School administrators, elementary and secondary	97	97

Table A-1, continued

Occupation	Scores Based On	
	Male Incumbents	All Incumbents
Managers and administrators, n.e.c., salaried		
Construction	81	81
Durable goods manufacturing	92	93
Nondurable goods, including not specified manufacturing	90	92
Transportation	81	85
Communications, utilities, and sanitary services	86	88
Wholesale trade	86	88
Retail trade		
Hardware, farm equipment, and building material retailing	76	82
General merchandise stores	78	79
Food stores	70	70
Motor vehicles and accessories retailing	74	80
Gasoline service stations	45	53
Apparel and accessories stores	81	77
Furniture and home furnishings and equipment stores	82	84
Other retail trade	76	79
Finance, insurance, and real estate	91	92
Business and repair services	87	89
Personal services	71	62
All other industries	90	91
Managers and administrators, n.e.c., self-employed		
Construction	67	69
Durable goods manufacturing	69	72
Nondurable goods, including not specified manufacturing	81	83
Transportation	65	67
Communications, utilities, and sanitary services	73	71
Wholesale trade	76	78
Retail trade		
Hardware, farm equipment, and building material retailing	73	75
General merchandise stores	68	60
Food stores	44	44
Motor vehicles and accessories retailing	73	75
Gasoline service stations	50	57
Apparel and accessories stores	80	74
Furniture and home furnishings and equipment stores	73	74
Other retail trade	66	63
Finance, insurance, and real estate	93	93
Business and repair services	71	75
Personal services	60	53
All other industries	74	74
Managers and administrators, except farm--allocated	67	67
Sales workers		
Advertising agents and salesmen	86	86
Auctioneers	68	69
Demonstrators	64	31
Hucksters and peddlers	41	28
Insurance agents, brokers, and underwriters	82	86
Newsboys	11	12
Real estate agents and brokers	84	81
Stock and bond salesmen	95	95
Salesmen and sales clerks, n.e.c.		
Sales representatives, manufacturing industries	86	88
Sales representatives, wholesale trade	76	81
Sales clerks, retail trade		
General merchandise stores	44	32
Food stores	30	24
Apparel and accessories stores	37	34
Other sales clerks, retail trade	45	37

Table A-1, continued

Occupation	Scores Based On	
	Male Incumbents	All Incumbents
Salesmen, retail trade	61	65
Salesmen of services and construction	77	67
Sales workers--allocated	44	34
Clerical and kindred workers		
Bank tellers	50	49
Billing clerks	56	48
Bookkeepers	64	52
Cashiers	32	29
Clerical assistants, social welfare	51	49
Clerical supervisors, n.e.c.	83	79
Collectors, bill and account	55	61
Counter clerks, except food	45	37
Dispatchers and starters, vehicle	62	63
Enumerators and interviewers	48	40
Estimators and investigators, n.e.c.	81	76
Expediters production controllers	70	72
File clerks	41	41
Insurance adjusters, examiners, and investigators	80	83
Library attendants and assistants	42	44
Mail carriers, post office	64	71
Mail handlers, except post office	39	41
Messengers, including telegraph and office boys	23	28
Meter readers, utilities	46	56
Office machine operators		
Bookkeeping and billing machine	51	47
Calculating machine	54	52
Computer and peripheral equipment	63	67
Duplicating machine	42	46
Keypunch	60	49
Tabulating machine	51	56
Office machine, n.e.c.	42	44
Payroll and timekeeping clerks	64	57
Postal clerks	66	68
Proofreaders	70	54
Real estate appraisers	88	91
Receptionists	44	43
Secretaries	66	56
Shipping and receiving clerks	41	50
Statistical clerks	66	59
Stenographers	81	58
Stock clerks and storekeepers	42	49
Teacher aides, except school monitors	42	37
Telegraph operators	64	67
Telephone operators	49	44
Ticket, station, and express agents	70	74
Typists	48	46
Weighers	40	44
Industry		
Manufacturing	67	57
Transportation, communications, and other public utilities	65	61
Wholesale and retail trade	44	41
Finance, insurance, and real estate	53	51
Professional and related services	47	29
Public administration	63	59
All other industries	51	41
Clerical and kindred workers--allocated	54	39

Table A-1, continued

Occupation	Scores Based On	
	Male Incumbents	All Incumbents
Craftsmen and kindred workers		
Automobile accessories installers	35	43
Bakers	24	34
Cabinetmakers	30	41
Carpet installers	41	51
Construction craftsmen		
Brickmasons and stonemasons	35	46
Bulldozer operators	23	34
Carpenters	33	42
Cement and concrete finishers	21	32
Electricians	66	70
Excavating, grading, and road machine operators,except bulldozers	30	41
Floor layers, except tile setters	41	48
Painters, construction, and maintenance	18	32
Paperhangers	28	39
Plasterers	33	42
Plumbers and pipe fitters	57	62
Roofers and slaters	18	32
Structural metal craftsmen	58	61
Tile setters	42	50
Cranemen, derrickmen, and hoistmen	39	46
Decorators and window dressers	53	46
Dental laboratory technicians	60	61
Electric power linemen and cablemen	66	70
Engravers, except photoengravers	46	50
Foremen, n.e.c.		
Construction	60	62
Manufacturing		
Metal industries	70	71
Machinery, except electrical	75	76
Electrical machinery, equipment, and supplies	78	78
Transportation equipment	77	77
Other durable goods	65	65
Food and kindred products	61	63
Textiles, textile products,and apparel	50	48
Other nondurable goods, including not specified manufacturing	78	72
Transportation	66	67
Communications, utilities, and sanitary services	76	77
Wholesale and retail trade	65	67
All other industries	65	66
Furniture and wood finishers	22	30
Furriers	44	46
Glaziers	50	56
Inspectors, scalers, and graders; log and lumber	26	36
Inspectors, n.e.c.	61	66
Jewelers and watchmakers	49	53
Locomotive engineers	69	69
Locomotive firemen	69	72
Mechanics and repairmen		
Air conditioning, heating, and refrigeration	54	61
Aircraft	68	72
Automobile body repairmen	37	47
Automobile mechanics	36	45
Data processing machine repairmen	78	85
Farm implement	33	44
Heavy equipment mechanics, including diesel	50	57
Household appliance and accessory installers and mechanics	50	58
Loom fixers	18	30

Table A-1, continued

	Scores Based On	
Occupation	Male Incumbents	All Incumbents
Office machine	61	69
Radio and television	56	60
Railroad and car shop	43	50
Mechanics, except auto, apprentices	53	60
Miscellaneous mechanics and repairmen, including mechanics, except auto, apprentices	52	58
Not specified mechanics and repairmen	51	56
Metal craftsmen, except mechanics		
Blacksmiths	26	37
Boilermakers	51	56
Forgemen and hammermen	42	48
Heat treaters, annealers, and temperers	47	53
Job and die setters, metal	50	54
Machinists	57	62
Millwrights	60	62
Molders, metal	30	38
Pattern and model makers, except paper	70	72
Rollers and finishers, metal	47	52
Sheetmetal workers and tinsmiths	59	63
Shipfitters	52	58
Tool and die makers	70	73
Millers; grain, flour, and feed	14	27
Motion picture projectionists	39	50
Opticians and lens grinders and polishers	62	61
Piano and organ tuners and repairmen	44	54
Power station operators	71	75
Printing craftsmen		
Bookbinders	52	40
Compositors and typesetters	61	64
Electrotypers and stereotypers	65	68
Photoengravers and lithographers	73	75
Pressmen and plate printers, printing	60	63
Shoe repairmen	11	18
Sign painters and letterers	39	48
Stationary engineers	60	64
Stone cutters and stone carvers	20	33
Tailors	22	28
Telephone installers and repairmen	68	74
Telephone linemen and splicers	60	69
Upholsterers	22	33
Craftsmen and kindred workers, n.e.c.	45	49
Former members of the armed forces	38	42
Craftsmen and kindred workers--allocated	36	44
Operatives, except transport		
Asbestos and insulation workers	58	61
Assemblers	41	41
Blasters and powdermen	26	36
Bottling and canning operatives	26	22
Chainmen, rodmen, and axmen; surveying	35	44
Checkers, examiners, and inspectors; manufacturing	42	47
Clothing ironers and pressers	12	11
Cutting operatives, n.e.c.	28	33
Dressmakers and seamstresses, except factory	12	18
Drillers, earth	36	44
Dry wall installers and lathers	45	51
Dyers	16	29
Garage workers and gas station attendants	19	20
Graders and sorters, manufacturing	20	17

Table A-1, continued

Occupation	Scores Based On	
	Male Incumbents	All Incumbents
Produce graders and packers, except factory and farm	04	05
Laundry and drycleaning operatives, n.e.c.	15	14
Meat cutters and butchers, except manufacturing	47	54
Meat cutters and butchers, manufacturing	31	33
Meat wrappers, retail trade	20	29
Metalworking operatives, except precision machine		
Filers, polishers, sanders, and buffers	19	30
Furnacemen, smeltermen, and pourers	35	43
Heaters, metal	42	49
Metal platers	37	45
Punch and stamping press operatives	37	40
Riveters and fasteners	26	28
Solderers	26	29
Welders and flame cutters	41	49
Milliners	27	19
Mine operatives, n.e.c.		
Coal mining	25	35
Crude petroleum and natural gas extraction	41	48
Mining and quarrying, except fuel	31	42
Mixing operatives	33	43
Oilers and greasers, except auto	31	41
Packers and wrappers, except meat and produce	25	24
Painters, manufactured articles	25	36
Photographic process workers	53	51
Precision machine operatives		
Drill press operatives	39	42
Grinding machine operatives	47	52
Lathe and milling machine operatives	53	59
Precision machine operatives, n.e.c.	53	56
Sailors and deckhands	23	36
Sawyers	08	19
Sewers and stitchers	11	14
Shoemaking machine operatives	08	15
Stationary firemen	38	45
Textile operatives		
Carding, lapping, and combing operatives	07	17
Knitters, loopers, and toppers	17	19
Spinners, twisters, and winders	09	16
Weavers	12	22
Textile operatives, n.e.c.	11	19
Winding operatives, n.e.c.	50	42
Industry		
Manufacturing		
Durable goods		
Lumber and wood products, except furniture	10	19
Furniture and fixtures	10	17
Stone, clay, and glass products		
Glass and glass products	42	44
Cement, concrete, gypsum, and plaster products	17	31
Other stone, clay, and glass products	21	32
Primary metal industries		
Blast furnaces, steel works, and rolling and finishing mills	44	51
Other primary iron and steel industries	27	37
Primary nonferrous industries	39	45
Fabricated metal industries, including not specified metal		
Cutlery, hand tools, and other hardware	26	32
Fabricated structural metal products	23	34
Screw machine products and metal stamping	26	32
Miscellaneous fabricated metal products and not specified metal	33	39

Table A-1, continued

Occupation	Scores Based On	
	Male Incumbents	All Incumbents
Machinery, except electrical		
Farm machinery and equipment	37	44
Construction and material handling machines	51	57
Metalworking machinery	52	54
Office and accounting machines and electronic computing equipment	54	50
Other machinery, except electrical	43	47
Electrical machinery, equipment, and supplies		
Household appliances	37	41
Radio, T.V., and communication equipment	52	46
Electrical machinery, equipment, and supplies, n.e.c.	40	40
Not specified electrical machinery, equipment and supplies	45	40
Transportation equipment		
Motor vehicles and motor vehicle equipment	49	52
Aircraft and parts	53	58
Other transportation equipment	29	38
Professional and photographic equipment and watches	50	43
Ordnance	70	46
Miscellaneous manufacturing industries	21	22
Durable goods--allocated	32	36
Nondurable goods		
Food and kindred products		
Meat products	20	19
Dairy products	38	46
Canning and preserving fruits, vegetables,and seafoods	08	09
Bakery products	24	31
Beverage industries	41	45
Other food and kindred products	21	30
Tobacco manufacturers	18	20
Apparel and other fabricated textile products		
Apparel and accessories	12	15
Miscellaneous fabricated textile products	09	16
Paper and allied products		
Pulp, paper, and paperboard mills	52	56
Miscellaneous paper and pulp products	40	38
Paperboard containers and boxes	27	33
Printing, publishing, and allied industries	44	41
Chemicals and allied products		
Industrial chemicals	60	65
Synthetic fibers	43	49
Soaps and cosmetics	49	41
Other chemicals and allied products	54	57
Petroleum and coal products	65	68
Rubber and miscellaneous plastic products		
Rubber products	48	48
Miscellaneous plastic products	32	29
Leather and leather products		
Tanned, curried, and finished leather	14	24
Footwear, except rubber	11	17
Leather products, except footwear	14	15
Nondurable goods--allocated	25	24
Not specified manufacturing industries	24	26
Nonmanufacturing industries		
Construction	30	32
Railroads and railway express service	19	32
Transportation, except railraods	52	57
Communications, utilities, and sanitary services	50	56
Wholesale trade	20	24
Retail trade	20	24
Business and repair services	29	37

Table A-1, continued

	Scores Based On	
Occupation	Male Incumbents	All Incumbents
Public administration	45	51
All other industries	24	28
Operatives, except transport--allocated	16	22
Transport equipment operatives		
Boatmen and canalmen	27	37
Bus drivers	36	40
Conductors and motormen, urban rail transit	60	63
Deliverymen and routemen	38	48
Fork lift and tow motor operatives	27	38
Motormen; mine, factory, logging camp, etc.	28	37
Parking attendants	18	25
Railroad brakemen	61	65
Railroad switchmen	60	65
Taxicab drivers and chauffeurs	26	35
Truck drivers	31	41
Transport equipment operatives--allocated	21	34
Laborers, except farm		
Animal caretakers, except farm	20	25
Carpenters' helpers	06	14
Construction laborers, except carpenters' helpers	13	24
Fishermen and oystermen	07	16
Freight and material handlers	25	35
Garbage collectors	08	22
Gardeners and groundkeepers, except farm	06	14
Longshoremen and stevedores	29	40
Lumbermen, raftsmen, and woodchoppers	04	12
Stock handlers	19	19
Teamsters	08	19
Vehicle washers and equipment cleaners	10	15
Warehousemen, n.e.c.	40	49
Industry		
Manufacturing		
Durable goods		
Lumber and wood products, except furniture	05	13
Furniture and fixtures	05	14
Stone, clay, and glass products		
Cement, concrete, gypsum, and plaster products	16	28
Structural clay products	06	17
Other stone, clay, and glass products	25	35
Primary metal industries		
Blast furnaces, steel works, and rolling and finishing mills	28	43
Other primary iron and steel industries	20	30
Primary nonferrous industries	28	40
Fabricated metal industries, including not specified metal	17	24
Machinery, except electrical	28	38
Electrical machinery, equipment, and supplies	27	32
Transportation equipment		
Motor vehicles and motor vehicle equipment	29	40
Ship and boat building and repairing	18	29
Other transportation equipment	21	32
Professional and photographic equipment and watches	25	28
Ordnance	21	37
Miscellaneous manufacturing industries	06	13

Table A-1, continued

	Scores Based On	
Occupation	Male Incumbents	All Incumbents
Manufacturing, durable goods--allocated	07	15
Nondurable goods		
Food and kindred products		
Meat products	16	23
Dairy products	33	34
Canning and preserving fruits, vegetables, and seafoods	05	10
Grain-mill products	13	26
Beverage industries	14	27
Other food and kindred products	06	16
Tobacco manufacturers	05	11
Textile mill products		
Yarn, thread, and fabric mills	05	13
Other textile mill products	06	15
Apparel and other fabricated textile products	08	14
Paper and allied products		
Pulp, paper, and paperboard mills	38	49
Other paper and allied products	18	25
Printing, publishing, and allied industries	18	18
Chemicals and allied products	31	40
Petroleum and coal products	36	48
Rubber and miscellaneous plastic products	29	35
Leather and leather products	06	14
Nondurable goods--allocated	03	09
Not specified manufacturing industries	12	21
Nonmanufacturing industries		
Railroads and railway express service	13	26
Transportation, except railroads	17	28
Communications, utilities, and sanitary services	13	25
Transportation, communications, utilities, and sanitary services--allocated	03	07
Wholesale trade	07	14
Retail trade	08	10
Business and repair services	14	20
Personal services	02	03
Public administration	07	19
All other industries	08	13
Laborers, except farm--allocated	07	15
Farmers and farm managers		
Farmers, owners and tenants	19	31
Farm managers	43	52
Farmers and farm managers--allocated	09	18
Farm laborers and farm foremen		
Farm foremen	22	34
Farm laborers, wage workers	02	04
Farm laborers, unpaid family workers	13	15
Farm service laborers, self-employed	30	37
Farm laborers and farm foremen--allocated	01	02
Service workers, except private household		
Cleaning service workers		
Chambermaids and maids, except private household	14	05
Cleaners and charwomen	07	09
Janitors and sextons	10	19
Food service workers		
Bartenders	36	42

Table A-1, continued

Occupation	Scores Based On	
	Male Incumbents	All Incumbents
Busboys	13	12
Cooks, except private household	18	14
Dishwashers	09	07
Food counter and fountain workers	17	17
Waiters	24	19
Food service workers, n.e.c.	16	15
Health service workers		
Dental assistants	40	41
Health aides, except nursing	34	38
Health trainees	35	42
Lay midwives	20	34
Nursing aides, orderlies, and attendants	32	28
Practical nurses	43	44
Personal service workers		
Airline stewardesses	68	69
Attendants, recreation and amusement	25	24
Attendants, personal service, n.e.c.	27	31
Baggage porters and bellhops	24	30
Barbers	31	40
Boarding and lodging housekeepers	33	25
Bootblacks	00	02
Child care workers, except private household	32	23
Elevator operators	12	21
Hairdressers and cosmetologists	46	35
Housekeepers, except private household	48	36
School monitors	40	30
Ushers, recreation and amusement	16	15
Welfare service aides	47	38
Protective service workers		
Crossing guards and bridge tenders	07	18
Firemen, fire protection	69	74
Guards and watchmen	32	43
Marshals and constables	52	60
Policemen and detectives		
Public	71	77
Private	54	59
Sheriffs and bailiffs	58	65
Service workers, except private household--allocated	11	15
Private household workers		
Child care workers, private household	10	10
Cooks, private household	06	02
Housekeepers, private household	06	03
Laundresses, private household	06	00
Maids and servants, private household	02	02
Private household workers--allocated	05	01

References

Acker, Joan, "Women and Social Stratification: A
    1973   Case of Intellectual Sexism." <u>Amer-</u>
               <u>ican Journal of Sociology</u>. 78:936-945.

Bose, Christine E., <u>Jobs and Gender: Sex and Occu-</u>
    1973   <u>pational Prestige</u>. Baltimore: Johns
               Hopkins University, Center for Metro-
               politan Planning and Research.

De Cesare, Constance B., "Changes in the Occupa-
    1975   tional Structure of U.S. Jobs,"
               <u>Monthly Labor Review</u>, 98:23-24.

De Jong, Peter Y. M. Brawer and S. Robin, "Patterns
    1971   of Female Intergenerational Mobility:
               A Comparison with Male Patterns of
               Intergenerational Mobility." <u>American</u>
               <u>Sociological Review</u>, 36:1033-1042.

Duncan, Otis D., "A Socioeconomic Index for All
    1961   Occupations," in <u>Occupations and</u>
               <u>Social Status</u> by Albert J. Reiss, Jr.,
               Otis D. Duncan, Paul K. Hatt, and
               Cecil C. North, New York: The Free
               Press of Glencoe, 109-138.

Garfinkel, Stuart H., "Occupations of Women and
    1975   Black Workers." <u>Monthly Labor Review</u>,
               98: 25-35.

Featherman, David L. and Robert H. Hauser, "Sex-
    1976   ual Inequalities and Socioeconomic
               Achievement in the U.S., 1962-1973."
               <u>American Sociological Review</u>, 41:
               <u>462-483</u>.

Hatt, Paul K., "Occupation and Social Stratifi-
    1950   cation." <u>American Journal of Soci-</u>
               <u>ology</u>, LV: 533-543.

Haug, Marie., "Social Class Measurement and
    1973   Women's Occupational Roles." <u>Social</u>
               <u>Forces</u>, 52:86-98.

Hedges, Janice M. and Stephen E. Bemis, "Sex
    1974   Stereotyping: Its Decline in the
               Skilled Trades." <u>Monthly Labor</u>
               <u>Review</u>,97:14-22.

Hodge, Robert W., Paul M. Siegel, and Peter H.Rossi,
    1964   "Occupational Prestige in the
                  United States, 1925-1963." Ameri-
                  can Journal of Sociology, 70:286-302.

McClendon, McKee J., "The Occupational Attainment
    1976   Processes of Males and Females."
                  American Sociological Review, 41:52-64.

Nam, Charles B. and Mary G. Powers, "Changes in the
    1968   Relative Status Level of Workers in
                  the United States, 1950-1960."
                  Social Forces, 48: 158-77.

Nam, Charles B. and Mary G. Powers, "Variations
    1965   in Socioeconomic Structure by Race,
                  Residence and the Life Cycle."
                  American Sociological Review, 30:
                  97-103.

Nam, Charles B., Mary G. Powers, and Paul C. Glick,
    1964   "Socioeconomic Characteristics of
                  the Population: 1960." Current
                  Population Reports, Series P23,
                  No. 12, Washington, D.C.: Govern-
                  ment Printing Office.

Nam, Charles B., John LaRocque, Mary G. Powers,
        and Joan J. Holmberg, "Occupational
    1975   Status Scores: Stability and
                  Change." Proceedings of the Social
                  Statistics Section of the American
                  Statistical Association. pp. 570-75.

Oppenheimer, Valerie K., The Female Labor Force in
    1970   the United States: Demographic and
                  Economic Factors Governing the
                  Growth and Changing Composition.
                  Berkeley, California: University
                  of California Press.

Oppenheimer, Valerie K., "Demographic Influence of
    1973   Female Employment and the Status
                  of Women." American Journal of
                  Sociology, 78:946-961.

Reiss, Albert J., Jr., Otis D. Duncan, Paul K.
        Hatt, and Cecil C. North, Occupations and
    1961   Social Status. New York: The Free
                  Press of Glencoe.

Sweet, James A., Women in the Labor Force. New
    1973   York: Seminar Press.

St. Marie, Stephen M, and Robert W. Bedwerzik,
    1976   "Employment and Unemployment During
                1975."Monthly Labor Review, 99:11-20.

Treiman, Donald J. and Kermit Terrell, "Sex and
    1975   the Process of Status Attainment:
                A Comparison of Working Women and
                Men." American Sociological Review,
                40:174-200.

Tyree, Andrea and Judith Treas, "The Occupational
    1974   Mobility of Women." American Socio-
                logical Review, 39:293-302.

U.S. Bureau of the Census. Census of Population:
    1963a   1960 Subject Reports. Occupational
                Characteristics. Final Report PC
                (2)-7A. Washington, D.C.: U.S. Gov-
                ernment Printing Office.

U.S. Bureau of the Census. Methodology and Scores
                of Socioeconomic Status. Working
    1963b   Paper No. 15. Washington, D.C.:
                U.S. Government Printing Office.

U.S. Bureau of the Census. 1970 Census of the
    1973   Population. Subject Reports. Occu-
                pational Characteristics. Final
                Report PC(2)7A. Washington, D.C.:
                U.S. Government Printing Office.

Vanneman, Reeve, "The Occupational Composition of
    1977   American Classes." American Journal
                of Sociology, 82:783-808.

Waite, Linda, "Working Wives: 1940-1960." American
    1976   Sociological Review, 41:65-80.

Wright, Erik Olin, "Class Structure and Occupa-
    1977   tion: A Research Note." University of
                Wisconsin, Institute for Research
                on Poverty, Discussion Paper No. 415-
                77.

Weisshoff, Francine B., "Women's Place in the
    1972   Labor Market." The American Economic
                Review, 62:161-66.

5. A Revised Socioeconomic Index of Occupational Status: Application in Analysis of Sex Differences in Attainment

Duncan's (1961) Socioeconomic Index (SEI) for occupations was originally constructed in an attempt to provide proxy "prestige" scores for detailed census occupational titles lacking a prestige rating in the 1947 North-Hatt Prestige Study (see Reiss, 1961). Duncan estimated these SEI scores by using a regression equation predicting occupational prestige from two major occupational attributes: 1950 education and 1949 income levels. Since the production of these "socio-economic"--or proxy prestige--scores, various prestige scales have become available incorporating most occupational titles (e.g., Siegel, 1971). Subsequently, systematic comparisons of the scale and metric properties of "prestige" and "socioeconomic" indices of occupations suggested that the two are not substantively identical. Indeed, Featherman, Jones, and Hauser (1975) argued that the SEI was the preferred index of the occupational hierarchy in metric analyses of occupational attainment processes; in that context, prestige scores of occupations were interpreted as "error-prone" proxies of the occupational attributes more faithfully reflected in the Duncan SEI (Featherman and Hauser, 1976b).

In this paper, we offer a revised version of the Duncan SEI. There are several reasons for doing so. The first and

We thank Professors Charles Nam and Mary Powers for providing their special tabulations from the 1970 census, Richard Janosik for preparing initial computer files and Mary Balistreri and David Dickens for additional analysis. Computer services were provided by the Center for Demography and Ecology, funded by PRC Grant No. 5P01-HD058760. Other support was provided by a grant from the N.I.A. No.A484600 144 Q736-4. This is reprinted from a chapter in Social Structure and Behavior, R. M. Hauser et al. (eds.), ©1982 by Academic Press, Inc.

most obvious lies in the passage of time since the original
construction of the scale. Not only has the occupational
classificatory scheme been altered since then, but the educational and income characteristics of the American labor
force--the two dimensions underlying the socioeconomic index--
have shifted since 1950. The two decades may also have seen
a shift in the relations between the educational and income
attributes of an occupation and its social standing (or
prestige). (There is also the possibility that the prestige
ranking of occupations may have changed over time. However
numerous studies have demonstrated that prestige rankings
are largely invariant over time, e.g., Hodge, Siegel, and
Rossi, 1964.) Second, the original construction of the SEI
rested on the educational and income characteristics of the
male labor force, rather than the total of men and women in
the labor force. We therefore offer two contemporary versions
of the Duncan SEI: one based on the educational and income
attributes of the male labor force and a second based on the
educational and income attributes of the total labor force.
Third, in the process of revising the socioeconomic index,
we also investigate whether or not certain arbitrary deci-
sions in the construction of the original scale served to
vest the Duncan index with some artifactual properties that,
as has been argued, have desirable consequences for the
analysis of occupational stratification vis-a-vis analysis
based on popular "prestige" indexes (e.g., Featherman and
Hauser, 1976; Treas and Tyree, 1979). In a set of alternative revisions of the Duncan SEI, we show that these desirable consequences for research are retained when based on
less arbitrary methods.

Finally, we use the revised and updated indexes to compare the occupational attainment processes for men and women
in middle adulthood. The conclusions one reaches regarding
sex differences are highly dependent on the scale and metric
properties on the index one uses. Contrasts are most
striking between prestige and socioeconomic indexes.

The 1950 Socioeconomic Index For All Occupations

The socioeconomic scores published in 1961 by Duncan
are the predicted scores from a regression equation linking
occupational prestige to educational and income levels. The
measure of occupational prestige was constructed using the
proportion of "good" and "excellent" ratings of occupation
titles by persons responding to the North-Hatt Prestige Study
carried out by the National Opinion Research Center (NORC)
in 1947. Duncan used the percentage of "good" and "excellent" ratings as the prestige measure--rather than the
weighted summation of all prestige ratings (i.e., the NORC

Prestige score) because it provided a scale with a greater
range that appeared to magnify the intermediate portion of
that range (Duncan, 1961:119). The educational measure con-
sisted of the age-standardized proportion of males within
each occupation with 4 or more years of high school in 1950,
and the income measure, the age-standardized proportion of
males with incomes of $3500 or more in 1949. The regression
procedure was based on the 45 occupation titles common to
the NORC study and the 3-digit 1950 census occupational
classificatory system. Without attempting to update the
relative educational and income characteristics of occupations to reflect change after 1950, or to incorporate alterations in the relative "prestige" or popular evaluation
of occupational titles, Blau and Duncan (1967) and Hauser
and Featherman (1977: Appendix B) reconciled the SEI scores
for 1950 occupational categories with changes in the 3-digit
census classificatory system in 1960 and 1970 respectively.
In effect, these transformations merely provided SEI scores
for the later occupational classificatory systems without
incorporating current information about the levels of and
relationships between occupational income, education and
prestige. Thus, while SEI scores are now available for
1970-basis census titles, they are tied to the relationships
found 30 years ago between occupational education, income
and prestige.

Updating of the 1950 Socioeconomic Index Using 1970-Basis Occupational Characteristics

Our updating of the 1950 SEI scores was guided by an
attempt to maintain close comparability between the 1950-
basis SEI scores and the revisions. As a result, we followed
the procedures used by Duncan (1961), with alterations introduced only when we felt it expedient to take advantage of
additional information available in 1970, or when it was not
possible or desirable to replicate Duncan's method exactly.
Published characteristics of occupations (e.g., U.S. Bureau
of the Census, 1973) proved an insufficient source of data
owing to the unavailability of a personal income (versus
earnings) measure. Existing 1-in-100 and 1-in-1000 public
use tapes were too limited by sample size to estimate occupational levels of education and income for detailed occupational titles.[1] Our computation of the 1970-basis socioeconomic index was made possible by special tabulations of

---

[1]Personal income was a sample item--asked of only a
fraction of all residents in 1970--further reducing the den-
sity of data for occupations represented in the public use
samples.

full 1970 census records that had been prepared by the Bureau
of the Census for other purposes.[2] These special tabulations
were necessary in order to move our analysis toward an exact
replication of Duncan's method of computation.

In the production of an updated version of the 1950
socioeconomic scores, we used three approaches. First, we
experimented with differing measures of the independent
variables, occupational income and education levels, and
examined their impact on the regression equation predicting
the SEI. Second, we reconstructed the dependent variable,
occupational prestige, to provide a closer approximation to
the criterion measure used by Duncan. Third, we reestimated
the SEI prediction equations, restricting the analysis to
the subset of occupation titles used by Duncan.

We experimented with four combinations of differing
income and educational measures to cope with the changing
income and educational characteristics of the American labor
force between 1950 and 1970. The first pair of measures,
"PTEDHS" and "PTIN5," are directly equivalent to the measures
used by Duncan. "PTEDHS" refers to the percentage of men
and women in an occupation with four or more years of high
school; "PTIN5," to the percentage with 1969 incomes of
$5,000 or more ($3500 adjusted for inflation by the consumer
price index). The second set of measures, "PTEDSC" and
"PTIN10," corresponds to Duncan's measures in that these
measures cut off approximately the same proportions of the
educational and income distributions in 1970 as Duncan's
measures did for the 1950 labor force: "PTEDSC" refers
to the percentage of men and women with one or more years of
college while "PTIN10" refers to the percentage of men and
women with incomes of $10,000 or more. Finally, the third
set, "PMEDSC" and PMIN10," refers to the percentage of men--
rather than both men and women--with one or more years of
college, and incomes of $10,000 or higher, respectively.

We obtained our first prestige measure from Siegel
(1971). These prestige scores are the result of the merging
of popular prestige ratings (i.e., weighted summations of
"excellent," "good," "average," etc. categories) from three
distinct social surveys: The 1963 replication of the 1947
NORC study, the 1964 Hodge-Siegel-Rossi study, and the 1965
supplementary study. The prestige ratings from these three
studies were first combined by means of regression analysis

---

[2]Professors Charles B. Nam and Mary Powers kindly made
these data available.

linking prestige ratings for occupational titles common to
two or more of these studies, translated into a common metric,
and then transformed into scores for all detailed 1960 census
occupational titles (Siegel, 1971: Ch. 2). These prestige
scores were then reconciled with 1970 census occupational
titles, using procedures outlined in Hauser and Featherman
(1977: Ch. 2).

For our second prestige measure, we approximated the
occupational prestige measure used by Duncan: The percentage of "good" and "excellent" ratings accruing to each
occupational title in the 1947 NORC prestige study. Unfortunately, although Siegel's scores were derived from a
weighted summation of the prestige categories, it was not
possible for us to separate the categories. We were,
therefore, unable to replicate Duncan's prestige measure
in the strictest sense. However, the 1947 NORC prestige
scores and the prestige measure used by Duncan are closely
linked; this relationship can be approximated by a third-
order equation (see Duncan, 1961:119, for a graphic illus-
tration). Therefore, we could estimate the proportion of
"good" and "excellent" ratings by working on the presump-
tion that the 1947 NORC prestige scores and the 1971 Siegel
prestige scores are analogous measures of prestige. We
first specified the relationship between the percentage
of "good" and "excellent" ratings (obtained from Reiss, 1961)
and Siegel's prestige scores for the 45 occupations for
which both measures existed, and then predicted the proportion of "good" and "excellent" ratings for all 1970 occupational titles using the relationship:

$$\text{PGOOD} = -2.575 \text{ PRESTIGE} + .09715 \text{ PRESTIGE}^2$$

$$- .00068 \text{ PRESTIGE}^3 + 25.20338; \ (R^2 = .987).$$

The first set of regression analyses are based on 426
occupation titles from the 1970 census occupational classification. Thirteen titles were not included. Of these 13,
11 were "allocated" categories (i.e., census returns with
no occupational entry are allocated during computer processing); the twelfth is the "unemployed" category; and
the thirteenth title, "former members of the armed forces,"
was omitted since it refers by convention to currently
unemployed individuals whose last occupation was in the
armed forces. The second set of regression analyses is
based on those occupational titles used by Duncan (1961).
Unfortunately of the forty-five 1960 titles used by Duncan,

Table 1. Prediction Equations for Estimating Revised Socioeconomic Scores for Occupations.

Dependent variable[a]	Independent variables[a]	N	Metric coefficients			Standardized coefficients			Standard error of estimate	β_{inc}/β_{ed}	Estimated SEI score[a]
			b_{inc}	b_{ed}	constant	β_{inc}	β_{ed}	R			
1. PRESTIGE	PTIN5, ptedhs	426	.157	.448	2.393	.238	.707	.842	8.700	.34	
2. PRESTIGE	PTIN10, ptedhs	426	.246	.378	10.329	.353	.600	.861	8.210	.59	
3. PRESTIGE	PTIN10, ptedsc	426	.165	.343	25.695	.237	.679	.865	8.105	.35	(TSEI1)
4. PRESTIGE	PTIN10, pmedsc	426	.229	.292	23.866	.336	.578	.864	8.133	.58	(MSEI1)
5. PGOOD	PTIN5, ptedhs	426	.204	.756	-23.599	.192	.739	.844	13.964	.26	
6. PGOOD	PTIN10, ptedhs	426	.386	.628	-12.578	.343	.614	.869	12.865	.56	
7. PGOOD	PTIN10, ptedsc	426	.232	.589	12.795	.206	.723	.883	12.204	.29	(TSEI2)
8. PGOOD	PMIN10, pmedsc	426	.338	.508	9.730	.307	.623	.881	12.313	.49	(MSEI2)
9. PRESTIGE	PTIN10, ptedsc	42	.328	.316	21.605	.443	.565	.927	7.478	.78	
10. PRESTIGE	PMIN10, pmedsc	42	.404	.248	19.544	.550	.445	.931	7.478	1.24	
11. PGOOD	PMIN10, pmedsc	42	.429	.599	5.399	.489	.518	.941	10.599	.94	(MSEI3)
12. PGOOD	PMIN3.5, pmedhs	45	.59[b]	.59[b]	-6.0[b]	.47[c]	.51[c]	.91[b]	15.5[b]	.92[c]	(DUNCAN)
13. PRESTIGE	PMIN5, pmedhs	323	--	--	--	.313[c]	.602[c]	.853[c]	--	.52[c]	

[a] See text for definitions of labels. [b] SOURCE: Duncan, 1961. [c] SOURCE: Siegel, 1971.

only 42 could be closely matched with 1970 occupational
titles.[3]

The results from these alternative specifications are
presented in Table 1.

The indicators used in the first equation, "PTIN5,"
and "PTEDHS," are, as noted before, directly equivalent
to those used by Duncan. They refer to the percentage of
workers in occupational groupings with incomes of $5,000
or more and high school graduation. They do differ, however,
in that our measures refer to the income and educational
attributes of the total labor force rather than just the
male labor force. The dependent variable used is the Siegel
Prestige Scale--"PRESTIGE." Unlike the results obtained
by Duncan, these two indicators of occupational prestige do
not share equally in the prediction of prestige. The
educational measure is by far the more powerful. One
plausible explanation lies in the lesser ability of the
income measure to differentiate between "higher" status
occupations and "lower" status occupations in 1970 than in
1950. The next equation (2) explores this possibility.
Using a more stringent income measure, "PTIN10"--the percentage of individuals with incomes of $10,000 or more--sub-
stantially increases the role of income in the prediction
of occupational prestige. If in a similar fashion we adjust
the education measure to take into account the educational
upgrading of the labor force between 1950 and 1970, i.e.,
considering the percentage of individuals with one or more
years of college rather than just completion of high school,
the effect of income drops (equation 3). It appears that
whereas education and income previously were about equally
important dimensions underlying occupational prestige, the
relative emphasis has shifted in the last two decades
towards education. No matter which combination of education
and income measures are used, income has a smaller effect
on the prestige of occupations.

In these three equations, however, the predictor
variables refer to the income and educational attributes of
both men and women in the labor force. What appears to be
a shift since 1950 in the relative importance of these two
criteria in the prediction of occupational prestige may be
due to our inclusion of the earnings characteristics of
women, since the variance of women's earnings is less than

---

[3]"College presidents," "auto service attendants," and
"machine operators" were the 1960 titles which could not
be matched.

that of men's earnings. This is partly the case. When
considering only men's characteristics and using cutoff
points in the income and educational distributions parallel
to those used by Duncan (i.e., "PMIN10" and "PMEDSC"), the
relative importance of income increases, although still not
to the level suggested by Duncan's results (see equation 4).

Of these four equations which can be used to generate
socioeconomic scores, the best--in terms of variance ex-
plained--are the two which rely on the combination of income
and education indicators parallel to those used by Duncan.
One is based on the income and educational characteristics
of the total labor force; the other, on the characteristics
of the male labor force. The only difference between these
two equations lies in the relative emphasis placed on the
role of education versus income in the prediction of
occupational prestige. As would be expected, the parameters
found in the "male" equation are a closer approximation to
those found by Duncan, although for these more recent data,
the effect of education is more prominent. When considering
the attributes of the total labor force, education is almost
three times as important as income.

This differential emphasis in the parameters between
the "male" equation and the "total" equation could be due
to a number of factors. First, it could be due to the
nature of the occupational classificatory scheme, which may
not differentiate between higher and lower female earners
as well as it does between higher and lower male earners.
It may be due to the concentration of large numbers of
women in relatively low-paying occupations. It could also
reflect a differing relationship between occupational
status[4] and the two objective occupational characteristics--
education and income--for female-dominated occupations.

So far, the procedures followed in the estimation of
the parameters differ in two major ways from the procedure

---

[4]Occupational prestige scores, the dependent variable
used in these equations, may differ for each occupational
title depending on whether or not we are considering the
total, or just the male, labor force. These differences
are not, however, due to the raters in the original
prestige studies differentiating between the prestige or
social standing of men versus women in the occupational
role. The differences are solely a function of the
weighting procedure which transformed the scores for 1960
occupational titles into scores for 1970 occupational
titles.

followed by Duncan. First, our dependent variable is not parallel to Duncan's; second, we used a far larger sample of occupational titles.

Duncan used the percentage of "good" and "excellent" ratings as his prestige measure for his dependent variable because of its desirable statistical properties. It also has the merit of paralleling in its construction the independent variables since it refers to the percentage of people who were willing to accord each occupational title a "social standing" or prestige ranking above some threshold. To investigate the possibility that our results are not solely a function of differing dependent variables, we reestimated the equations using as the dependent variable, a measure constructed from the Siegel Prestige Scores: the predicted percentage of "good" and "excellent" ratings--"PGOOD."

In at least one sense, these reestimated equations prove better. Due to the slightly higher correlation between the independent variables and this prestige construct, the proportion of variance explained by these equations is consistently higher than in the corresponding equation using 1971 Siegel Prestige Scores (Table 1, equations 5-8). Although the patterns found in the first four equations concerning the relative importance of education versus income (note the beta coefficients in Table 1) persist when using this prestige construct rather than the raw prestige scores, the relative importance of education has been further augmented. This result emerges even though the dependent variable now more closely corresponds to Duncan's prestige measure in this set of equations. Thus our earlier conclusions appear to be corroborated; the education characteristics of occupations have apparently assumed greater importance for the social standing or prestige that raters attribute to occupations.

However, Duncan was confined to a sample of 45 occupations for the construction of the 1961 socioeconomic scale. As Duncan himself noted, this small sample is not a representative one. Professional and service occupations are over-represented, while operatives and laborers are under-represented. In an effort to portray any possible ramifications of these sample biases, Siegel (1971) estimated the relationship between occupational prestige and 1960 educational and income characteristics for 323 occupational titles (Table 1, EQ. 13). In this instance, the educational variable was approximately twice as important as the income variable. But when the analysis was restricted to the same 45 occupations used by Duncan, the results were parallel to those obtained by Duncan. Siegel concluded that "the

Table 2. Socioeconomic and Prestige Scores for Major Occupational Groups, 1970 Census Classification.

Occupational group	Socioeconomic scores[a]						Prestige scores[a]	
	DUNCAN	MSEI3	MSEI2	TSEI2	MSEI1	TSEI1	PRESTIGE	PGOOD
Professional	74.65	76.49	68.63	66.47	59.69	58.13	61.03	72.45
Managerial	61.95	55.83	51.07	48.93	49.65	48.22	50.54	55.39
Sales	50.54	44.95	42.30	36.11	43.93	40.04	35.88	28.88
Clerical	44.56	32.35	31.99	28.74	37.38	35.29	36.35	28.45
Crafts	31.70	25.09	25.63	25.95	33.92	34.07	38.16	31.62
Operatives	18.58	15.84	18.24	18.23	29.25	29.19	28.76	16.25
Transport	19.50	18.54	20.37	21.71	30.69	31.50	30.55	18.19
Laborers	8.96	12.98	15.99	18.72	27.71	29.42	19.19	7.14
Farm owners and managers	14.22	20.82	22.29	23.91	31.81	32.79	40.73	35.56
Farm laborers	7.90	10.74	14.19	17.33	26.53	28.50	19.17	7.01
Service (exc. priv. hsld.)	17.95	18.80	20.81	21.05	30.64	30.77	26.08	15.97
Service-- priv. hsld.	7.46	10.53	14.04	15.47	26.41	27.36	18.90	6.81
Scale characteristics								
Minimum	3.0	7.15	11.13	13.88	24.79	26.51	9.30	6.10
Maximum	96.0	100.89	88.65	90.45	72.15	73.27	81.20	92.86
Standard deviation	24.71	27.43	22.76	22.73	13.80	13.75	16.02	25.89

[a]See designation of scale labels in TABLE 1 (last column) and text.

apparent increase in the importance of education as a determinant of the social evaluation of occupations (between 1950
and 1960)...is due to the biases of the sample...used in the
earlier period" (1971:15). If we too restrict the regression
analysis to the same subset of occupational titles and use
indicators of occupational prestige, income, and education
analogous to those used in 1961, we reproduce the basis for
Siegel's conclusions. The income and educational criteria
now share equally in the prediction of occupational prestige
scores (Table 1, EQ. 12). Thus, the apparent increase in
the importance of the educational criteria noted earlier
appears to be a function of the biases in the smaller set of
occupational titles.

Any one of the 11 equations presented in Table 1 could
be used to generate 1970 socioeconomic scores. Faced with
these options, we kept for consideration those equations in
which the educational and income criteria most closely
paralleled Duncan's. Equations 3, 4, 7 and 8 also had the
advantage of explaining more of the variance in occupational
prestige than those that we discarded (eqs. 1, 2, 5, 6).
For purposes of comparison, we also computed scores from the
equation based on only the "Duncan" occupations (eq. 11).
The unweighted means, standard deviations, and ranges for
the scales generated from these alternative equations are
presented in Table 2.

Using the 1950 basis Duncan SEI as a standard, it seems
clear that the least satisfactory candidates for an updated
socioeconomic index are those relying on the equations using
Siegel prestige scores as the dependent variable, MSEI1 and
TSEI1 (EQS. 3 and 4 in Table 1). Not only are the ranges
limited, but neither of these two scales differentiates
among "crafts," "operatives," "transport," "service," and
"farm owners and managers." The two scales, MSEI2 and TSEI2,
based on the constructed prestige measure ("PGOOD" in eqs. 7
and 8 in Table 1) do somewhat better; there is a regular
downward rank progression from professional through
managerial, sales, clerical and crafts, transport, farm
owners and service, with laborers and private household
service workers clustered at the bottom. However, it is
the scale constructed from the small sample of "Duncan"
occupations, MSEI3 (from eq. 11 in Table 1), that differentiates most clearly among the major occupational groups,
particularly those at the bottom of the socioeconomic
distribution. Again we note an impact of selectivity among
occupations on which the prediction equation for MSEI3 was
estimated. Here the effect is to maximize relative to the
other options for prediction, the "socioeconomic" differences
among occupational groups. This consequence should be borne

Table 3. Correlation Coefficients Among Scales of Occupational Standing of Current (Above Diagonal) and Family Head's
(Below Diagonal) Occupations: U.S. Men Aged 25-64 in March
1973.

Variables[a]	1	2	3	4	5
1. Siegel PRESTIGE scores	--	.877	.891	.889	.891
2. DUNCAN socioeconomic index	.779	--	.944	.942	.944
3. Revised MSEI1	.823	.935	--	.999	.999
4. Revised MSEI2	.815	.933	.999	--	.999
5. Revised MSEI3	.821	.934	.999	.999	--

[a]Siegel PRESTIGE scores are based on popular assessments
of the social standing of detailed Census titles circa
1964-65; DUNCAN socioeconomic index reflects 1950-basis
educational and income characteristics of 45 detailed occupational titles; MSEI1, 2 and 3 are revised socioeconomic
scores reflecting 1970-basis characteristics (see TABLE 1
for computation).

in mind as we apply these scales in a regression analysis of
the occupational attainment process, since this feature of a
socio-economic index--the ability to differentiate among
major occupational groups--is often regarded as desirable.
Also, this feature may be the basis for the larger correlations observed in analyses comparing SEI and prestige scales,
since it could be associated with the lesser errors made by
the SEI in capturing differences in occupational social
standing and interoccupational mobility (Hodge and Rossi,
1978; Featherman, Jones and Hauser, 1975; Treas and Tyree,
1979).

Analysis of Occupational Achievement: Implications of the Choice of an Index of Occupational Standing

Comparisons among the various scales of occupational
standing--the 1965 NORC prestige score (hereafter, PRESTIGE);
the Duncan SEI (Duncan) based on 1950 occupational characteristics, and three updated versions of the socioeconomic
index (MSEI1, MSEI2, MSEI3) based on 1970 occupational
characteristics--in models of occupational attainment are
made using the 1973 occupational changes in a generation
(OCG) survey of men aged 25 to 64 in the experienced civilian
labor force during the month of March (Featherman and Hauser,
1978). In these comparisons, all occupational index values
are based on 1970 census 3-digit codes for detailed occupations.[5]

The coefficients reported in Table 3 are estimates of
the product-moment correlations between the five indexes
(PRESTIGE, DUNCAN, MSEI1, MSEI2, MSEI3) of individuals'
occupations. The correlations above the diagonal refer to
the OCG respondent's current occupation (or last occupation

---

[5]Recall that the use of the 1970 occupational classificatory system for the Siegel PRESTIGE and Duncan SEI
scores reflects only changes since 1950 and 1960 in the
classifying and coding practices of the Bureau of the Census.
The recombination of the Siegel scores and the original
Duncan SEI scores did not involve an updating of occupational and income characteristics, or their reweighting, to be
consistent with changes in these features of occupations
since 1950. Rather, it involved a mapping of the former
occupation classifications on the 1970 system and the
calculation of weighted average Siegel and Duncan scores
according to population distributions of the roughly four
hundred 1970-basis codes. This procedure and scale scores
are reported in Hauser and Featherman (1977: Ch. 2 and
Appendix B).

Table 4. Standardized Regression Coefficients Relating Measures of Current Occupational Status to Indicators of Social Background, Schooling, and First Job Status: Men Aged 20-65 in March 1973.

Independent variable	Siegel PRESTIGE	DUNCAN 1950-basis	Revised Socio-economic index		
			MSEI1	MSEI2	MSEI3
Family head's education	.002[a]	-.010[a]	-.014	-.014	-.014
Family head's occupation	.041	.060	.059	.058	.058
Farm origin	.009[a]	-.019	-.007[a]	-.008[a]	-.007[a]
Number of siblings	-.013	-.022	-.019	-.019	-.019
Intact (vs. broken) family	.004[a]	.007[a]	.005[a]	.005[a]	.005[a]
Race (black vs. other)	-.084	-.074	-.058	-.055	-.056
Education	.303	.295	.267	.264	.266
First job	.392	.406	.493	.503	.498
R^2	.440	.484	.546	.554	.550

[a]Coefficient less than twice the size of its standard error.

within the previous five years), whereas the correlations
below the diagonal refer to the father's (or other family
head's) occupation when the respondent was about 16 years
old.

Table 3 leads to several summary observations. First,
despite the varying educational and income criteria which
were used to generate the three updated socioeconomic
scales, the correlations between them approach unity, suggesting that in the context of socioeconomic attainment they
are essentially interchangeable. Second, the three updated
socioeconomic scales share a greater commonality with the
1950-based Duncan SEI than with the Siegel prestige scale.
Third, the differences between the socioeconomic scales and
the prestige scale are slightly larger in the case of family
head's occupation than in respondent's current occupation.
It is likely that the last two observations stem from the
well-documented distinction between the "prestige" and the
"socioeconomic" status of farm occupations and from minor
differences in the metric properties of "prestige" versus
"socioeconomic" indexes (Featherman and Hauser, 1976; Treas
and Tyree, 1979). Whatever the basis of the relative sizes
of correlations among the indexes, they convey an interesting
implication for analysis of occupational achievement:
namely, that temporal changes in the ranking of occupational
"socioeconomic status" since 1950 have been smaller than
contemporaneous differences in occupational "prestige" and
"socioeconomic" status.

Notwithstanding small differences in correlation, the
conclusions about the effects of social background, length
of schooling, and status at full-time entry into the labor
force on current occupational attainment are similar
whichever scale of occupational status is employed. This
consistency is most marked in the assessment of relative
effects, reported in Table 4 as a series of standardized
regression coefficients. However, the socioeconomic indexes
apparently explain more of the variance in attainment than
does the prestige index. This comparative distinction has
been interpreted to mean that the allocative processes of
occupational mobility within and between generations are
less well demarcated by the prestige index (e.g., Featherman
et al., 1975; Treas and Tyree, 1979). Whether this result
rests on a substantive difference between what is reflected
by one index versus the other is moot, since "prestige" and
"socioeconomic status" are difficult to measure by simple
global means such as these. Indeed, the two concepts may
overlap, or neither may conform closely to what socioeconomic or prestige scales actually rank among occupations
(see Spenner, 1977; Goldthorpe and Hope, 1972; and Treiman,

1977 for further discussion of these unresolved points). Failing a definitive answer to this important substantive question, one that requires more carefully designed social psychological experiments than have been attempted (see Coxon and Jones, 1978, for example), one might assume temporarily a simple empiricist interpretation. That is, the difference between the two indexes is chiefly one of relative errors in measurement with the SEI being a somewhat more valid hierarchical index of occupational standings (here the German, Stände, is apt) when applied to mobility processes.

   This empirical distinction is clearer in the 3 columns of regressions in Table 4 employing the revised socioeconomic indexes. There the R^2 values are 10 points greater than in the equation involving PRESTIGE. In addition, these larger values are at least six points greater than in the corresponding equation computed on the 1950-basis Duncan SEI. Thus, the relative research advantage of using a "socioeconomic" index has apparently increased as a consequence of revising the Duncan SEI by using 1970 occupational characteristics.

   Despite the general similarity of relative effects that are estimated by the five equations in Table 4, there are some differences that deserve note. PRESTIGE scores tend to emphasize the effect of education relative to the effect of parental occupation to a greater extent than do any of the socioeconomic indexes. The ratio of the net effects is 7.3 ↖ (.303:.041) in column 1 and ranges between 4.5 and 4.9 in the other columns. Likewise, the strength of the race effect is greater than the paternal occupation effect by a larger margin in the PRESTIGE equation; it is twice the size (and opposite in sign) in column 1 and about of equal size (and opposite in sign) in all socioeconomic regressions. Finally, all of the revised socioeconomic indexes tend to enhance the relative effects of first full-time occupational status vis-a-vis the effects of education: the ratios of beta coefficients are about 1.9 in the last three columns of Table 4; they are roughly 1.3 in the first two columns.

   We do not attach any substantive significance to these differences. They are impossible to sort out without convincing evidence that what one index measures is conceptually and operationally distinct from another. Instead we think of these relative differences as manifestations of the instruments themselves—artifacts of methods to be construed as calibrations of one instrument against another. That there are differences that one could be tempted to interpret is important to note, for the reviewer of the literature on occupational achievement should not mix

indiscriminately detailed numerical findings from research
employing prestige scales with those using a socioeconomic
index. Likewise, the analyst of occupational processes who
uses a global measure of standing like a socioeconomic index
or prestige scale should calibrate the estimated effects
against conceptually alternative scales. If there is no
substantive difference to guide the choice of indexes, and
no consensus of preference on methodological or other
grounds, then perhaps all relative effects ought to be estimated using both indexes. Or, at least some "confidence
limits" should be put around interpretations that reflect
the artifacts entailed by the crudeness of the measurement
of the concepts at issue. To do otherwise is to perpetrate
false precision.

   To continue the comparison among the indexes of occupational standing, we shall assume that metric units of the
various indexes have interpretable meaning so that the
indexes have ordinal properties. These are stronger assumptions than were necessary to interpret the relative effects
in Table 4, but they do permit a comparison across the indexes at the level of individual metric variables. We make
this comparison solely for didactic purposes. Table 5 provides the metric regression coefficients corresponding to
the standardized coefficients presented in Table 4. The
regressions in Table 5 can be thought of as estimating the
effects of a set of independent variables on what is, for
all purposes, a set of occupational variables that are
simple linear transformations of each other. Certainly,
that interpretation is implied by the nearly perfect correlation among the revised socioeconomic indexes (Table 3).
Even the common variances shared by the least similar
rankings the PRESTIGE scale and 1950 basis Duncan SEI, of
current occupation (77%) and father's occupation (61%) suggest that one variable is essentially a linear transformation
of the other. Indeed, analysts frequently view correlations
as reported in Table 3 as indicating good grounds for empirical and conceptual indifference to the use of a prestige
versus a socioeconomic index of occupational standing. Our
didactic purpose in Table 5 is to document the error of that
indifference.

   The means and standard deviations presented in Table 5
are consistent with the assumption that what is indexed by
these several variables of occupational standing is the same.
Mean differences are within the range often regarded as substantively insignificant (Siegel, 1971:95-97). The range of
variation about these identical means is notably different
in the cases of PRESTIGE (column 1) and MSEI1 (column 3)
regressions, both of which are based on indexes where an

Table 5. Metric Regression Coefficients Relating Measures of Current Occupational Status to Indicators of Social Background, Schooling, and First Job Status: Men Aged 25-64 in March 1963.

Independent variables[a]	Occupational status measures				
	Siegel PRESTIGE	DUNCAN 1950-basis	Revised socioeconomic index		
			MSEI1	MSEI2	MSEI3
Family head's education	.009 (.022)[b]	-.058 (.037)	-.043 (.018)	-.072 (.029)	-.086 (.035)
Family head's occupation	.045 (.006)	.067 (.007)	.073 (.007)	.074 (.007)	.074 (.007)
Farm origin	.295 (.181)	-1.050 (.311)	-.192 (.143)	-.360 (.233)	-.404 (.282)
Number of siblings	-.067 (.029)	-.192 (.049)	-.087 (.023)	-.138 (.038)	-.168 (.046)
Intact (vs. broken) family	.164 (.196)	.456 (.326)	.166 (.156)	.252 (.252)	.314 (.306)
Race (black vs. other)	-3.548 (.227)	-5.390 (.378)	-2.151 (.180)	-3.341 (.292)	-4.153 (.354)
Education	1.264 (.030)	2.136 (.051)	.987 (0.25)	1.596 (.040)	1.942 (.049)
First job	.356 (.006)	.403 (.007)	.492 (.006)	.500 (.006)	.496 (.006)
Constant	11.846	2.309	6.909	1.698	-2.620
Error of estimate	10.465	17.436	8.329	13.512	16.404
Mean	40.08	39.81	35.03	35.75	32.10
Standard deviation	13.99	24.27	12.36	20.23	24.46

[a]See text and Featherman and Hauser (1978) for definition of variables.

[b]Standard errors in parentheses.

explicit "prestige" score was used as the criterion of
standing (see the earlier discussion of Table 1). The
variation associated with the Duncan SEI (column 2) and
MSEI3 (column 5) is slightly greater than with the others
and seems connected to the use of a small subset rather than
the full list of occupations in estimating the prediction
equation for the derived socioeconomic scores (again refer
to the discussion attending Table 1). It is possible to
think of these statistics as indicating a set of variables
measuring the same concept but with different degrees of
precision such that the variances of some (vis., PRESTIGE
and MSEI1) are attenuated more than the variances of others.
However, this hypothetical circumstance should not affect
the structural (metric regression) coefficients so long as
the errors that lead to attenuation are uncorrelated with
those associated with the independent variables. (However
unreasonable this assumption, given the presence of first
job and family head's occupational statuses in all these
equations, it is a highly conventional one and is implicit
in all ordinary least-squares regressions regardless of the
choice of one over another occupational index.)

If we assume that the equations in Table 5 provide
replicate estimates, then we are faced with the sometimes
rather wide variation in metric effects. This variation
often exceeds sampling error and consequently might tempt
the analyst to interpret them. For example, rearing in a
family headed by a farmer (or farm laborer, manager, or
foreman) has a small negative effect on current occupation
in the DUNCAN regression but is essentially zero (by conventions of statistical significance) in all other equations.
Far larger statistical and perhaps substantive differences
appear in the effect of being black (versus white or other
racial distinction). The DUNCAN regression tends to estimate the largest racial handicap to achieved standing. This
same equation also tends to emphasize the effect of education as an antecedent to occupational attainment, especially
by comparison with the PRESTIGE-based equations (columns
1 and 3).

Despite these illustrative differences in estimated
effects, there are few, if any, systematic distinctions among
the equations that suggest unambiguous conceptual or substantive features of the various indexes. Differences as
large and in the same direction as between the PRESTIGE and
the DUNCAN regressions (columns 1 and 2) can also be found
among the revised socioeconomic regressions; the effects of
race and education are illustrative. The only exception to
this generalization may be the estimates for the first job
variable, for which the effects are consistently higher in

the three equations for the revised socioeconomic index (columns 3-5) than elsewhere. But this later difference rests on the assumption that one is willing to interpret the metric coefficients to more than one decimal place for substantive purposes.

In a fundamental sense, there are no substantive conclusions about the process of occupational achievement that can be drawn from the comparisons of the metric regression equations in Table 5. The dependent variables are as different as dollars and cents--both of which refer to income or money but differ in their metrics, means, and standard deviations. The conclusion to be taken from these regressions--and the reason for reporting them--is a didactic one concerning the use of indexes of occupational standing or status. High correlations among occupation variables created by prestige and socioeconomic indexes should not lead the analyst to an indifference about the empirical implications of the choice for a specific research problem. In the case of standardized variables (as in Table 4), estimates of relative effects are essentially, although not entirely, unaffected by the choice. This suggests that the main difference among the indexes is primarily a metric one--a difference of their means and standard deviations. It follows that the metric regressions in Table 5 reflect differences for the same reasons. Thus, if an important type of analysis of occupational process involves the estimation of structural coefficients--as students of stratification frequently calculate when they compare societies or compare across years in a time-series for a single nation-- then the choice of a metric for occupational standing cannot be arbitrary. Under no circumstances should these comparisons be made when more than one index is used, even when these indexes are as apparently similar as the 1950-basis DUNCAN and MSEI1, MSEI2, and MSEI3, or as are the latter three among themselves.

Analyzing Sex Differences In Attainment With Different Occupational Indexes

Previous research reports sex differences in occupational attainment and in the processes that link these achievements with characteristics of social background, length of schooling, and full-time occupations in the early work history, (e.g., Featherman and Hauser, 1976a; McClendon, 1976; Sewell, Hauser, and Wolf, 1980). Yet reported differences are not consistently replicated across studies. For example, Sewell, et al. (1980) conclude that women's continued reliance on educational training and credentials, rather than accumulated job experience, differentiates their course of occupational attainment from that of men. By contrast, Tyree and Treas (1979) suggest that it is men who continue to convert their formal schooling into better occupations and whose early occupational attainments are of lesser relative importance for later achievements than is schooling.

Unfortunately, these differences are difficult to reconcile, for they rest on different bodies of data, sample definitions, and the use of different scales of occupational standing. In this section, we examine the effects of choice of occupational index on the relative occupational attainments of men and women.

There are several reasons for supposing that sex differences in attainment may manifest the effects of metric in the analysis. First, almost all previous research on this topic has used an occupational status scale derived from the characteristics of men, e.g., the Duncan index. One can question how well such an index captures the relevant dimensions of attainment for women. Second, since women are concentrated in relatively fewer occupations than men--especially those in the middle of the status hierarchy--estimation of effects of variables in attainment models for women may be more sensitive to how a particular status index ranks these occupations.

Tables 6 and 7 present standardized and metric regression coefficients (respectively) for simple recursive models of occupational attainment for men and women. The sample reflects a broad subset of the cohort of 1957 Wisconsin high school seniors that has been followed through 1975 by Professors William H. Sewell and Robert M. Hauser (Sewell and Hauser, 1980). We included all respondents who reported ever having a full-time job in the paid labor force and who had no missing data on social background, education, and current (or most recent) occupation in the paid labor force (N = 6991). Since our purpose is limited to the examination of the consequences of the choice of occupational metric, we limit our discussion of these tables to the relative effects of education and first job on current occupation. As in the earlier portions of this paper, we compare the 1950-basis DUNCAN, the PRESTIGE, and the several revised indexes of occupational socioeconomic status. Of the latter, we shall give special attention to the significance of using indexes estimated from male incumbents (viz., TSEI2).

A major difference in conclusions would be reached about the paths to attainment by men versus women if one

Table 6. Standardized Regression Coefficients Relating Measures of Current Occupational Status to Indicators of Social Background, Schooling and First Job Status for Wisconsin Men and Women

	DUNCAN		MSEI2		MSEI3		TSEI2		PRESTIGE	
	Men	Women	Men	Women	Men	Women	Men	Women	Men	Women
Family head's education	.037	.037	.036	.043	.035	.044	.026[a]	.035	.025[a]	.035[a]
Family head's occupation	.042	.009	.025[a]	-.023[a]	.028	-.022[a]	.041	-.016[a]	.038	-.018[a]
Farm origin	-.092	-.034	-.060	-.040	-.061	-.040	-.032	-.023[a]	-.031	-.029[a]
Number of siblings	-.003[a]	-.003[a]	-.012[a]	-.028[a]	-.011[a]	-.028[a]	-.030[a]	-.017[a]	-.031	-.018[a]
Intact (vs. broken) family	.016[a]	.035	.011[a]	.036	.011[a]	.038	.016[a]	.040	.018[a]	.040
Education	.182	.275	.296	.364	.293	.362	.299	.240	.308	.244
First Job	.447	.301	.415	.291	.417	.289	.362	.388	.354	.360
R^2	.425	.277	.511	.390	.512	.387	.427	.336	.425	.307

[a]Coefficient less than twice its standard error.

Table 7. Metric Coefficients Relating Measures of Current Occupational Status to Indicators of Social Background, Schooling and First Job Status for Wisconsin Men and Women

	DUNCAN		MSEI2		MSEI3		TSEI2		PRESTIGE	
	Men	Women	Men	Women	Men	Women	Men	Women	Men	Women
Family head's education	.261 (.101)	.232 (.111)	.222 (.081)	.225 (.086)	.258 (.098)	.274 (.104)	.167 (.092)	.249 (.119)	.098 (.054)	.140 (.071)
Family head's occupation	.041 (.015)	.079 (.016)	.027 (.014)	-.021 (.014)	.031 (.015)	-.020 (.015)	.043 (.014)	-.018 (.018)	.036 (.012)	.017 (.015)
Farm origin	-5.770 (.828)	-1.718 (.861)	-3.252 (.635)	-1.692 (.632)	-3.960 (.764)	-2.057 (.762)	-1.817 (.724)	-1.307 (.873)	-1.060 (.432)	-.968 (.525)
Numbers of siblings	-.031 (.065)	-.253 (.123)	-.096 (.096)	-.181 (.095)	-.111 (.115)	-.217 (.114)	-.259 (.111)	-.149 (.133)	-.163 (.066)	-.092 (.080)
Intact (vs. broken) family	1.408 (1.756)	2.416 (1.063)	.816 (.852)	2.078 (.824)	.994 (1.020)	2.629 (.990)	1.248 (.980)	3.113 (1.151)	.844 (.586)	1.835 (.696)
Education	1.708 (.175)	3.080 (.204)	2.410 (.160)	3.428 (.188)	2.865 (.193)	4.102 (.226)	2.598 (.168)	3.044 (.236)	1.593 (.099)	1.819 (.139)
First Job	.408 (.019)	.330 (.019)	.373 (.018)	.304 (.021)	.374 (.018)	.303 (.021)	.304 (.016)	.423 (.020)	.289 (.015)	.404 (.205)
Constant	6.053	-14.564	-5.978	-19.859	-10.274	-28.216	-4.654	-21.354	9.730	-1.282
Error of estimate	18.654	17.294	14.898	13.366	17.892	16.091	17.210	18.758	10.236	11.275

used PRESTIGE rather than the 1950-basis DUNCAN index.
According to the DUNCAN-based regressions, the effect of
education and of first job on women's current occupational
attainment are about equal; for men, the relative effect
of first job is about two and one-half times the effect of
formal education (Table 6). Similarly, the comparison of
the metric regression coefficients for men's and women's
education indicates that women in middle adulthood derive
a greater benefit from each year of schooling than men;
from the two first job coefficients, one concludes that
men benefit more favorably from prior occupational attainments than do women (Table 7). However, with the same
analyses run with the PRESTIGE index, the relative effects
of men's first jobs and schooling appear to be nearly equal,
whereas for women the larger effect would seem to come from
previous or first job experience (Table 6). Thus while the
metric regression coefficients for education are about equal
for the sexes, the analysis suggests that women draw somewhat greater benefit from first jobs than men (Table 7).
(We ignore for brevity the other differences between the
sexes and the fact that standard errors of coefficients are
typically larger for women than for men in these data.)

Considering the two revised indexes, MSEI2 and MSEI3,
one finds nearly identical outcomes in portraying how
women attain their current occupations vis-a-vis men. As
in the DUNCAN regressions, the differences suggest that men
draw more heavily on their prior job experiences and attainments than on schooling for occupational attainment in middle adulthood. Women, with perhaps less overall continuity
in employment in the paid economy, profit relatively more
from their formal education than from factors associated
with early work histories. Thus, the pattern of results
based on the socioeconomic indexes is consistently
reproduced as the DUNCAN index is revised and updated, although it is notable that for both sexes the revised
indexes, MSEI2 and MSEI3, account for more variance (R^2)
than do either DUNCAN or PRESTIGE. Perhaps the new indexes
commit fewer errors in the ranking of occupational standing.

All of the indexes we have discussed to this point,
the socioeconomic indexes in particular, have been estimated
from characteristics of the male labor force. TSEI2, however, reflects the same computational logic as MSEI2 but is
based on the total labor force. One might suppose that it
is a more desirable, common instrument to use in assessing
the relative occupational achievements of the sexes. It
could be more accurate in scoring the occupations dominated
by women in which the few male incumbents might provide an
erroneous estimate of the occupation's relative standing.

And in other occupations, the male-based estimation procedure tends to miss the impact of women's educational and
income characteristics on the occupation's place in the
status hierarchy.

The sex comparison under analysis through TSEI2 looks
more like the pattern associated with the prestige metric
than with the socioeconomic metric. Women show a greater
differential impact of first job over education on their
current occupations at mid-life than men (Table 6), and the
sexes seem similar by their patterns of relative effects
(standardized coefficients). The metric coefficients for
education and first job, based on TSEI2, imply that women
benefit more than men from each of these characteristics,
a pattern reminiscent of that revealed by the PRESTIGE results (Table 7).

The differences between the results suggested by TSEI2
and MSEI2, MSEI3 and DUNCAN are not a result of indexes
being based on differing subsets of occupations, for the
results based on MSEI2 and MSEI3 are virtually identical.
Nor are they accountable on the basis of different emphases
in the prediction equations that underlie the indexes (as
reported in Table 1) for the same reasons. It seems more
likely that the contrasting results between TSEI2 and the
socioeconomic indexes derived from the characteristics of
the male labor force stem from the different treatment
(i.e., ranking) of occupations at the upper end of the
status distribution (e.g., among semiprofessional and
professional occupations) and/or at the boundary between
white-collar and blue-collar jobs where women are heavily
clustered. Although the range and variability of occupational standing as indicated by MSEI2 and TSEI2 are similar,
a major difference does occur in the standing accorded to
sales work (see Table 2), a common category for women that
accomodates the often episodic attachment to the paid labor
force. In these data, over half of the women are engaged
in current and first jobs that can be classified as clerical
or retail sales (Sewell et al. 1980: Table 4). Of the
women who do shift occupations, we can assume that many
simply change between clerical and retail sales. Note that
the statuses assigned to these categories are much more
similar on PRESTIGE and TSEI2 than on MSEI2 and other male-
based socioeconomic indexes (Table 2).

This interpretation is consistent with the sex differences in the relative importance of first job status
vis-a-vis education for occupational attainment (Table 6),
for sales is often a quite temporary first job category for
men (see Featherman and Hauser, 1978: Table e.8). Most

men with first jobs in sales are in non-retail employment.
Moves out of this category typically involve entrances into
managerial work. The MSEI2 and DUNCAN indexes place these
categories much closer in status than do TSEI2 and PRESTIGE.
Thus, we expect that the larger relative effect of first
job status vis-a-vis education for men, in comparison to
women, on the male-based socioeconomic indexes reflects
sex differences in who works at what occupations. The contrasting sex pattern of differences yielded by PRESTIGE and
TSEI2 versus MSEI2 and DUNCAN, seems to reflect the different ranks assigned to key occupations in which the sexes are
not evenly distributed.

Which set of results is to be believed? There is no
fully defensible answer. If one argues that TSEI2 is a more
appropriate index to use in the study of women's attainment
than MSEI2, one must reconcile that choice with the observation that MSEI2 explains more variance in current
occupational differences for women (as well as for men)
than any other index. The same observation applies if one
argues that a common rather than a sex-specific scale
should be used in sex comparative analyses.

Choosing a Metric of Occupational Standing

Our purpose in analyzing a simple set of regression
models of occupational attainment was to demonstrate that
parameter estimates are not indifferent to the choice of
the index of social standing. This is so even when indexes
are so similar in their ranking of occupations that correlations among them approach unity. Lacking conceptual reasons
for choosing one index over another, the analyst is faced
with artifactual variation among statistical estimates that
ought to be reflected in the confidence vested in the numerical results that are based on a single index. Unfortunately, the state of the art in stratification research is that there is no consensus about substantive
reasons for using a prestige versus a socioeconomic index.
Thus, we close this discussion with a pragmatic argument.

We recommend the choice of a "socioeconomic" index of
occupational standing over a prestige index for the study
of mobility and attainment processes, whenever the analyst
has an option. This recommendation reflects a considerable
body of empirical evidence demonstrating that mobility
processes are clearly revealed by indexes such as the
DUNCAN SEI and the updated versions we have
constructed by existing "prestige" indexes. Whether or not
this recommendation generalizes to the study of other social
processes is problematic and requires ad hoc investigations.

In an earlier paper (Stevens and Featherman, 1981), we recommended the updated version of the Duncan socioeconomic index, MSEI2, among the socioeconomic indexes as the best scale of occupational status, especially in research among men. We also suggested that TSEI2 might be considered for general use where both men and women in the labor force were being studied. In light of the comparative performance of the scales in analyzing men's and women's occupational attainments that we have reported in the present paper, we are more skeptical about the practical utility of TSEI2. We have, however, included the TSEI2 index in the appendix for others who may wish to make their own assessments.[6]

We believe that the development of a common index of occupational roles that would apply equally to all incumbents is still a desirable goal in stratification research. TSEI2, based on educational and income characteristics of all persons in each detailed Census occupation category, was intended to achieve that objective. However, TSEI2 apparently misallocates the ranks of occupations and their relative social "distances" in the study of occupational mobility and status attainment processes. By the criterion of explained variance, this misallocation is somewhat greater for men than for women, vis-a-vis results using the MSEI2 index. We therefore think our effort was unsuccessful in the attempt to develop a common index and the failure may lie in two possibilities.

First, the classification of job tasks and titles that persons report to the Census into detailed occupational categories may not properly capture the "real" occupational structure. That is, insofar as two workers classified into nominally the same occupation perform a different set of tasks, more precision is necessary in order to reflect the detailed division of labor as a set of homogeneous categories. That TSEI2 makes errors for both men and women implies that for neither sex does it identify as homogeneous a set of occupation-based status categories as MSEI2.

Second, there may not be a unitary definition of homogeneous occupational positions such that ranks on some dimen-

---

[6]For purposes of consistency across indexes in logical range (values between 1 and 100), the index values of MSEI3 (only) as listed in the appendix were adjusted from the originally predicted values by subtracting a constant of 5. This adjustment merely affects the mean reported in Table 5 by a corresponding amount as the constant. Results in Tables 3-5 reflect this adjustment; those in Table 2 do not.

sion of the occupational structure are independent of the
characteristics of incumbents. If this is the case, then
even the most faithful representation of the occupational
structure will fail to yield status estimates for an occupation's position in the social structure that is invariant--
that is a characteristic of social structure versus one that
reflects both the position's location in some structural
hierarchy and some characteristic of a particular incumbent,
eg. sex. We have assumed that there is not a parallel or dual
structure of occupations with women in them but rather that
the occupational structure is unitary.

We cannot judge between these two possibilities at this
juncture. The best strategy for future research seems to
recommend an initial search for more homogeneous role or
finely detailed job definitions that capture more information
about task differentiations that entail status differences.
This may mean the development of more function or task-based
definitions of occupations (eg. head-work/handwork; job
authority) or some other definitions linked to a specific
theory of social structure (eg. position in the political
economy or relationships of production). At the moment,
status attainment research uses the status scores as proxy
estimates for position in the social structure. It may be
better to code occupational positions more specifically and
directly in terms of some conception of that structure (i.e.,
functional; class relational) and to allow the "attainments"
(eg. deference, earnings) to reflect the effects of a role's
place in the structure.

Meanwhile the estimation of socioeconomic status scores
for occupations should remain experimental. Our repetition
of Duncan's basic strategy for estimating socioeconomic status
scores has not yielded a satisfactory index derived from the
education and income characteristics of the total labor force.
One could abandon the goal of replication. For example, using
wage rates, rather than income, in the estimation equations
for the socioeconomic scores might eliminate some errors in
TSEI2 that arise from the differentials in part-time versus
full-time work by men and women in the same occupation.

Should these strategies fail, or other evidence demonstrate that a unitary conception of occupational structure is
untenable, alternative procedures to develop an index appropriate for comparative analysis should be pursued. This might
lead to "functionally equivalent" scales of status in which,
in the comparison of men and women, a given occupation might
provide a female incumbent with a different level of status
than a male. Such an index would be quite difficult to construct, unless a common reference point were available to

calibrate the men's against the women's scale (or vice versa).
Currently available prestige scales for women's occupations
or women in occupations do not satisfy this criterion.

For the moment, we recommend that the updated socioeconomic index, MSEI2, be used as a practical convention.
We hasten to remind our colleagues that what we shall learn
about occupational stratification through the use of this
scale is no more or less index-specific than for another
index. This recommends that we take seriously the need for
standardized conventions if we are to be able to compare
findings across studies and to build a cumulative social
science in this field.

Appendix A

Table A-1. 1970 Based Socioeconomic Indexes for Detailed
Census Occupational Categories.

Census occupational category	MSEI2	TSEI2	MSEI3
001 Accountants	70.17	64.68	73.33
002 Architects	78.16	80.11	83.15
Computer Specialists			
003 Computer programmers	63.57	66.05	65.35
004 Computer systems analysts	75.39	74.10	80.02
005 Computer specialists, n.e.c.	73.01	71.19	77.15
Engineers			
006 Aeronautical and astronautical engineers	83.21	83.53	89.57
010 Chemical engineers	85.39	87.14	91.97
011 Civil engineers	75.33	76.79	79.87
012 Electrical and electronic engineers	78.32	79.04	83.59
013 Industrial engineers	71.62	72.02	75.51
014 Mechanical engineers	76.21	76.84	81.10
015 Metallurgical and materials engineers	81.92	80.34	87.94
020 Mining engineers	74.22	75.49	78.56
021 Petroleum engineers	80.55	82.32	86.12
022 Sales engineers	77.08	78.16	82.08
023 Engineers, n.e.c.	75.27	76.36	79.85
024 Farm management advisors	77.74	80.25	82.33
025 Foresters and conservationists	47.48	49.57	45.84
026 Home management advisors	47.10	65.83	45.28
Lawyers and judges			
030 Judges	79.87	79.68	85.42
031 Lawyers	86.96	88.42	93.81
Librarians, archivists, and curators			
032 Librarians	65.23	65.46	66.83
033 Archivists and curators	57.14	61.22	57.30
Mathematical specialists			
034 Actuaries	84.37	80.37	90.55
035 Mathematicians	84.33	84.39	90.55
036 Statisticians	71.45	65.12	74.91
Life and physical scientists			
042 Agricultural scientists	62.73	63.80	64.36
043 Atmospheric and space scientists	77.70	74.58	82.91
044 Biological scientists	76.95	76.73	81.27
045 Chemists	75.56	77.76	79.89
051 Geologists	85.59	87.35	92.12
052 Marine scientists	80.72	82.48	86.30
053 Physicists and astronomers	85.16	87.00	91.64
054 Life and physical scientists, n.e.c.	81.72	80.05	87.37

Table A-1, continued

Census occupational category	MSEI2	TSEI2	MSEI3
055 Operations and systems researchers and analysts	65.28	64.94	67.89
056 Personnel and labor relations workers	66.21	59.88	68.87
Physicians, dentists, and related practitioners			
061 Chiropractors	77.88	80.19	82.49
062 Dentists	88.49	89.57	95.72
063 Optometrists	84.16	85.73	90.44
064 Pharmacists	80.35	81.10	85.68
065 Physicians, medical and osteopathic	87.14	88.37	93.99
071 Podiatrists	81.94	82.89	87.55
072 Veterinarians	85.46	86.60	91.95
073 Health practitioners, n.e.c.	67.90	71.66	70.40
Nurses, dietitians, and therapists			
074 Dietitians	39.56	43.38	36.30
075 Registered nurses	46.62	46.41	44.65
076 Therapists	56.93	59.94	56.95
Health technologists and technicians			
080 Clinical laboratory technologists and technicians	52.99	54.96	52.08
081 Dental hygienists	53.47	67.25	53.81
082 Health record technologists and technicians	53.47	50.75	52.65
083 Radiologic technologists and technicians	45.98	39.20	44.08
084 Therapy assistants	39.66	36.37	36.21
085 Health technologists and technicians	51.90	45.58	50.89
Religious workers			
086 Clergymen	62.10	66.03	62.92
090 Religious workers, n.e.c.	57.61	57.08	57.55
Social scientists			
091 Economists	81.02	80.70	86.65
092 Political scientists	84.75	81.09	91.15
093 Psychologists	81.06	82.48	86.34
094 Sociologists	73.79	78.33	77.49
095 Urban and regional planners	77.21	79.63	81.85
096 Social scientists, n.e.c.	73.51	74.64	77.16
Social and recreation workers			
100 Social workers	64.39	66.14	65.85
101 Recreation workers	52.30	54.12	51.23

Table A-1, continued

Census occupational category	MSEI2	TSEI2	MSEI3
Teachers, college and university			
102 Agriculture teachers	82.58	85.71	88.26
103 Atmospheric, earth, marine, and space teachers	81.82	85.04	87.23
104 Biology teachers	81.67	83.80	87.05
105 Chemistry teachers	81.96	85.03	87.42
110 Physics teachers	80.41	84.22	85.56
111 Engineering teachers	83.30	84.88	89.25
112 Mathematics teachers	79.43	82.46	84.24
113 Health specialties teachers	86.63	80.74	93.36
114 Psychology teachers	84.20	85.53	90.22
115 Business and commerce teachers	83.03	82.91	88.81
116 Economics teachers	84.10	87.11	90.09
120 History teachers	80.04	83.61	84.97
121 Sociology teachers	79.15	82.28	83.87
122 Social science teachers, n.e.c.	82.13	85.04	87.64
123 Art, drama, and music teachers	78.42	79.74	83.03
124 Coaches and physical education teachers	78.57	81.43	83.21
125 Education teachers	85.34	86.20	91.74
126 English teachers	79.15	80.81	83.85
130 Foreign language teachers	77.74	78.97	82.12
131 Home economics teachers	74.84	73.13	79.16
132 Law teachers	88.65	90.45	95.89
133 Theology teachers	76.14	80.48	80.08
134 Trade, industrial, and technical teachers	66.90	68.84	69.21
135 Miscellaneous teachers, college and university	79.02	81.93	83.73
140 Teachers, college and university, subject not specified	75.22	77.13	79.08
Teachers, except college and university			
141 Adult education teachers	59.33	59.56	60.25
142 Elementary school teachers	68.99	70.88	71.15
143 Prekindergarten and kindergarten teachers	50.32	58.51	48.75
144 Secondary school teachers	73.02	75.14	76.20
145 Teachers, except college and university, n.e.c.	48.92	51.64	47.46
Engineering and science technicians			
150 Agriculture and biological technicians, except health	37.65	39.10	33.92
151 Chemical technicians	45.71	48.48	43.66

Table A-1, continued

Census occupational category	MSEI2	TSEI2	MSEI3
152 Draftsmen	46.26	48.48	44.52
153 Electrical and electronic engineering technicians	45.01	45.73	43.26
154 Industrial engineering technicians	43.46	43.77	41.40
155 Mechanical engineering technicians	49.95	49.50	49.48
156 Mathematical technicians	54.79	57.39	55.03
161 Surveyors	36.54	39.43	32.77
162 Engineering and science technicians, n.e.c.	43.47	45.32	41.11
Technicians, except health, and engineering and science			
163 Airplane pilots	68.66	68.65	72.10
164 Air traffic controllers	52.62	50.11	53.12
165 Embalmers	52.12	56.94	51.22
170 Flight engineers	62.08	61.45	64.28
171 Radio operators	34.22	32.77	30.09
172 Tool programmers, numerical control	57.76	58.60	58.73
173 Technicians, n.e.c.	41.04	42.78	38.38
174 Vocational and educational counselors	75.57	77.81	79.59
Writers, artists, and entertainers			
175 Actors	55.62	56.95	55.56
180 Athletes and kindred workers	43.06	45.16	40.54
181 Authors	70.34	71.43	73.58
182 Dancers	41.20	29.82	38.16
183 Designers	62.31	60.47	64.20
184 Editors and reporters	69.51	67.36	72.51
185 Musicians and composers	40.70	45.69	37.52
190 Painters and sculptors	54.58	54.68	54.64
191 Photographers	42.54	42.69	40.21
192 Public relations men and publicity writers	69.09	67.43	72.25
193 Radio and television announcers	50.91	55.36	49.78
194 Writers, artists, and entertainers, n.e.c.	55.67	55.69	55.91
195 Research workers, not specified	71.28	73.57	74.37
196 Professional, technical, and kindred workers-allocated	56.71	56.75	56.98
201 Assessors, controllers, and treasurers; local public administration	43.43	38.70	41.24

Table A-1, continued

Census occupational category	MSEI2	TSEI2	MSEI3
202 Bank officers and financial managers	66.48	62.13	69.21
203 Buyers and shippers, farm products	33.63	34.31	29.65
205 Buyers, wholesale and retail trade	48.70	45.80	47.84
210 Credit men	56.60	50.89	56.95
211 Funeral directors	58.33	60.47	59.06
212 Health administrators	68.80	61.90	71.97
213 Construction inspectors, public administration	38.91	39.63	36.10
215 Inspectors, except construction, public administration	44.89	44.92	43.24
216 Managers and superintendents, building	40.74	38.43	38.02
220 Office managers, n.e.c.	56.34	48.48	56.99
221 Officers, pilots, and pursers; ship	36.65	35.28	33.73
222 Officials and administrators; public administration, n.e.c.	59.78	57.09	61.25
223 Officials of lodges, societies, and unions	53.17	52.47	53.45
224 Postmasters and mail superintendents	45.23	39.84	43.89
225 Purchasing agents and buyers, n.e.c.	56.73	54.52	57.55
226 Railroad conductors	36.42	33.75	33.66
230 Restaurant, cafeteria, and bar managers	36.80	32.51	33.41
231 Sales managers and department heads, retail trade	45.36	41.58	43.75
233 Sales managers, except retail trade	69.25	68.09	72.89
235 School administrators, college	80.14	79.49	85.59
240 School administrators, elementary and secondary	84.98	83.39	91.36
245 Managers and administrators, n.e.c.	50.89	49.13	50.66
246 Managers and administrators, except farm-allocated	41.07	40.07	38.55
260 Advertising agents and salesmen	60.93	58.71	62.38
261 Auctioneers	35.94	34.40	32.79
262 Demonstrators	41.68	25.69	39.13
264 Hucksters and peddlers	32.79	25.64	28.26
265 Insurance agents, brokers, and underwriters	54.57	53.43	54.78
266 Newsboys	16.43	19.40	8.49
270 Real estate agents and brokers	55.28	50.92	55.72

Table A-1, continued

Census occupational category	MSEI2	TSEI2	MSEI3
271 Stock and bond salesmen	72.53	71.93	76.45
281 Sales representatives, manufacturing industries (Ind. 107-399)	58.50	56.96	59.64
282 Sales representatives, wholesale trade (Ind. 017-058, 507-599)	47.30	47.22	46.09
283 Sales clerks, retail trade (Ind. 608-699 except 618, 639, 649, 667, 668, 688)	30.06	25.37	24.90
284 Salesmen, retail trade (Ind. 607, 618, 639, 649, 667, 668, 688)	35.17	35.31	31.37
285 Salesmen of services and construction (Ind. 067-078, 407-499, 707-947)	48.86	42.21	47.90
296 Sales workers-allocated	33.29	28.67	28.97
301 Bank tellers	33.46	27.38	28.64
303 Billing clerks	29.95	24.62	24.64
305 Bookkeepers	40.79	29.65	37.78
310 Cashiers	25.57	21.16	19.26
311 Clerical assistants, social welfare	42.35	34.75	39.60
312 Clerical supervisors, n.e.c.	54.16	44.14	54.57
313 Collectors, bill and account	36.28	35.86	32.17
314 Counter clerks, except food	29.10	25.38	23.55
315 Dispatchers and starters, vehicle	29.11	28.92	24.09
320 Enumerators and interviewers	44.26	37.27	41.65
321 Estimators and investigators, n.e.c.	53.82	46.15	53.85
323 Expediters and production controllers	37.05	35.90	33.61
325 File clerks	28.30	24.85	22.55
326 Insurance adjusters, examiners, and investigators	58.51	56.05	59.08
330 Library attendants and assistants	43.71	45.10	40.61
331 Mail carriers, post office	25.09	27.84	18.95
332 Mail handlers, except post office	25.50	26.16	19.31
333 Messengers and office boys	20.46	24.40	13.19
334 Meter readers, utilities	20.84	23.88	13.79
Office machine operators			
341 Bookkeeping and billing machine operators	35.39	24.41	31.14
342 Calculating machine operators	36.92	22.05	33.07
343 Computer and peripheral equipment operators	37.07	37.22	33.25
344 Duplicating machine operators	25.96	26.40	19.77
345 Key punch operators	32.15	22.88	27.43

Table A-1, continued

Census occupational category	MSEI2	TSEI2	MSEI3
350 Tabulating machine operators	30.27	28.05	24.92
355 Office machine operators, n.e.c.	26.29	23.73	20.26
360 Payroll and timekeeping clerks	33.41	27.38	29.00
361 Postal clerks	29.92	30.25	24.83
362 Proofreaders	43.71	35.25	41.49
363 Real estate appraisers	64.33	64.93	66.52
364 Receptionists	37.33	29.00	33.26
Secretaries			
370 Secretaries, legal	47.79	34.73	46.03
371 Secretaries, medical	44.21	35.57	41.76
372 Secretaries, n.e.c.	45.99	31.75	44.25
374 Shipping and receiving clerks	19.49	21.93	12.20
375 Statistical clerks	37.24	31.28	33.65
376 Stenographers	50.66	30.02	50.22
381 Stock clerks and storekeepers	22.93	25.26	16.29
382 Teacher aides, exc. school monitors	40.85	31.56	37.20
383 Telegraph messengers	20.46	24.40	13.19
384 Telegraph operators	29.02	28.48	23.89
385 Telephone operators	33.98	21.89	29.82
390 Ticket, station, and express agents	38.04	39.28	34.61
391 Typists	28.69	25.23	23.09
392 Weighers	19.15	20.33	11.90
394 Miscellaneous clerical workers	40.22	32.93	37.22
395 Not specified clerical workers	34.13	27.74	29.78
396 Clerical and kindred workers- allocated	29.65	27.19	24.44
401 Automobile accessories installers	19.81	22.03	12.67
402 Bakers	18.48	19.22	11.16
403 Blacksmiths	19.35	20.72	12.30
404 Boilermakers	26.07	25.55	20.78
405 Bookbinders	24.65	19.88	18.77
410 Brickmasons and stonemasons	22.15	22.62	15.86
411 Brickmasons and stonemasons, apprentices	21.51	23.63	14.82
412 Bulldozer operators	18.29	19.54	11.05
413 Cabinetmakers	19.04	20.89	11.83
415 Carpenters	21.43	22.58	14.87
416 Carpenter apprentices	17.74	21.31	9.96
420 Carpet installers	21.65	23.07	15.18
421 Cement and concrete finishers	20.08	21.10	13.25
422 Compositors and typesetters	28.11	28.02	23.01
423 Printing trades apprentices, exc. pressmen	18.34	22.06	10.71

Table A-1, continued

Census occupational category	MSEI2	TSEI2	MSEI3
424 Cranemen, derrickmen, and hoistmen	21.80	21.98	15.49
425 Decorators and window dressers	33.18	32.22	28.66
426 Dental laboratory technicians	33.12	32.58	28.99
430 Electricians	31.94	31.04	27.90
431 Electrician apprentices	23.53	26.78	17.00
433 Electric power linemen and cablemen	28.94	28.14	24.29
434 Electrotypers and stereotypers	32.32	30.72	28.48
435 Engravers, exc. photoengravers	23.62	23.47	17.41
436 Excavating, grading, and road machine operators; exc. bulldozer	21.16	21.74	14.65
440 Floor layers, exc. tile setters	22.53	23.13	16.27
441 Foremen, n.e.c.	36.89	34.81	33.91
442 Forgemen and hammermen	22.32	22.27	16.12
443 Furniture and wood finishers	18.59	19.95	11.17
444 Furriers	24.14	24.22	18.14
445 Glaziers	24.53	24.62	18.78
446 Heat treaters, annealers, and temperers	21.44	22.08	14.95
450 Inspectors, scalers, and graders; log and lumber	18.50	20.43	11.09
452 Inspectors, n.e.c.	30.28	30.83	25.47
453 Jewelers and watchmakers	25.49	26.31	19.69
454 Job and die setters, metal	22.68	22.72	16.56
455 Locomotive engineers	38.42	34.77	36.24
456 Locomotive firemen	31.36	30.52	27.23
461 Machinists	24.05	24.49	18.12
462 Machinist apprentices	20.27	23.69	13.03
Mechanics and repairmen			
470 Air conditioning, heating, and refrigeration	26.24	26.38	20.80
471 Aircraft	32.18	31.83	28.07
472 Automobile body repairmen	20.52	21.57	13.78
473 Automobile mechanics	19.19	20.95	12.06
474 Automobile mechanic apprentices	14.59	17.87	6.22
475 Data processing machine repairmen	48.70	49.08	47.85
480 Farm implement	17.36	19.94	9.70
481 Heavy equipment mechanics, incl. diesel	23.03	23.64	16.89
482 Household appliance and accessory installers and mechanics	22.50	24.26	16.03
483 Loom fixers	11.13	13.88	2.15
484 Office machine	27.90	30.04	22.49
485 Radio and television	27.54	29.36	22.06

Table A-1, continued

Census occupational category		MSEI2	TSEI2	MSEI3
486	Railroad and car shop	17.87	19.60	10.47
491	Mechanic, exc. auto, apprentices	24.43	24.83	18.30
492	Miscellaneous mechanics and repairmen	24.96	26.40	19.03
495	Not specified mechanics and repairmen	25.71	26.87	20.01
501	Millers; grain, flour, and feed	16.77	18.58	9.13
502	Millwrights	29.17	27.58	24.72
503	Molders, metal	17.71	18.66	10.31
504	Molder apprentices	20.82	23.90	13.74
505	Motion picture projectionists	29.95	32.75	24.92
506	Opticians, and lens grinders and polishers	30.28	29.21	25.43
510	Painters, construction and maintenance	18.58	20.71	11.28
511	Painter apprentices	15.38	18.91	7.13
512	Paperhangers	22.65	23.40	16.29
514	Pattern and model makers, exc. paper	33.74	31.49	30.24
515	Photoengravers and lithographers	37.66	34.33	34.94
516	Piano and organ tuners and repairmen	30.11	33.12	24.96
520	Plasterers	20.92	21.55	14.37
521	Plasterer apprentices	17.92	20.28	10.60
522	Plumbers and pipe fitters	28.09	27.24	23.27
523	Plumber and pipe fitter apprentices	21.44	24.42	14.56
525	Power station operators	34.65	33.59	31.19
530	Pressmen and plate printers, printing	26.16	25.70	20.77
531	Pressman apprentices	19.97	22.80	12.80
533	Rollers and finishers, metal	25.16	23.87	19.70
534	Roofers and slaters	17.97	19.73	10.59
535	Sheetmetal workers and tinsmiths	26.54	26.12	21.30
536	Sheetmetal apprentices	19.66	23.12	12.30
540	Shipfitters	22.30	23.21	15.93
542	Shoe repairmen	15.50	17.29	7.49
543	Sign painters and letterers	23.72	25.80	17.48
545	Stationary engineers	28.08	28.34	23.06
546	Stone cutters and stone carvers	17.50	19.63	9.92
550	Structural metal craftsmen	29.06	27.99	24.48
551	Tailors	18.52	19.13	11.26
552	Telephone installers and repairmen	32.46	32.59	28.33

Table A-1, continued

Census occupational category	MSEI2	TSEI2	MSEI3
554 Telephone linemen and splicers	26.85	28.12	21.39
560 Tile setters	21.98	22.68	15.61
561 Tool and die makers	34.64	32.61	31.36
562 Tool and die maker apprentices	24.27	27.24	17.97
563 Upholsterers	16.23	17.89	8.40
571 Specified craft apprentices, n.e.c.	22.12	23.11	15.64
572 Not specified apprentices	a	a	a
575 Craftsmen and kindred workers, n.e.c.	a	a	a
580 Former members of the Armed Forces	28.21	32.47	22.42
586 Craftsmen and kindred workers-allocated	22.49	23.88	16.16
601 Asbestos and insulation workers	29.22	28.01	24.66
602 Assemblers	17.57	17.70	9.96
603 Blasters and powdermen	17.91	19.55	10.48
604 Bottling and canning operatives	17.17	17.61	9.48
605 Chainmen, rodmen, and axmen; surveying	23.19	27.10	16.48
610 Checkers, examiners, and inspectors manufacturing	25.05	21.21	19.14
611 Clothing ironers and pressers	14.02	14.74	5.66
612 Cutting operatives, n.e.c.	16.56	17.59	8.30
613 Dressmakers and seamstresses, except factory	18.74	18.41	11.36
614 Drillers, earth	20.65	21.41	13.92
615 Dry wall installers and lathers	23.65	23.74	17.75
620 Dyers	15.33	17.79	7.26
621 Filers, polishers, sanders, and buffers	16.12	17.51	8.29
622 Furnacemen, smeltermen, and pourers	19.56	20.69	12.58
623 Garage workers and gas station attendants	16.27	19.73	8.22
624 Graders and sorters, manufacturing	17.16	15.94	9.43
625 Produce graders and packers, except factory and farm	14.65	15.28	6.31
626 Heaters, metal	25.04	24.29	19.58
630 Laundry and dry cleaning operatives, n.e.c.	17.59	16.91	9.94
631 Meat cutters and butchers, exc. manufacturing	20.97	22.04	14.26
633 Meat cutters and butchers, manufacturing	18.48	18.36	11.27

Table A-1, continued

Census occupational category	MSEI2	TSEI2	MSEI3
634 Meat wrappers, retail trade	16.55	15.10	8.55
635 Metal platers	18.18	19.94	10.77
636 Milliners	21.96	17.68	15.86
640 Mine operatives, n.e.c.	18.16	20.24	10.73
641 Mixing operatives	17.19	19.32	9.55
642 Oilers and greasers, exc. auto	18.69	20.00	11.50
643 Packers and wrappers, except meat and produce	15.42	16.07	7.28
644 Painters, manufactured articles	16.33	17.99	8.56
645 Photographic process workers	31.90	28.46	27.24
Precision machine operatives			
650 Drill press operatives	17.10	18.25	9.46
651 Grinding machine operatives	20.82	21.21	14.20
652 Lathe and milling machine operatives	21.28	22.16	14.67
653 Precision machine operatives, n.e.c.	22.24	22.17	15.93
656 Punch and stamping press operatives	17.07	17.54	9.46
660 Riveters and fasteners	14.16	15.93	5.80
661 Sailors and deckhands	19.91	21.71	12.92
662 Sawyers	13.80	16.39	5.36
663 Sewers and stitchers	14.78	14.48	6.58
664 Shoemaking machine operatives	11.83	14.29	2.94
665 Solderers	16.63	15.90	8.86
666 Stationary firemen	20.32	20.99	13.52
Textile operatives			
670 Carding, lapping, and combing operatives	11.44	14.12	2.48
671 Knitters, loopers, and toppers	14.92	15.42	6.76
672 Spinners, twisters, and winders	11.80	13.98	2.91
673 Weavers	11.62	14.32	2.69
674 Textile operatives, n.e.c.	12.67	14.76	3.98
680 Welders and flame-cutters	19.76	20.66	12.83
681 Winding operatives, n.e.c.	18.32	17.17	11.05
690 Machine operatives, miscellaneous specified	18.43	18.86	11.12
692 Machine operatives, not specified	18.00	18.63	10.57
694 Miscellaneous operatives	18.34	19.30	10.91
695 Not specified operatives	18.93	19.43	11.70
696 Operatives, except transport-allocated	18.01	17.97	10.56
701 Boatmen and canalmen	22.02	23.09	15.59
703 Bus drivers	21.16	21.47	14.40

Table A-1, continued

Census occupational category	MSEI2	TSEI2	MSEI3
704 Conductors and motormen, urban rail transit	24.60	25.12	18.74
705 Deliverymen and routemen	21.19	23.16	14.42
706 Fork lift and tow motor operatives	15.65	17.94	7.69
710 Motormen; mine, factory, logging camp, etc.	16.46	18.36	8.73
711 Parking attendants	19.17	23.11	11.65
712 Railroad brakemen	27.84	27.42	22.87
713 Railroad switchmen	23.86	25.09	17.79
714 Taxicab drivers and chauffeurs	19.44	22.46	12.11
715 Truck drivers	20.09	21.10	13.28
726 Transport equipment operatives-allocated	17.94	19.89	10.49
740 Animal caretakers, exc. farm	19.25	23.18	11.76
750 Carpenters' helpers	14.74	18.04	6.40
751 Construction laborers, exc. carpenters' helpers	15.90	18.50	7.93
752 Fishermen and oystermen	18.90	20.65	11.70
753 Freight and material handlers	17.02	19.59	9.24
754 Garbage collectors	15.03	17.24	6.95
755 Gardeners and groundskeepers, exc. farm	16.06	19.24	8.02
760 Longshoremen and stevedores	21.80	22.62	15.38
761 Lumbermen, raftsmen, and woodchoppers	15.36	17.69	7.32
762 Stock handlers	16.99	19.99	9.05
763 Teamsters	15.47	17.73	7.47
764 Vehicle washers and equipment cleaners	14.28	17.16	5.89
770 Warehousemen, n.e.c.	18.98	21.96	11.55
780 Miscellaneous laborers	15.08	17.49	6.94
785 Not specified laborers	14.84	17.77	6.53
796 Laborers, except farm-allocated	16.37	19.06	8.44
801 Farmers (owners and tenants)	22.19	23.81	15.70
802 Farm managers	31.92	33.64	27.40
806 Farmers and farm managers-allocated	21.60	23.52	14.90
821 Farm foremen	22.62	25.49	15.99
822 Farm laborers, wage workers	13.79	16.77	5.26
823 Farm laborers, unpaid family workers	15.54	19.02	7.31
824 Farm service laborers, self-employed	20.46	22.04	13.67

Table A-1, continued

Census occupational category		MSEI2	TSEI2	MSEI3
	Cleaning service workers			
846	Farm laborers and farm foremen- allocated	14.41	17.41	6.01
901	Chambermaids and maids, except private household	15.74	15.24	7.60
902	Cleaners and charwomen	14.52	15.97	6.16
903	Janitors and sextons	15.80	18.51	7.72
	Food service workers			
910	Bartenders	22.71	23.96	16.06
911	Busboys	15.23	19.04	6.89
912	Cooks, except private household	18.06	17.52	10.43
913	Dishwashers	16.35	19.03	8.21
914	Food counter and fountain workers	18.52	20.43	10.83
915	Waiters	22.38	18.88	15.42
916	Food service workers, n.e.c., except private household	17.55	17.81	9.68
	Health service workers			
921	Dental assistants	34.22	27.15	29.79
922	Health aides, exc. nursing	27.11	25.65	21.16
923	Health trainees	33.95	45.49	29.24
924	Lay midwives	28.54	23.58	22.78
925	Nursing aides, orderlies, and attendants	21.09	19.52	13.86
926	Practical nurses	24.20	24.94	17.67
	Personal service workers			
931	Airline stewardesses	35.17	51.51	31.51
932	Attendants, recreation and amusement	24.89	28.84	18.51
933	Attendants, personal service, n.e.c.	23.37	27.09	16.66
934	Baggage porters and bellhops	19.25	23.22	11.71
935	Barbers	18.19	20.45	10.75
940	Boarding and lodging house	31.16	26.69	26.11
941	Bootblacks	11.56	14.91	2.59

Table A-1, continued

Census occupational category		MSEI2	TSEI2	MSEI3
942	Child care workers, exc. private household	24.40	23.06	17.82
943	Elevator operators	14.23	16.78	5.86
944	Hairdressers and cosmetologists	26.91	19.10	21.41
945	Personal service apprentices	13.18	15.99	4.47
950	Housekeepers, exc. private household	35.54	29.19	31.40
952	School monitors	35.67	26.08	31.08
953	Ushers, recreation and amusement	16.97	23.01	8.97
954	Welfare service aides	36.60	28.48	32.59
	Protective service workers			
960	Crossing guards and bridge tenders	14.72	16.72	6.48
961	Firemen, fire protection	32.73	32.35	28.78
962	Guards and watchmen	21.05	23.61	14.16
963	Marshals and constables	31.38	33.12	26.67
964	Policemen and detectives	37.07	37.98	33.73
965	Sheriffs and bailiffs	31.02	33.33	26.21
976	Service workers, exc. private household-allocated	19.51	19.64	12.25
980	Child care workers, private household	13.09	17.98	4.39
981	Cooks, private household	16.93	15.33	8.98
982	Housekeepers, private household	16.51	15.38	8.55
983	Laundresses, private household	19.31	15.62	12.01
984	Maids and servants, private household	13.44	14.71	4.81
986	Private household workers-allocated	13.35	13.81	4.86

NOTE: Source tapes provided by the U.S. Census did not include data for these two titles. Consequently, updated scores could not be computed. See Hauser and Featherman (1977:326) for approximations: 572:39.00 (MSEI2); 575:25.70 (MSEI2)/ 25.30 (TSEI2).

REFERENCES

Blau, Peter M. and Otis Dudley Duncan
1967   The American Occupational Structure. New York: John Wiley and Sons.

Coxon, Anthony and Charles Jones
1978   The Images of Occupational Prestige: A Study in Social Cognition. New York: St. Martin's Press.

Duncan, Otis
1961   "A socioeconomic index for all occupations." Pp. 109-138 in A. J. Reiss, Jr., Occupations and Social Status. New York: Free Press.

Featherman, David L., F. Lancaster Jones and Robert M. Hauser
1975   "Assumptions of social mobility research in the United States: the case of occupational status." Social Science Research 4:329-60.

Featherman, David L. and Robert M. Hauser
1976a   "Sexual inequalities and socioeconomic achievement in the United States, 1962-1973." American Sociological Review 41:462-83.

1976b   "Prestige or socioeconomic scales in the study of occupational achievement?" Sociological Methods and Research 4:402-422.

1978   Opportunity and Change. New York: Academic Press.

Goldthorpe, John and Keith Hope
1972   "Occupational grading and occupational prestige." Pp. 19-80 in John Goldthorpe and Keith Hope (eds.), The Analysis of Social Mobility: Methods and Approaches. Oxford: Clarendon Press.

Hauser, Robert M. and David L. Featherman
1977   The Process of Stratification: Trends and Analyses. New York: Academic Press.

Hodge, Robert W., Paul M. Siegel and Peter H. Rossi
1964   "Occupational prestige in the United States, 1925-63." American Journal of Sociology 70:286-302.

McClendon, McKee J.
1976   "The occupational status attainment processes of males and females." American Sociological Review 41:52-64.

Reiss, Albert J.
    1961   Occupations and Social Status. New York:
            Free Press.

Siegel, Paul M.
    1971   Prestige in the American Occupational Structure.
            Unpublished Doctoral Dissertation. University
            of Chicago.

Sewell, William H. and Robert M. Hauser
    1980   "The Wisconsin longitudinal study of social and
            psychological factors in aspirations and
            achievements." Research in Sociology of Education
            and Socialization Volume 1. Greenwich, Conn.:
            JAI Press.

Sewell, William H., Robert M. Hauser, and Wendy C. Wolf
    1980   "Sex, schooling, and occupational status."
            American Journal of Sociology 86:551-84.

Spenner, Kenneth I.
    1977   From Generation to Generation: The Transmission
            of Occupation. Unpublished Ph.D. Dissertation.
            University of Wisconsin-Madison.

Stevens, Gillian and David L. Featherman
    1981   A revised socioeconomic index of occupational
            status. Social Science Research 10:364-92.

Treas, Judith and Andrea Tyree
    1979   "Prestige versus socioeconomic status in the
            attainment processes of American men and women."
            Social Science Research 8:201-21.

Treiman, Donald J.
    1977   Occupational Prestige in Comparative Perspective.
            New York: Academic Press.

U.S. Bureau of the Census
    1973   Census of Population: 1970. Subject Reports,
            Final Report PC(2)-7A Occupational Characteristics.
            Washington, D.C.: U.S. Government Printing Office.

6. Women, Men, and Socioeconomic Indices: An Assessment

Introduction

The increasing labour force participation of North American women has been accompanied by a growing interest in the conceptualization and measurement of sex differences in labour force attainments. In sociology, students of sex differences in occupational status now question the use of the usual socioeconomic indices (S.E.I.) which arrange census occupations in a hierarchy according to the labour force characteristics of male incumbents only. The use of such socioeconomic indices to represent occupations is questionable both because the sex composition of the labour force has changed to include more women and because the studies which use the socioeconomic indices to compare men and women find similarities which contrast with other evidence concer-

Revision of a paper presented at the January 1981 meeting of the American Association for the Advancement of Science, Toronto, Canada. The authors thank Paula England, Jerry Jacobs and John Myles for their helpful comments on various drafts of this paper. Research presented in this paper was funded by grants from the President's Fund, the Dean of Social Sciences and the Office of Graduate Studies, Carleton University. The study was also funded by the research grant portion of the Canadian Social Science and Humanities Research Council Sabbatical Fellowships awarded to Professors Boyd and McRoberts who were visiting scholars at Harvard University and Statistics Canada, respectively, during 1980-81. The data analyzed were collected by the 1973 Canadian Mobility Study of whom the principal investigators were: Monica Boyd, Hugh A. McRoberts and John Porter (Carleton University); John Goyder (University of Waterloo); Frank E. Jones and Peter C. Pineo (McMaster University).

ning sex segregation of occupations, autonomy of work, promotional opportunities and pay levels. This paper begins with a general review of the criticisms of socioeconomic indices as used in studies of male/female labour force inequality. Particular attention is given to the use of socioeconomic indices which are calculated from the characteristics of male workers in studies of male/female inequalities. We first review and assess the consequences of using prestige studies as a basis for the derivation of socioeconomic indices. We then consider the recent proposals to incorporate the characteristics of women as well as men into the construction of socioeconomic indices. Here, we empirically assess sex differences in the status attainment process when occupations are scaled according to a female specific hierarchy of socioeconomic status.

Socioeconomic Indices and Sexual Inequality

Socioeconomic indices were developed to overcome the absence of information on the social standing of all occupations in a given society. In the past, various prestige studies requested respondents to rank order a selected group of occupations, the purpose being to generate a hierarchy based on social consensus (see Reiss, 1961; Pineo and Porter, 1967). By now it is well established that the ranking of occupations in such studies is determined largely by the economic properties of the occupations included (see Reiss, 1961:23-42), and the term "prestige" may be a misnomer to the extent that the properties of authority and deference do not appear to be the most important criteria used in ranking occupations.

Although these prestige studies provided a mechanism by which to approximate an individual's position in the stratification system, the list of occupational titles to be ranked was generally small, partly because of respondent fatigue and because of the practical impossibility of obtaining knowledgeable rankings over all occupations existing in a society. In order to overcome this limitation, the rankings generated by the prestige studies became the basis for predicting the rankings of a much larger group of occupations. Although several variations of this resultant index predominate in North American research with reference to the United States (Duncan, 1961a; Featherman and Hauser, 1978) and to Canada (Blishen, 1967; Blishen and McRoberts, 1976), these indices are similar in construction. First, prestige rankings of a limited number of occupations or titles done by national samples of respondents are obtained (Pineo and Porter, 1967; Reiss, 1961). Where possible, these occupational titles then are matched with census occupational titles. Next, a prediction equation is obtained by regressing the prestige of these matched occupational titles on the proportion of men in those occupations who earn above a specified amount and who exceed a specified level of education (Figure 1). The resultant regression equation (Figure 1, Equation 2) is used to estimate scores (Y) for all census occupations for which education and income data exist (X_1, X_2). It is generally conceded that the resulting socioeconomic scale distributes occupations along a dimension of socioeconomic "goodness" or desirability rather than along dimensions of authority or deference (Goldthorpe and Hope, 1972; Featherman, Jones and Hauser, 1975; Featherman and Hauser, 1967a; Reiss, 1961).

Why should such an index be considered problematic for research on sexual inequality? Initial answers are provided by socioeconomic attainment studies. During the 1960s and 1970s researchers made abundant use of socioeconomic indices in order to study the differential occupational status of men and to illuminate the process whereby such occupational status differences are attributable to family of origin characteristics and subsequent educational and first job attainments. The growth of the female labour force provided the impetus for the inclusion of women in such status attainments models (Boyd, 1982; Featherman and Hauser, 1976b; Marini, 1980; McClendon, 1976; Sewell, Hauser and Wolf, 1980; Treiman and Terrill, 1965; Treas and Tyree, 1979). These studies generally show striking similarity among men and women in how background resources such as family of origin characteristics, and education affect the acquisition of occupational status. Although several studies (Boyd, 1982; Marini, 1980; Sewell, Hauser and Wolf, 1989) confirm the lower career mobility of women compared to men, virtually all North American research observes that the occupational status of women in the labour force on the average is equal to, if not higher, than the average status observed for males. Such similarity between the sexes in occupational status and in the effects of family background and other occupationally-relevant resources on occupational socioeconomic achievement contrast sharply with the sex segregation of occupations, and the sexual inequalities in income, promotional opportunities, on-the-job training and autonomy observed in other studies. As stated by one critic (Huber, 1980:7), "the analomies in the S.E.I. indicate that something badly needs to be fixed."

Exactly what is wrong and needs to be fixed in the S.E.I. is interpreted in various ways. Some of the discon-

$$Y_i = f(X_{1i}, X_{2i}) \qquad\qquad \text{Eq. 1}$$

Where Y_i is the ranking assigned to a particular occupation on the basis of a study in which respondents are asked to sort and rank a limited number of occupations (see Pineo and Porter, 1976; Reiss, 1961; Siegel, 1971); where X_{1i} is the percentage of male incumbents in the ith occupation who attained or exceeded a specified educational level; and where X_{2i} is the percentage of male incumbents in the ith occupation who attain or exceed a specified level of earnings. X_i and X_2 are calculated from census data. The resultant regression equation

$$Y = a + b_1X_1 + b_2X_2 \qquad\qquad \text{Eq. 2}$$

is subsequently used to assign ranking scores (Y) to all census occupations for which the requisite education and income percentages exist.

Figure 1. The Construction of Socioeconomic Indices

tent with the use of socioeconomic indices to examine male
and female labour force inequalities reflects a discontent
with the model of status attainment. The virtues and lia-
bilities of the status attainment paradigm per se are well
documented (Acker, 1978, 1980; Coser, 1975; Crowder, 1974;
Featherman, 1976; Horan, 1978; Huber, 1980; Treiman, 1976)
and will not be covered in this paper. Most of the concerns
and criticisms over the use of the S.E.I. in depicting the
status of women derive from three additional sources: the
summary nature of the index; the conceptual properties of
the index; and the assumption of a male work world which is
built into the construction of the indices initially provided
by Duncan (1961a) and Blishen (1967).

   Summary measures are often used in stratification research because of the resultant simplicity in assigning and
locating an individual position in a stratification system
(Haller and Bills, 1979). However, by definition, summary
measures force the researcher to work with only one measure,
which may in fact be a composite of several indicators and
which may differ systematically across different sections of
the population. These general characteristics of summary
measures form the basis for more specific complaints against
the socioeconomic index. As noted earlier, the S.E.I. is
obtained by combining the two measures (education and income) which are specific to an occupation, and which appear
to be highly predictive of the social standing of occupations
(see Duncan, 1961a). By design, this procedure is problematic for students of sex stratification in several ways.
First, the procedure ignores location of work roles which
are unpaid, such as housewife (see Acker, 1980), although
several studies attempt to remedy the problem (Bose, 1973;
Bose, 1980; Dworkin, 1981; Eichler, 1977; Nilson, 1978;
Olsen, 1979). Secondly, by virtue of being a summary measure, this procedure also masks the different education-
income configurations which characterize occupations. There
is evidence that these configurations differ by sex. Women
tend to be in occupations which are characterized by more
education and lower incomes than are occupations filled by
men (Blishen and Carroll, 1978). These inequalities are
minimized in the construction of socioeconomic indices.
Under the method of calculations, the same score can be assigned to two different occupational categories such as
graduate nursing and aircraft mechanics and repairing occupations either because the education and income measures
for the occupations are similar or because unequal but
counterbalancing combinations of weighted education and
income measures exist (Figure 1, Equation 2). What is of
interest to students of stratification is the sexual inequality in these specific socioeconomic measures, and critics

derive little comfort from the knowledge that both nursing
and aircraft mechanic occupations are socioeconomically
better than are babysitting and pelt processing occupations.

A second but similar body of criticism originates from
the conceptual properties of S.E.I. We suggest that the
failure to recognize the scaling properties of the S.E.I. in
fact underlie much of the exasperation over the insensitivi-
ties of the S.E.I. in measuring sexual inequalities. Studies
using socioeconomic indices and those using other variables
can provide different parameters of male/female inequalities
simply because different dependent variables scale different
dimensions of the stratification system. Socioeconomic indices are measures of the socioeconomic goodness or desirability of occupations, represented to a large extent by
the resources (education) and rewards (income) associated
with occupations (see Acker, 1980; Featherman and Hauser,
1976a; Featherman, Jones and Hauser, 1975; Haller and Bills,
1979). They do not scale features of the various jobs which
exist within broad occupational categories. This is an important distinction because many of the male/female labour
force inequalities which are observed are characteristics
of jobs, not occupations. Men and women in identical occupations (or identically scored occupations) can be in different jobs with different sources and levels of income,
fringe benefits, autonomy, and promotional opportunities.
In this sense, some of the properties of the S.E.I. may have
been misinterpreted or overlooked by its critics who seek
to use the S.E.I. as a single all-purpose stratification
variable. Socioeconomic indices describe an individual's
location along a hierarchy of socioeconomic desirability,
nothing more, nothing less. Such scales are useful in indicating how far individuals move from a starting point.
And in combination with the status attainment paradigm, such
scales are also informative in depicting the process by which
the intergenerational and intragenerational mobility of individuals occurs. But because such scales are summary measures of occupational goodness, they will not measure many
more specific components of inter-group inequalities between
men and women in the labour force.[1] "Fixing" the S.E.I. will

1. Male/female differences are not completely masked, however. Status attainment research using S.E.I. documents reduced career mobility of women relative to men (Boyd, 1982;
Marini, 1980); Sewell, Hauser and Wolf, 1980). Such depressed intragenerational mobility for women is consistent with
the absence of internal labour markets and career traject-
ories in predominantly female occupations. But the S.E.I.
by its very construction does not permit testing for these
specific factors.

not resolve the difficulties arising from the summary nature of the index or from its conceptual properties. Two alternatives would be first, the creation of a new and different summary measure which is more sensitive to other labour force dimensions of male/female equalities and secondly, the study of specific indicators of labour force inequality such as income, job autonomy and sex segregation. Much of the North American research on male/female inequalities has moved in the latter direction (e.g., Boyd and Humphreys, 1979; McLaughlin, 1978; Wolf and Fligstein, 1979).

In addition to criticisms which evolve from the S.E.I. as a summary measure of socioeconomic goodness, criticisms also originate from the absence of women in the scale construction. This absence exists either because male incumbents or male dominated occupations are the stimuli in the prestige studies and/or because the S.E.I. scores are calculated subsequently from the income and educational characteristics of occupations held by males in the labour force. In the latter case, the occupational specific educational and income characteristics of male incumbents are used to assign scores to "female" occupations such as secretarial occupations. These procedures are problematic to the extent that they induce error in the S.E.I. with respect to how it measures the position of women along the axis of stratification which it scales. If such errors exist, previous comparisons of men and women in the labour force which use the S.E.I. may be inaccurate.

The response to this body of criticism is to create a more valid measure of occupational status which recognizes the labour force characteristics of women. However, attempts to "bring women back in" are varied in approach and rationale. Recent research has generally taken one of two directions in regard to improving the measurement of the relative standing of men and women within the general S.E.I. format. One body of research focuses on the left hand side of Equation 1 in Figure 1, and it seeks to determine if rankings assigned to occupations have a sexual component. The second direction of recent research is to modify the socioeconomic index to include the female labour force characteristics in the calculation of the S.E.I. scores for census occupations. With only a few exceptions in the United States (Bose, 1973; Heyns and Gray, 1973), these modifications do not incorporate the possibility that the sex of the perceived occupational incumbent can affect the occupational rankings generated by a "prestige" study. Instead, the modifications consist of altering the data for the right hand side of the equations in Figure 1 (e.g., the education and income data).

How problematic is the exclusion of women in S.E.I.
scales for studies of male/female inequalities? Answering
this question requires first an assessment of whether or not
the problem indeed exists, and secondly an evaluation of how
their existence might alter our understanding of sex differences in the labour force. For organizational purposes,
this review first examines the attempts to "bring women back
in" to prestige studies (the left hand side of Equation 1,
Figure 1), and then it discusses recent attempts to modify
the calculation of the S.E.I. by including occupational
characteristics of female incumbents (the right hand side of
Equation 2, Figure 1).

Women and Prestige Studies

As shown by Figure 1, the starting point for the calculation of socioeconomic indices are rankings of a limited
number of occupations which were generated by a given "prestige" study (see Reiss, 1961; Pineo and Porter, 1967). The
difficulties associated with such prestige studies both in
general and in the construction of socioeconomic indices
have been commented upon from the outset (Blishen, 1967;
Blishen and McRoberts, 1976; Duncan, 1961a, 1961b; Haug,
1972, 1977; Haug and Sussman, 1971; Pineo and Porter, 1967;
Reiss, 1961: Chapter 1; Siegel, 1971: Chapter 2). Quite
apart from other concerns with respect to the measurement
of occupational status, two specific issues are pertinent
for studies of male/female inequality using S.E.I. scores.
First, to what extent are the lists of occupations which
are employed in prestige studies either representative of
the universe of occupations or representative of the distribution of female occupations in the labour force? Secondly,
does a sexual component to the rating task exist which affects the evaluation of the occupation?

The first question arises from the early 1947 NORC
study (Reiss, 1961) which deliberately omitted the titles
of female-sex labelled occupations, such as secretaries.
As a result, the rank ordering of occupations produced by
that study are not representative by sex or of the universe
of all occupations. Subsequently, the National Opinion Research Center did obtain rankings of both male and female
dominated occupations from three surveys in the 1960s
(Siegel, 1971: Chapter 2) as did the Canadian Porter-Pineo
(1967) study. The inclusion of female occupational titles
renders the occupational rankings produced somewhat more
representative by sex than the listing produced by the
early 1947 study. The increase between 1947 and the 1960s
in the number of occupational titles which respondents are

asked to rank also improves the representativeness of the
underlying occupational hierarchy being assessed, and it increases the number of matches with census titles used in calculating the socioeconomic index. As a result the prediction
equation for the American S.E.I. has changed (see Stevens and
Featherman, 1981).

A second issue pertinent to the S.E.I. concerns the possible existence of a sexual component to the rating of occupations. If this situation exists, then there are two occupational hierarchies rather than one and this suggests the
need for sex-specific S.E.I. prediction equations. The
studies which investigate this possibility ask a number of
interrelated questions but two questions predominate: Are
male and female incumbents differentially evaluated or are
occupations differentially evaluated on the basis of sex composition? The first question is addressed by examining the
"within" occupation effect of sex on prestige rankings of
occupations (England, 1979) which occurs when an occupation
with a designated female incumbent (e.g., mailwoman) has a
different ranking than the same occupation with a male incumbent (mailman). With respect to the issue of whether or
not rankings differ according to the sex of the incumbent,
the evidence is mixed. A study based on the ranking of 93
occupations (including househusband and housewife) by 180
respondents in Kitchener, Ontario indicates that designating
the sex of the incumbent does affect the ranking of occupations (Guppy and Siltanen, 1977; Eichler, 1977). However,
American studies which also are based on small local samples
are more mixed, finding both no support (Bose, 1973 - cited
in England, 1979; Heyns and Gray, 1973) and evidence (Nilson,
1976; Powell and Jacobs, 1980; Walker and Bradley, 1973) for
the argument that male incumbent occupations and female incumbent occupations are differentially ranked.

The variability of these results may be attributable to
uncontrolled characteristics of local samples or to differences in research designs. However, quite apart from the
general conclusion reached by a review of male and female
incumbents across all occupations, some of these studies do
observe that female incumbents of strongly male-labelled
occupations and male incumbents of female-labelled occupations tend to be assigned a ranking which differs from that
normally assigned the sex appropriate incumbent (Bose, 1973;
Eichler, 1977; Guppy and Siltanen, 1977; Nilson, 1976; Olsen,
1979). The findings are not consistent across studies either
in magnitude or direction. Nonetheless, they imply that the
general perceptions of the <u>appropriate</u> sex incumbent may act
as a criterion of occupational rankings.

What is the appropriate sex for the incumbent of an occupation is highly related to the sex composition of that
occupation. A second question found in investigations into
the sexual component to prestige ranks asks whether or not
the sex composition of all occupations are related to their
rankings. This relationship could occur for either or both
of two reasons: 1) those occupations which are assigned a
lower rank happen to be those into which women are recruited
or steered; and/or alternatively; (2) occupations which em-
ploy mostly women are docked some increment of social standing in accordance with the general societal tendency to place
greater evaluation on the tasks performed by men (see England, 1979:254-257). Here again, evidence is mixed. In
Canada, Guppy and Siltanen (1977) find a negative association (r = .24) between the proportion of an occupation that
is female and the occupation's rank. In the United States,
Bose (1973) observes that female-typed jobs have lower prestige than do male-typed jobs but the difference is considered small (Acker, 1978). Other studies find that the percent
of an occupation which is female exerts an insignificant
effect on prestige scores, net of other variables, and/or
that zero order correlations are very weak (England, 1979;
Siegel, 1971).

What do these studies suggest about sex-specific evaluations of occupations and are these findings likely to
modify the prestige component of socioeconomic indices?
From a review of this research, a pattern emerges in which
studies using global measures (means, correlations) calculated over a large number of occupational titles are less
likely to support the sexual component of prestige argument
than are analyses which examine a limited number of strongly
sex labelled occupations. This pattern implies that commen-
tators are correct in noting that sex of the incumbent can
affect the evaluation of the work role in certain occupations. But the pattern also suggests that over the entire
occupational distribution the sex of the incumbent is not an
obvious source of bias in occupational evaluation, the implication being that separate prestige rankings for male and
female incumbents would not markedly improve the socioeconomic scaling of occupational standing. We note that even
if two sex-specific rankings were produced and incorporated
into the S.E.I., this fine tuning will likely have little
effect on the actual socioeconomic indices produced. Indices are based on the percentage of the sample giving a
"good" or "excellent" response to the question on ranking a
specific occupation (Duncan, 1961a; 1961b) or on other summary measures (Pineo and Porter, 1967). The resultant parameters are so broad that any attempt to fine tune the instru-

ment is unlikely to lead to much change in the resulting
analyses. We suggest that the largest modification to date
in the construction of the S.E.I., as currently designed,
results from the increase in the number and representativeness of occupational titles, both ranked by evaluators in
the "prestige studies" and also matched with occupational
census titles.

Socioeconomic Indices and Women

In addition to occupational "prestige" scores, income
and education measures specific to occupations are also used
to generate socioeconomic indices for the full set of census
occupations (see Figure 1). Thus, the actual calculation of
the S.E.I. scales introduces two additional questions.
First, what is the reference population used to generate the
prediction equation (Figure 1, Equation 1)? Secondly, from
what population are the income and educational characteristics taken and inserted into the S.E.I. prediction equation
(Figure 1, Equation 2)?

Two decades ago, the answers were patently obvious.
Since the labour force was composed largely of men, both
the prediction equation and the actual S.E.I. scores were
constructed from the occupational-specific education and
income characteristics of men in the labour force. By the
1970s this conceptualization of an all male work world was
inaccurate and it was sharply critiqued in stratification
research (Acker, 1973, 1978, 1980). By implication, the
S.E.I. needs to be altered because in its exclusion of women,
it incorrectly measures the location of occupations along a
socioeconomic hierarchy. In the current literature, at
least three ways exist for revising the socioeconomic index
to correct for this possible error, each with its own rationale and strategy for better representing women in the construction of the index. One approach calculates the socioeconomic indices using the total population as the reference
population. A second approach stresses the construction of
socioeconomic scales which are sex-specific. And a third
approach is a hybrid of the two, advocating the construction
of socioeconomic scales from a single prediction equation
but using sex-specific education and income parameters to
generate the index scores. With only a few exceptions,
based on local studies (e.g., Bose, 1973; Heyns and Gray,
1973) these approaches take as given the rankings of occupations produced by prestige studies, and they focus instead
on modifications of the calculation of the prediction equation and/or the calculation of the S.E.I. for the universe
of census occupations.

The first approach which brings women into the construction of socioeconomic indices does so largely on methodological grounds. The argument is that the prediction of the
S.E.I. may be error prone if it is calculated solely from the
characteristics of men. Such error results from failure of
certain occupational characteristics to be representative of
the actual set of characteristics, such as when the income
and educational characteristics of male secretaries are used
in the construction of the S.E.I. (Powers and Holmberg, 1978;
Stevens and Featherman, 1981). A consequence of this practice appears to be inflated socioeconomic indices for occupations in which females are heavily concentrated (Jacobs,
1981; Powers and Holmberg, 1978).

One way of minimizing this "error" in the construction
of S.E.I. is to input the educational and income characteristics of the total labour force instead of the male labour
force. Powers and Holmberg (1978) pioneered this use of the
total population in their recalculation of the occupational
status scale, which unlike the socioeconomic index does not
use rankings provided by prestige scales as a starting point
(see Nam, Powers and Glick, 1964; United States Bureau of the
Census, 1963). More recently, Stevens and Featherman (1981)
have developed a socioeconomic index which is based on the income and educational characteristics of the total population.

A different strategy and rationale for modifying the
socioeconomic indices to include women is represented in recent work by Blishen and Carroll (1978). Using Canadian data
these researchers calculate a second prediction equation
(Figure 1, Equation 2) based on the educational and income
characteristics of women in each census occupational category. The result is a socioeconomic index with women as the
reference population. In combination with the earlier
Blishen-McRoberts (1976) scale, which was produced with men
as the reference population, this new Blishen-Carroll index
means that sex-specific socioeconomic indices can be generated.

What is the rationale for the production of sex-specific
socioeconomic indices? Blishen and Carroll (1978) never explicitly provide one although their emphasis is consistent
with the second of the two rationales which we suggest below.
One reason for creating a second S.E.I. is simply to provide
a different approximation to the underlying socioeconomic
hierarchy which is scaled by S.E.I. measures. This rationale
is similar to the one presented for creating a scale based on
the total population since the effort assumes a socioeconomic
hierarchy of occupations, which may be imperfectly described
by an S.E.I. measure calculated solely from male characteristics. The second rationale departs from this assumption of
an underlying socioeconomic hierarchy which is the same for

men and women. Instead, the creation of a female-based
S.E.I. is motivated by the argument that although both indices scale occupations according to a hierarchy of desirability and socioeconomic goodness, sex-specific hierarchies
exist. Occupations which are scaled as high in socioeconomic
status for men may not be those scaled as high for women and
vice versa. This particularly seems to be the case for occupations in which women predominate versus those in which men
concentrate. Inspection of the top forty occupations according to the Blishen-Carroll (1978) and Blishen-McRoberts
(1976) indices shows that the Blishen-Carroll scale derived
from female characteristics elevates considerably the rank
of occupations such as nursing supervisors, dieticians, ele-
mentary and kindergarten teachers, librarians and archivists,
and it depresses the rankings of occupations such as nuclear
engineer, petroleum engineer, metallurgical engineer, archi-
tects and financial management occupations. These changes
in rankings are consistent with the view that occupations
which are desirable or good for men are not necessarily the
occupations which are socioeconomically good for women, and
vice versa.

Two factors might account for the existence of these
sex-specific hierarchies of socioeconomic goodness. First,
the socioeconomic standing of occupations for women may reflect a different set of criteria used to evaluate the "goodness" of occupations for women than men. Acker (1980) suggests that the generalized respect which women earn as wives
and mothers is one of the components of the occupational
standing assigned to predominantly female occupations. Secondly, the socioeconomic desirability or goodness of occupations may vary by sex because the configuration of occupation-
ally-specific socioeconomic characteristics differ for men
and women. For example, according to the 1971 Census of the
Canadian population, roughly the same proportion of men and
women in the non-governmental administrative and management
groups of occupations had a high school education or better
(approximately 70 percent), but the average male income for
this group was nearly 160 percent higher than the female income in the same group of occupations. Such education-
income disparities are reflected in a more general way in
the equations which Blishen and McRoberts (1976) and Blishen-
and Carroll (1978) present. In particular, the relatively
large magnitude of the income coefficient in the female
equation suggests that given their incomes, women need more
education in order to generate the same status levels as men
for a specific occupation. In the face of such differences,
it seems difficult to argue that identical occupations have
the same level of socioeconomic desirability independently
of the sex of the incumbent.

A third approach to altering the socioeconomic indices
to include women is illustrated in work by Jacobs (1981) who
calculates socioeconomic indices from a single prediction
equation but uses sex specific income and educational distributions to predict the S.E.I. scores for all occupations.
Jacobs contends that the derivation of weights in the prediction equation (Figure 1, Equation 2) from the characteristics
of the male labour force does not in itself mislocate occupations along a given hierarchy. Rather error is generated
when male labour force characteristics are inserted into the
prediction equation to generate the S.E.I. for women in the
labour force. As a result, Jacobs (1981) advocates inserting
male labour force characteristics into a prediction equation
to generate S.E.I. scores for men and inserting female educational and income characteristics into the same prediction
equation to calculate scores for women.

What is the rationale for this third approach? According to Jacobs (1981), a socioeconomic index which is calculated from the educational and income characteristics of
either the total or male labour force inhibits the analysis
of intraoccupational inequality. Assigning a single score
to each occupation forces men and women (or blacks and whites)
with the same occupation to be identically scored even though
men and women might have different standing in these occupations. In order to capture "these between-sex" differences,
Jacobs recommends that sex-specific socioeconomic indices be
generated from the education and income characteristics of
men and women using a single prediction equation for weighting education and income. Although this is a rationale conceptually oriented to showing sex differences in "prestige",
it parallels the argument that a sex-specific hierarchy
exists. Jacobs goes on to devise a number of male and female specific prediction equations, using a variety of different measures of occupational specific educational and
income measures. Operationally, his research is a hybrid
between work by Stevens and Featherman (1981) and Blishen
and Carroll (1978).

An Empirical Assessment

It is clear from the preceding discussion that by the
1980s a number of alternatives exist in regard to recalcul-
ating the socioeconomic index to include women. Although
these attempts differ in conceptualization and operationali-
zation, they are similarly motivated by the increased labour
force participation of women and the desire to better measure the degree of sexual inequality in the labour force. Has
this attention to women in fact provided an improved under-

standing of the status of men and women in the labour force?
In particular, does the recalculation of socioeconomic indices for occupations alter previous findings of studies on
male/female occupational achievement?

Table 1 summarizes the results of several studies which
use socioeconomic indices to depict the occupational status
of men and women in the Canadian and American labour force.
The first four rows of Table 1 display the relative status
of men and women using the Duncan (1961a, 1961b) socioeconomic index and the Blishen-McRoberts (1976) index which are
calculated solely from the characteristics of the male
labour force in the United States and Canada. The observed
pattern is an often criticized one (Acker, 1980; Huber, 1980)
in which the average socioeconomic index for women is higher
than the average socioeconomic status observed for men. But
the relatively higher socioeconomic status of women persists
even with the Blishen-Carroll index which is calculated
solely from the occupational-specific educational and income
characteristics of women in the Canadian labour force. In
contrast, the pattern of relative advantage for women sharply reverses when the total population is the reference population for the educational and occupational characteristics.
When the educational and income characteristics of occupations
for the total labour force are used to generate occupational
status scores,[2] men have on the average a status score which
is nearly eleven points higher than the average score for
women (Table 1). This reversal occurs largely because the
inclusion of women in the calculation of the occupational
status scores tends to decrease the ranking of occupational
categories in which women are over-represented and increases
the scores for those occupational groupings in which men concentrate (see Cooney, Clague and Salvo, 1980; Powers and
Holmberg, 1978).

The relative disadvantage of women is also revealed when
comparisons are made between the male labour force population,
using male derived indices and the female labour force population, using female derived indices. For the United States
data, socioeconomic indexes are calculated for women and men

---

2. As noted earlier, Stevens and Featherman (1981) have produced prediction equations for the production of socioeconomic indices which are based on the characteristics of the
total labour force. When our paper was written, comparisons
of men and women using a total population index were not
available, and the data in Table 1 draws upon the research of
Cooney, Clague and Salvo (1980) which relies on the slightly
different Powers-Holmberg (1978) socioeconomic measure.

Table 1. Mean Socioeconomic Status for Various Socioeconomic Indexes[a] by Sex for Canada and the United States

Indices and Country	Means		
	Males	Females	Difference
Male-Derived Index			
Duncan S.E.I., U.S.A. 1970[b]	38.6	40.3	-1.7
Duncan S.E.I., U.S.A. 1973[c]	37.9	38.9	-1.0
Blishen-McRoberts, Canada 1970[d]	41.0	42.4	-1.4
Blishen-McRoberts, Canada 1973[e]	43.9	46.7	-2.8
Female-Derived Index			
Blishen-Carroll, Canada 1970[d]	41.1	42.3	-1.2
Blishen-Carroll, Canada 1973[e]	43.3	45.9	-2.6
Total Population Status Scores			
Powers-Holmberg, U.S.A. 1970[b]	54.1	43.4	+10.7
Sex Specific Indices			
Jacobs, U.S.A. 1970[f]	39.4	31.7	+7.7
Blishen-McRoberts-Carroll Canada 1973[g]	47.1	30.4	+16.7

[a] Includes occupational status scores calculated from the methodology developed by Nam et al. (1964) and Powers and Holmberg (1978).

[b] Experienced labour force (including blacks and whites) taken from Cooney, Clague and Salvo, 1980: Table 1.

[c] Married spouse present persons in the labour force, ages 20-64. Taken from Featherman and Hauser, 1976b: Table 1.

[d] Total labour force population excluding 26,680 women and 163,035 men in occupations not classified by the 1970 census. Taken from Blishen and Carroll (1978:356).

[e] Full-time paid native born population ages 25-64 calculated by the authors from 1973 Canadian Mobility Survey data.

[f] Total experienced civilian labour force (Jacobs, 1981).

[g] Same population and data base described in fn. e. Blishen-Carroll and Blishen-McRoberts indexes are transformed to conform to a range of 0-100, as discussed in fn. 3 in the text. The Blishen-McRoberts index is used to calculate the status for the male labour force and the Blishen-Carroll index is used with reference to the female labour force.

using the same prediction but sex specific educational and income measures (Jacobs, 1981). For Canadian data, both the prediction equation and the income and educational measures are sex specific. The resultant male and female specific socioeconomic indices have been transformed, however, since differences in the prediction equations (see Blishen and Carroll, 1978; Blishen and McRoberts, 1976) mean that even for occupations with identical educational and income measures the Blishen-Carroll index will always assign a higher socioeconomic index than will the male derived Blishen-McRoberts index.[3]

Overall, the data contained in Table 1 suggest that sex differentials in socioeconomic status vary in direction and magnitude depending on the measure. Women have a lower socioeconomic status than do men on the average when socioeconomic measures are calculated from the characteristics of the total labour force or are specific to each sex. This lower status of women relative to men is more consistent with the lower pay of occupations and other characteristics of work done by women. Thus sex specific measures or alternatively measures calculated from the characteristics of the total population, may have considerable appeal for students of sex stratification who challenge the apparent similarity between the sexes in regard to socioeconomic status.

Table 1 compares the status of men and women in the labour force only with respect to occupational outcomes. But occupational outcomes are only one way to gauge sex differences in the labour force. The fact that men and women can arrive at similar (or different) socioeconomic statuses in similar (or different) ways is the focus of the status attainment investigations into male/female labour force inequalities. In combination with the data in Table 1, this focus leads to a reconsideration of sex differences in the status attainment process, using various socioeconomic indices. Of special interest, given the pattern of male/female differences in socioeconomic indexes in Table 1, is whether or not the recalculation of socioeconomic indices to include women alters the previous findings of male/female status attainment studies.

---

3.   There are several transformations which deal with calibration problems of this type, ranging from simple linear transformations through to percentiles, standard z scores to exponential transformations. We have selected a linear transformation which constrains each scale to a range of 0 to 100. This transformation is intuitively appealing as it preserves all the basis scaling features of the original Blishen-McRoberts and Blishen-Carroll indices.

Table 2. Zero Order Correlations, Means and Standards Deviations for a Model of Occupational Attainment Using Blishen-McRoberts and Blishen-Carroll Socioeconomic Indices for Full Time Native Born Males and Females Age 25-64 in the 1973 Canadian Labour Force

Males \ Females	Zero Order Correlations					Male	
	X	$V^{(b)}$	U	W	Z	Means	s.d.
Blishen-McRoberts Scores							
X	–	.488	.458	.351	.346	7.34	3.90
V_b	.510	–	.395	.402	.399	34.69	12.98
U	.363	.270	–	.643	.618	10.91	3.65
W	.275	.239	.638	–	.675	38.40	14.19
Z	.263	.235	.600	.697	–	43.87	15.00
Means, Female	7.85	36.20	11.77	44.71	46.70		
s.d.	3.93	13.26	2.75	12.70	12.68		
Blishen-Carroll Scores							
X	–	.497	.460	.314	.323	7.37	3.92
V_b	.509	–	.400	.339	.337	34.84	13.15
U	.363	.271	–	.603	.591	11.02	3.68
W	.277	.227	.644	–	.669	39.16	13.67
Z	.274	.243	.634	.761	–	43.41	14.63
Means, Female	7.85	36.18	11.77	44.40	45.92		
s.d.	3.93	13.25	2.75	14.19	14.46		

Table 2, continued

Note: Variables are: X, father's education; V, S.E.I. for father's occupation; U, respondent's education; W, S.E.I. for respondent's first job; Z, S.E.I. for respondent's current occupation.

a Zero order correlations are presented above the diagonal for males and below the diagonal for females.

b Father's occupation coded using the Blishen-McRoberts socioeconomic index. Occupation refers to the occupation of the father or the head of household when the respondent was age 16.

c Because several census occupations exist for which there are no female incumbents, and for which no Blishen-Carroll scores exist, the Canadian Mobility study respondents who hold these occupations were omitted from the analysis using Blishen-Carroll scores. This affects about 9.3 percent of the Blishen-weighted male sample (see Table 1). Analyses were conducted deleting these men from the Blishen-McRoberts based equations as well, but since the conclusions were essentially unaltered, the data from the Blishen-McRoberts scale is presented for the larger population.

In the remainder of this paper we report initial results from our investigation into the substantive impact of using the female based Blishen-Carroll in male/female status comparisons. The data are taken from the Canadian Mobility Study, which is similar in design to the Occupational Changes in a Generation Surveys I and II (Blau and Duncan, 1967; Featherman and Hauser, 1978; Hauser and Featherman, 1977). The survey was funded by the Canada Council, and it was fielded in July 1973 as a supplement to the Statistics Canada Labour Force Survey. Questionnaires were distributed to all male and female members of the household or sampling unit who were 18 years of age and over and who were not intending to return to school. Subsequent research revealed a high item nonresponse to the question on current occupation for part-time female workers, and therefore, our analysis is based on a comparison of full-time paid men and women between the ages of 25 and 64 (Boyd, 1980a; 1982). Further, because the experiences of foreign born and native born differ (Boyd, 1980b, 1980c), the analysis focuses only upon comparisons of native born men and women in the July 1973 labour force.

Table 2 presents the means, standard deviations and zero order correlations for a standard male/female model in which occupational attainment, measured by the Blishen-McRoberts and the Blishen-Carroll indexes is regressed on respondents' first job status, education[4] and paternal education and socioeconomic status.[5] In keeping with the rationale for the creation of sex-specific socioeconomic indexes, the effect of creating a female specific index can be assessed in two ways. The first approach assumes that the Blishen-McRoberts and the Blishen-Carroll indexes are slightly different calibrations

---

4.   Respondents' and fathers' education are derived from questions concerning level of schooling attained which were recoded to approximate years of schooling.

5.   Fathers' socioeconomic status is coded in Blishen-McRoberts scores regardless of how current and first job statuses are scaled. Two reasons exist for this reliance on the Blishen-McRoberts scores to represent the occupation of the father or head of household. First, the reliance is appropriate since the father's occupation refers to a time when the labour force was a much more exclusively male preserve than it is today. Secondly, because the most developed model of status attainment is one which traces the impact of family of origin variables on attainments over the life cycle, we decided to keep the scaling of fathers' occupation constant in order to attribute the observed status attainment differences to variations in the scaling of the endogenous variables.

of the underlying socioeconomic hierarchy of occupations.
Neither index is error free since in their construction the
Blishen-McRoberts index ignores the occupational specific
characteristics of the female labour force and the Blishen-
Carroll index ignores the characteristics of the male labour
force. But most North American status attainment studies use
the male-derived Duncan (1961a) or Blishen-McRoberts (1976)
indices to compare the achievements of men and women. This
practice has generated considerable concern over how well
such indices represent the socioeconomic hierarchy for women,
and it sheds some doubt on the resultant male/female models
of status attainment. What happens to male/female comparisons when this error is reversed, such that the female-derived Blishen-Carroll index is used to examine the attainments
of men as well as women? This question requires comparing
the status attainment of men and women, first using one index
and then the other. Such metric-specific sex comparisons
should indicate if the use of the female-derived index substantially alters our understanding of sex differences in
status attainment.

Male/female differences in the attainment of current
socioeconomic status first are analyzed using the Blishen-
McRoberts male-based index, and the results are presented in
Columns 1 and 2 of Table 3. Detailed comparisons of these
sex differences in the attainment process are made elsewhere
by Boyd (1980a, 1982). A comparison of the male and female
regression equations for current occupations, measured by
the Blishen-McRoberts index, suggests that the status attainment process for women is more linked to recent rather than
past achievements. Compared to men, paternal socioeconomic
status has less of an effect on the socioeconomic status of
women. In contrast the socioeconomic status of the first
job has a greater impact on subsequent socioeconomic achievements compared to men, a finding which also is observed in
the United States (Sewell, Hauser and Wolf, 1980) and which
is consistent with the sex segregated nature of the occupational work world.

These results contrast only slightly with those obtained
from a male/female model of attainment which assigns occupational scores from the Blishen-Carroll index which is calculated solely from the characteristics of women in the labour
force (Table 3, Columns 3 and 4). When first and current
occupations are coded according to the Blishen-Carroll index
instead of the Blishen-McRoberts index, sex differences in
the impact of fathers' socioeconomic status on current socioeconomic status disappear to be replaced by significant sex
differences in the intercepts (Table 3, Columns 3 and 4).
These intercept differences indicate the existence of a sex

Table 3. Coefficients for a Model of Current Occupational
Attainment Using Blishen-McRoberts and Blishen-Carroll Socioeconomic Indices for Full-Time Native Born Men and Women, Age
25-64, in the 1973 Canadian Labour Force

| | Socioeconomic Index | | | |
| | Blishen-McRoberts | | Blishen-Carroll | |
	Male	Female	Male (a)	Female
Standardized Coefficients				
X	.008	.008	.014	.001
V[b]	.101	.037	.058	.043
U	.287	.251	.271	.236
W	.447	.526	.481	.599
Metric Coefficients (c)				
X	.030*	.027*	.054*	.003*
	(.037)	(.056)	(.038)	(.057)
V	.117	.036	.065*	.047*
	(.011)	(.016)	(.011)	(.017)
U	1.187*	1.157*	1.077*	1.240*
	(.045)	(.088)	(.045)	(.092)
W	.422	.525	.514	.610
	(.011)	(.019)	(.011)	(.017)
Constant	8.491*	8.101*	8.754	2.529
R^2	.522	.528	.506	.616

Note: Variables are: X, father's education; V, S.E.I. for
father's occupation; U, respondent's education; W, S.E.I. for
respondent's first job.

[a] See Table 2, footnote (c).

[b] See Table 2, footnote (b).

[c] Standard errors given in parentheses.

* Not significantly different at p > .05. Comparisons made
  for columns (1) vs (2); (3) vs (4).

effect which operates to the disadvantage of women. But
aside from these changes, the overall impression is one of
robustness in the male/female models of attainment. Despite
the S.E.I. employed, the direct effect of education on socioeconomic attainment is the same for men and women, and the
socioeconomic status of first job has a greater effect on the
current socioeconomic status of women compared to men. Given
this stability, we conclude that the choice of which S.E.I.
index should be employed to study sex difference in attainments is very much up to the discretion of the researcher.
This conclusion is also supported by the analysis of Blishen
and Carroll (1978).

The preceding discussion is based on the assumption that
both the Blishen-McRoberts and the Blishen-Carroll indexes
represent slightly different calibrations of a single underlying socioeconomic hierarchy of occupations. The second alternative rationale for comparison of the two indexes stresses the existence of two sex-specific socioeconomic status
hierarchies. This perspective has intuitive appeal because
it indirectly acknowledges the effects of sex segregation of
occupations (see England, 1979:261). If because of sex segregation, men and women work in parallel but sex specific
occupational hierarchies (England, 1979), then occupations
which are socioeconomically good or desirable for men will
differ somewhat from those which are desirable or good for
women. The existence of this sex specific status hierarchy,
in turn implies that the attainments of men and women should
be compared with the assumption of these separate status hierarchies built into the analysis. This requires comparing the
occupational attainments of males using the Blishen-McRoberts
index and the occupational attainments of women, using the
Blishen-Carroll index (Table 3, Columns 1 and 4).[6] Such a
comparison sharpens the earlier observed sex differences in
the process of socioeconomic attainment. Unlike males in the
labour force, the socioeconomic status of women is more affected by the status of first job, and less influenced by the
socioeconomic status of the father. Further, the effect of
being female, net of the other variables in the model, operates to about a 6 point disadvantage for women compared to
men. These findings are consistent with the existence of a
sex segregated work world which initially allocates women

----

6. For those researchers who are uncomfortable in comparing
magnitudes across two different S.E.I. indices, we note that
both indices are produced by identical cutoff levels of education and income (see Blishen and Carroll, 1978). As a result, any differences in metric reflect sex specific scaling
properties.

into a concentrated number of female occupations and which is
associated with a truncated range of occupational mobility
for women.   Overall, our results provide some ammunition for
those critics who are dissatisfied with the use of a male-
based socioeconomic scale to represent the socioeconomic position of women in the labour force.   Tables 1 and 3 indicate
that sex differences both in status levels and in the status
attainment process are the sharpest when the male population
is assigned male derived socioeconomic indices (e.g., Duncan,
1961a, 1961b; Blishen and McRoberts, 1976) and when the female population is assigned female derived indices (e.g.,
Blishen-Carroll, 1978).   Such comparisons, however, assume
the existence of sex-specific socioeconomic hierarchies.

Conclusion

The increasing labour force participation of North American women has been accompanied by an increasing interest in
the conceptualization and measurement of sex stratification.
In keeping with this general interest, this paper investi-
gates the substantive and theoretical implications of research which utilize socioeconomic indices to compare the
occupational attainments of men and women in the labour
force.   We argue that most of the concerns and criticisms
over the use of the S.E.I. in depicting the status of women
derive from several sources: a dissatisfaction with the
status attainment paradigm; the summary nature of the socioeconomic index; the conceptual properties of the S.E.I.; and
the assumption of a male work force which forms the basis of
the S.E.I. construction.   This paper focuses on the various
attempts to bring women back into the construction of socioeconomic indices.   We first assess the issues pertaining to
the occupational rankings which are produced by prestige
studies and then used to generate an equation to predict the
S.E.I. of occupations.   Our review suggests that reliance on
occupational prestige rankings specific to each sex will not
likely modify the socioeconomic indices produced.   Rather,
we suggest that a major modification to the S.E.I. results
from the use of a larger list of occupations to be ranked by
respondents, and matched with census occupations.   Such a
reliance creates a ranking which includes sex typed occupations in which women predominate as well as those in which
men concentrate.

The remainder of the paper focuses upon the use of the
educational and income characteristics of occupations in calculating socioeconomic indices.   The past practice is to calculate socioeconomic indices from the occupation-specific
educational and income characteristics for the male labour
force.   Recent modifications to this practice have been the

production of socioeconomic scales based on the total labour
force population, or the development of a socioeconomic index
calculated from the education and income characteristics of
occupations using the female population as the reference population. Reflecting these developments, we compare the socioeconomic attainments of men and women in the labour force.
Our analysis indicates that the average socioeconomic status
of women compared to men is higher when socioeconomic status
is defined according to a socioeconomic index calculated
wholly from the labour force characteristics of men or calculated wholly from the characteristics of women. This higher relative status for women may reflect the error introduced
when socioeconomic indices are calculated solely from the
characteristics of one sex and used to describe the status
of the other sex. Women have a lower average socioeconomic
status than men when socioeconomic measures are used which
are calculated from the characteristics of the total labour
force. The lower status of women relative to men also exists
when the female status is defined by an S.E.I. calculated
from the characteristics of women and compared to the S.E.I.
for men, calculated wholly from the occupational characteristics of men.

Use of any of these several indices which include women
involves an assumption about the sex-specificity of the hierarchy of socioeconomic goodness which socioeconomic indices
purport to scale. If a single hierarchy is assumed for all
labour force participants, the appropriate analytical strategy is to compare men and women using the identical index for
each sex. We initially adopt this orientation in our assessment of the sex differences in status attainment process,
first using the male derived Blishen-McRoberts index to compare sex specific models and then using the female derived
Blishen-Carroll index to compare male and female differences.
We find the sex differences in the status attainment process
are altered only slightly by the use of one index or the
other. The fact that the Blishen-McRoberts and Blishen-
Carroll indices produce slightly different parameters for
male and female models of attainment is not surprising since
both have a component of error associated with their scaling
of male or female dominated occupations.

An alternative approach in examining male/female models
of attainment is to compare the male attainment process using
the male-derived Blishen-McRoberts index to the female attainment process, using the female-derived Blishen-Carroll index.
This procedure assumes the existence of two sex-specific
hierarchies rather than a single socioeconomic hierarchy of
occupations. Under this conceptualization, occupations which
are socioeconomically good or desirable for men are not nec-

essarily those which are so for women, and vice versa. When
this assumption is adopted, the sex differences in the attainment process sharpen relative to those observed when only a
single socioeconomic hierarchy is assumed.

The question of course is where to proceed with respect
to research on socioeconomic indices. Because of the characteristics of our own data set, this paper did not assess extensively the consequences of using a socioeconomic index
which is calculated from the income and educational characteristics of the total labour force. Using an index which
has the total labour force as the reference population should
minimally provide parameters of male-female inequalities in
the status attainment process which differ from our results.
However, students of sex stratification may wish to go beyond
the confines of such an investigation in two ways. First,
by design, an analysis which uses an S.E.I. with a total
labour force reference population does not explicitly take
into account a sex-specific hierarchy of occupations. Whether or not such hierarchies exist and what their implications are for research into male-female inequalities is a
major issue of debate. Our own study has only scratched the
surface of this larger debate which will require additional
theoretical and empirical research for its solution.

However, even this debate assumes the acceptance of a
summary measure such as the S.E.I. as representing an individual's position in a stratification system. As noted elsewhere by students of stratification (Duncan, 1961b; Treas and
Tyree, 1979) the socioeconomic index is only one of multiple
labour force related measures. It is not surprising that a
second direction of current and future research is to move
beyond the initial insights provided by this summary measure.
Such research examines separately the various socioeconomic
characteristics of occupations as well as the job related
characteristics. Unlike studies using the socioeconomic
index, this research will tell us very little about the earlier stages of attainment. But with its emphasis on the
complexity of the work world, it promises to provide additional insight into the various dimensions of sexual inequality.

BIBLIOGRAPHY

Acker, Joan
   1973   Women and Social Stratification. American Journal
           of Sociology 78 (January):936-945.

   1978   Issues in the Sociological Study of Women's Work,
           pp. 134-161 in Ann H. Armstrong and Shirley Harkess
           (eds) Women Working, Palo Alto, California: The
           Mayfield Publishing Company.

   1980   Women and Stratification: A Review of Recent Liter-
           ature. Contemporary Sociology 9 (January):25-39.

Blau, Peter and Otis Dudley Duncan
   1967   The American Occupational Structure. New York:
           John Wiley.

Blishen, Bernard R.
   1967   A Socioeconomic Index for Occupations in Canada.
           Canadian Review of Sociology and Anthropology 4:
           41-53.

Blishen, Bernard R. and Hugh A. McRoberts
   1967   A Revised Socioeconomic Index for Occupations in
           Canada. Canadian Review of Sociology and Anthro-
           pology 13(1):71-79.

Blishen, Bernard R. and William K. Carroll
   1978   Sex Differences in a Socioeconomic Index for Occu-
           pations in Canada. Canadian Review of Sociology
           and Anthropology 15:352-371.

Bose, Christine E.
   1973   Jobs and Gender: Sex and Occupational Prestige.
           Baltimore: Center for Metropolitan Planning and
           Research, Johns Hopkins University.

   1980   Social Status of the Homemaker. pp.69-88 in Sarah
           Fenstermaker Berk (ed). Women and Household Labor.
           Beverley Hills, California: Sage Publications Inc.

Boyd, Monica
   1980a Educational and Occupational Attainments of Native
           Born Canadian Men and Women. Unpublished manusc-
           ript.

   1980b Immigration and Male Occupational Attainment in
           Canada. Unpublished manuscript.

   1980c The Double Negative: Female Immigrants in the
           Canadian Labour Force. Presented at the annual
           meeting of the Population Association of America.
           Denver, Colorado.

Boyd, Monica
  1982   (Forthcoming)   Sex Differences in the Occupational
          Attainment Process: Canada.   Canadian Review of
          Sociology and Anthropology 19 (February).

Boyd, Monica and Elizabeth Humphreys
  1979   Labour Markets and Sex Differences in Canadian In-
          comes.   Discussion Paper No. 143.   Ottawa: Economic
          Council of Canada.

Cooney, Rosemary Santana, Alice S. Clague and Joseph J.
  1980   Salvo Multiple Dimensions of Sexual Inequality in
          the Labor Force. Review of Public Data Uses
          8:279-293.

Coser, Lewis
  1975   Two Methods in Search of a Substance.   American
          Sociology Review 40:691-700.

Crowder, N. David
  1974   A Critique of Duncan's Stratification Research.
          Sociology 8 (January):19-45.

Duncan, Otis Dudley
  1961a   A Socioeconomic Index for all Occupations. Pp. 109-
          138 in Albert J. Reiss Jr.   Occupations and Social
          Status.   New York: The Free Press.

  1961b   Properties and Characteristics of the Socioeconomic
          Index. Pp. 139-161 in Albert J. Reiss Jr.   Occupa-
          tions and Social Status.   New York: The Free Press.

Dworkin, Rosalind J.
  1981   Prestige Ranking of the Housewife Occupation. Sex
          Roles 7:59-63.

Eichler, Margrit
  1977   The Prestige of the Occupation Housewife. Pp. 151-
          175 in Patricia Marchak (ed). The Working Sexes.
          Vancouver, British Columbia: University of British
          Columbia, The Institute of Industrial Relations.

England, Paula
  1979   Women and Occupational Prestige: A Case of Vacuous
          Sex Equality.   Signs 5 (Winter):252-265.

Featherman, David L.
  1976   Coser's ... "In Search of Substance".   The American
          Sociologist 11 (February):21-27.

Featherman, David L. and Robert M. Hauser
  1976a   Prestige or Socioeconomic Scales in the Study of
          Occupational Achievement?   Sociological Methods and
          Research 4 (May):402-422.

1976b   Sexual Inequalities and Socioeconomic Achievement in the United States, 1962-1973. American Sociological Review 41:462-483.

1978   Opportunity and Change. New York: Academic Press.

Featherman, David L., F. Lancaster Jones and Robert M. Hauser
  1975   Assumptions of Social Mobility Research in the United States: The Case of Occupational Status. Social Science Research 4 (December):329-360.

Goldthorpe, John and Keith Hope
  1972   Occupational Grading and Occupational Prestige. Pp. 19-80 in John Goldthorpe and Keith Hope (eds). The Analysis of Social Mobility: Methods and Approaches. Oxford: Clarendon Press.

Guppy, L.N. and Janet L.S. Hanen
  1977   A Comparison of the Allocation of Male and Female Occupational Prestige. Canadian Review of Sociology and Anthropology 14(3):320-330.

Haller, Archibald O. and David B. Bills
  1979   Occupational Prestige Hierarchies: Theory and Evidence. Contemporary Sociology 8 (November): 721-734.

Hauser, Robert M. and David L. Featherman
  1977   The Process of Stratification: Trends and Analyses. New York: Academic Press.

Haug, Marie R.
  1972   Social Class Measurement: A Methodological Critique. Pp. 429-451 in G.W. Thielbar, S.D. Feldman (eds). Social Inequality. Boston: Little, Brown and Co.

  1977   Measurement in Social Stratification. Annual Review of Sociology 3:51-79. Palo Alto: Annual Reviews, Inc.

Haug, Marie R. and Marvin R. Sussman
  1971   The Indiscriminate State of Social Class Measurement. Social Forces 49:549-563.

Heynes, Barbara and John Gray
  1973   A Socioeconomic Index for Women's Occupations. Unpublished paper. University of California, Berkeley and Sussex University, England.

Horan, Patrick
  1978   Is Status Attainment Research Atheoretical? American Sociological Review 43 (August): 534-541.

Huber, Joan
    1980   Ransacking Mobility Tables. Contemporary Sociology
            9 (January):5-8.

Jacobs, Jerry
    1981   On Comparing the Social Standing of Men and Women.
            Manuscript. Department of Sociology, Harvard
            University.

Marini, Margaret Mooney
    1980   Sex Differences in the Process of Occupational
            Attainment: A Closer Look. Social Science Res-
            earch 9 (December):307-361.

McClendon, Meker J.
    1976   The Occupational Attainment Processes of Males and
            Females. American Sociological Review 41:52-64.

Nam, Charles B., Mary G. Powers and Paul C. Glick
    1964   Socioeconomic Characteristics of the Population,
            1960. Current Population Reports, Series P23, No.
            12, Washington, D.C., United States Government
            Printing Office.

Nilson, Linda B.
    1976   The Occupational and Sex Related Components of
            Social Standing. Sociology and Social Research
            60 (April):328-336.

    1978   The Social Standing of a Housewife. Journal of
            Marriage and the Family (August):541-548.

Olson, Janice Ann
    1979   Gender Effects of Occupational Prestige. Ph.D.
            Dissertation. Department of Sociology, Cornell
            University.

Pineo, Peter C. and John Porter
    1967   Occupational Prestige in Canada. Canadian Review
            of Sociology and Anthropology 4:24-40.

Powell, Brian and Jerry Jacobs
    1980   Sex Differences in Occupational Prestige. Paper
            presented at the annual meetings of the American
            Sociological Association, New York.

Powers, Mary G. and Joan J. Holmberg
    1978   Occupational Status Scores: Changes Introduced by
            the Inclusion of Women. Demography 15 (May): 183-
            204.

Reiss, Albert Jr. (ed)
    1961   Occupations and Social Status. New York: The
            Free Press.

Sewell, William H., Robert M. Hauser and Wendy C. Wolf
    1980   Sex, Schooling and Occupational Status. American
            Journal of Sociology. 86 (November):555-583.

Siegel, Paul M.
    1971   Prestige in the American Occupational Structure.
            Unpublished doctoral dissertation. University of
            Chicago.

Stevens, Gillian and David L. Featherman
    1981   (Forthcoming) A Revised Socioeconomic Index of
            Occupational Status. Social Science Research 10
            (November).

Treas, Judith and Andres Tyree
    1979   Prestige Versus Socioeconomic Status in the Attain-
            ment Processes of American Men and Women. Social
            Science Research 8:201-221.

Treiman, Donald J.
    1976   A Comment on Professor Lewis Coser's Presidential
            Address 11 (February):27-33.

Treiman, Donald and Kermit Terrill
    1975   Sex and the Process of Status Attainment: A Com-
            parison of Working Men and Women. American Socio-
            logical Review, 40:174-200.

United States Bureau of the Census
    1963   Methodology and Scores of Socioeconomic Status.
            Working Paper No. 15. Washington, D.C.: United
            States Government Printing Office.

Walker, C. and D. Bradley
    1973   Women and Occupational Prestige. Paper presented
            at the Annual Meeting of the American Sociological
            Association, New York.

Wolf, Wendy C. and Neil D. Fligstein
    1979   Sex and Authority in the Workplace: The Causes of
            Sexual Inequality. American Sociological Review
            44 (April):235-252.

Rosemary Santana Cooney, Alice Sokolove Clague, Joseph J. Salvo

7. Status Attainment of Young White Men and Women: Two Socioeconomic Measures

In contrast to studies documenting well-known sex differences in earnings and pervasive patterns of occupational segregation, studies of occupational status have consistently reported that the mean occupational status score for women is approximately equal to that for men and that the process linking family background characteristics and education to occupational achievement is similar for both men and women (Treiman and Terrell, 1975; Featherman and Hauser, 1976a; McClendon, 1976). This paradox has renewed theoretical discussion of the complex characteristics associated with an occupational position. No single summary index has yet been devised that simultaneously captures the multiple dimensions of occupation--e.g., status, authority, task requirements, and potential for career mobility-relevant to understanding the broader issue of sexual inequality in the labor force (Acker, 1980; Cooney et al., 1980).

In the literature focusing specifically on occupational status attainment, the issue of multiple dimensions of occupation has surfaced in connection with the selection of an appropriate measure of occupational status. While occupational attainment research has employed prestige scales and socioeconomic status scores, recent evaluations of these indicators have argued, on both theoretical and methodological grounds,

The authors wish to acknowledge the institutional support provided by the Hispanic Research Center, NIMH Grant No. RO1-MH30569-04.

The views expressed in this paper are those of the authors and do not necessarily reflect those of the Bureau of the Census or the United Nations.

161

that the socioeconomic dimension of occupation is more central
than prestige to research on the relationship between family
background characteristics and current occupational status
(Featherman and Hauser, 1976b; Treas and Tyree, 1979, Treiman,
1977). Yet even if we limit our evaluation of occupational
status to the Featherman and Hauser (1976a) and McClendon
(1976) studies which rely on a socioeconomic measure, the
paradox of similar occupational status levels and similar
occupational attainment processes for both men and women
persists.

One approach to understanding the above paradox is to
recognize that the occupational attainments of women and men
may differ over the life cycle. If women start out in higher
status jobs and experience little career mobility, while men
experience a rise in occupational status over the life cycle,
then the earlier studies which are based on the broad age
range of working men and women may mask important sex differentials (Wolf and Rosenfeld, 1978). Two recent studies which
focus on middle-aged samples challenge earlier conclusions
that the level and process of occupational status attainment
are similar for men and women (Sewell et al., 1980; Treas and
Tyree, 1979). Their findings indicate that the status of
women's first job is higher than men's; men experience career mobility from first to current job while women do not;
and the relationship of family background characteristics to
education, subsequent first job and finally to current job
reflects sex differences in the attainment process.

While recognizing the merits of the above approach, there
is a need to look more closely at the socioeconomic measure.
The socioeconomic measure that has consistently been used in
all the above studies is Duncan's Socioeconomic Index (SEI).
It is widely recognized that the construction of the SEI is
calibrated on the education and income characteristics of
male incumbents in an occupation. The methodological problems of applying such scores to women have been addressed
by reporting high correlations between the SEI calculated
separately on males and females (Featherman and Hauser,1976a;
McClendon, 1976). High correlations do not, however, address
the issue of whether the status scores assigned to each occupation are equivalent.

An alternate socioeconomic measure based on the work of
Nam and his associates shows that despite a high correlation
(r=98) between scores based on male incumbents in an occupation and scores based on the total incumbents (both male and
female),the inclusion of women importantly affects the ranking of the middle range occupational categories (Nam et al.,
1963; Nam and Powers, 1968; Nam et al., 1975; Powers and

Holmberg, 1978). More importantly, these shifts affect the mean occupational status scores calculated on individual males and females as demonstrated in Cooney et al. (1980). The mean occupational status of all employed men and women in 1970 and 1977 is similar when the male-bases SEI scores are used. In contrast, the mean occupational status of all employed men and women is different, with men showing higher occupational status than women, when socioeconomic scores based on the total incumbents in an occupation are used. These substantively different conclusions cannot be simply dismissed by procedural differences in calculating the socioeconomic measure of Duncan as compared to Nam and his associates. The correlation between the male versions of these two socioeconomic scores is reported to be .97 (Nam and Powers, 1968).

The purpose of this paper is to investigate whether substantive conclusions regarding the occupational status attainment of men and women are affected by the socioeconomic measure used. The level and process of occupational attainment will be analyzed using both the male-based Duncan SEI scores and Nam/Powers total status scores. Earlier research already suggests that the level of occupational attainment of women relative to men is affected by the socioeconomic measure. Samples of young white men and women from the National Longitudinal Survey of Labor Market Experience provide the data for this study.

Sex and Occupational Status Attainment Research

A careful analysis of findings from the four major studies noted above, dealing with sex and occupational status (SEI) attainment reveals both major consistencies and contradictions. There are, however, differences in the samples and in the variables analyzed in each of the studies which make it difficult to obtain precise comparisons. While both Featherman and Hauser (1976a) and McClendon (1976) include a broad age range in their samples, the McClendon samples includes white men and women regardless of marital status, while the Featherman and Hauser's sample includes married, spouse present men and their wives regardless of race. Sewell et al.'s analysis (1980) is based on white high school seniors who graduated in Wisconsin in 1957 and were subsequently reinterviewed 18 years later. Treas and Tyree (1979) use a broader middle-aged group of men and women, aged 30 through 44.[1] In addition to sample comparability problems, there are

---

[1]Their analysis is done separately for black and nonblacks. To facilitate comparisons with the earlier studies we will focus on the nonblack results.

also differences in the number and kinds of variables included
in the analyses. Because the significance of independent variables is influenced by interrelationships with other independent variables in the model, substantively different conclusions may result from non-comparable models.[2] With these
cautions in mind, we turn our attention to the findings of
these four studies. The reader is reminded that all the research reviewed here utilizes the male-based SEI scores to
measure occupational status.

Both Featherman and Hauser (1976a) and McClendon (1976)
find that the mean level of occupational status for men and
women is similar, but that there is less variation in women's
status than men's status. The current occupation of Treas and
Tyree's (1979) middle-aged cohort agrees with both of these
findings, while the Sewell et al. study (1980) shows that
current job status is higher for men than women. The Sewell
et al. (1980) findings do agree with the other research finding that the women's occupational status is less variable than
men's occupational status. Additional information on first
job, available only from the studies of middle-aged cohorts,
shows consistent findings. Women start out at higher status
jobs than men and, once again, variability in status is more
limited among women than among men. Comparing first job to
current job, both studies show that men experience upward
mobility while the pattern for females shows no mobility.

Because of the important role education plays in mediating
the impact of family background characteristics on respondent's
occupational status, all of these studies include an analysis
of the impact of family background on educational achievement.
Before summarizing these findings, it is important to note
that the mean educational achievement of women is similar to
men, with the exception of the Sewell et al. (1980) study
where the sampling design focused only on persons with at

---

[2]The Sewell et al. (1980) research includes not only the
most comprehensive set of family background characteristics,
but also numerous social psychological variables. The investigators do, however, provide reduced-form equations in
Tables 8 and 9 for education that focus on family background
variables. The reduced-form equations for both first and
current job are more difficult to compare to earlier studies
because education only appears in equations confounded by
the social psychological variables. Because the focus of
our research and the ealier studies on sex differences in
occupational status attainment is on family background,
our discussion of Sewell et al.'s work is limited to these
variables.

least a high school degree. The variability in educational achievement is more limited among women who tend to complete high school without acquiring additional education.

In spite of the different model specifications and the different samples, father's education, father's occupational status, mother's education and the number of siblings consistently showed the significant expected effect for both men and women whenever they were included in the analysis. (For the reader's benefit, findings on both the educational and occupational attainment process from these four studies are shown in Table 1.) On the other hand, findings for farm origin varied. In Featherman and Hauser (1976a), the negative effect of farm origin was evident for both sexes, while for Sewell et al. (1980) farm origin had no effect on the educational attainment of men but had a significant positive effect for women. Only the Sewell et al. article included mother's employment status, that is, whether or not the mother was employed while the respondent was growing up. Mother's employment status showed no significant effect on the educational attainment of either sex.

While the above findings demonstrate that many family background variables significantly affect the educational attainment of both men and women in the same direction (i.e., the higher the father's education, the higher the child's education), these data do not address the complex question: Does the effect of family background characteristics on education vary for males and females? That is, does father's education have a significantly greater effect on the son's education than on the daughter's education? Neither the Featherman and Hauser (1976a) nor Treas and Tyree (1979) articles reported doing interaction tests. In both articles, however, information on the standard errors associated with the independent variables in the male and female equations enabled us to hand-calculate significance tests using the formula described by Chiswick and Chiswick (1975:213).

When we reanalyzed the Featherman and Hauser (1976a) study, one of the most frequently cited studies used to document similarities in the education and occupational attainment process, we did find sex interaction effects. While readers may question not only the generalizability of their sample which includes husbands and their wives but also the small number of variables used, the fact remains that for these data sex differences in the coefficients for father's occupation, farm origin and number of siblings on educational attainment do not occur by chance. Moreover, the finding that father's occupation has a significantly greater positive

Table 1. Summarization of Findings From Earlier Studies[a].

	Featherman and Hauser (1976a)			McClendon (1976)			Treas and Tyree (1979)			Sewell, Hauser, Wolf (1980)		
	Men	Women	Sex Interaction	Men	Women	Sex Interaction	Men	Women	Sex Interaction	Men	Women	Sex Interaction
Education												
Father's Education	+	+		+	+	NS	+	+	M+	+	+	M+
Father's Occupational Status	+	+	M+	+	+	NS	+	+	M+	+	+	M+
Mother's Education				+	+	NS				+	+	W+
Mother's Employment Status										NS	NS	M+
Rural Origin	-	-	M-							NS	+	W+
Number of Siblings	-	-	M-	-	-	M-				-	-	NS
Initial Occupation												
Education							+	+	W+	+	NS	M+
Father's Education							+	NS	NS	-	NS	NS
Father's Occupational Status							+	+	M+	+	NS	M+
Mother's Education										NS	NS	NS
Mother's Employment Status										+	NS	M+
Rural Origin										-	NS	M-
Number of Siblings										-	-	NS
Current Occupation												
Initial Occupation				+	+	NS	+	+	W+	+	+	M+
Education	+	+	W+	NS	NS	NS	+	+	M+	+	+	W+
Father's Education				+	NS	NS	NS	NS	NS	NS	NS	NS
Father's Occupational Status	+	+	M+	+	NS	NS	+	+	M+	+	NS	M+
Mother's Education										NS	NS	NS
Mother's Employment Status										NS	NS	NS
Rural Origin	-	-	NS							-	-	NS
Number of Siblings	-	-	W-	NS	-	W-				+	NS	M+

+ = Significant positive   NS= Not significant   W+= Greater positive effect for women   W-= Greater negative effect for women

- = Significant negative   M+= Greater positive effect for men   M-= Greater negative effect for men   Blank= Variable not included

a) The equations used to construct the table are as follows: From Featherman and Hauser (1976a), Table 4 for Education and Table 6, Eqs. 2a, 2b for Current Occupation; from McClendon (1976), Table 3 for both Education and Current Occupation; from Treas and Tyree (1979), Table 4 for Education, Initial Occupation and Current Occupation; from Sewell et al. (1980), Table 8, Eqs. 1, 11, 18 for Education, Initial Occupation and Current Occupation for Men; Table 9, Eqs. 1, 11, 18 for Education, Initial Occupation and Current Occupation for Women.

impact for men is also supported by the Sewell et al. (1980) and Treas and Tyree (1979) articles, while the significantly greater negative effect of sibling size for males is also supported by McClendon's (1976) work. Thus three studies suggest that the effect of father's occupation on child's education varies by sex; only the McClendon (1976) study disagrees. The sibling size interaction is supported by two studies; only the Sewell et al. (1980) article disagrees. Three studies examined father's education. In two of the studies, father's education has a significantly more positive effect on the education of sons than daughters. Only the McClendon (1976) study disagrees.

The evidence for the remaining sex interactions is contradictory or is limited to one study. Featherman and Hauser's (1976a) results suggest more negative consequences of farm origin for male than female educational achievement. In contrast, Sewell et al. (1980) find that farm origin has no effect for men, but a significantly different and positive effect for women. With respect to mother's education, Sewell et al. (1980) find a significantly more positive effect on the education of women than men, while McClendon (1976) finds no real differences. Only the Sewell et al. article provides data on sex interactions for mother's employment status. Although the effect of employment of the mother on educational attainment is not significant for either sex, the coefficients are significantly different with the employment of the mother favoring the higher education of the son rather than the daughter. Although there are contradictory findings among the studies, the weight of evidence from the Featherman and Hauser (1976a), Treas and Tyree (1979) and Sewell et al. (1980) studies raise serious questions regarding the widely accepted conclusion that the process linking family background characteristics to educational attainment is similar for men and women.

The analyses of occupational status attainment are more difficult to summarize because the two earliest studies include only current job, while the two more recent studies include both first and current job. Consistent with earlier research, education has the expected significant effect on occupational status and is relatively more important than family background characteristics in affecting the occupational status attainment of both sexes. This statement is true whether we focus on the current occupation of the samples with a broader age range, used by Featherman and Hauser (1976a) and McClendon (1976), or the first and current job of the samples of middle-aged groups used by Treas and Tyree (1979) and Sewell et al. (1980). With respect to the later studies, first job shows consistent significant expected effects on current job for both sexes and is also relatively more important than family background characteristics. Thus, both of the respondent's characteristics, education and first job, show significant relationships in the same direction for men and women. Before we discuss sex interactions, we will examine the significance and direction of family background characteristics on occupational status attainment for men and women.

The most consistent findings on the relationship between family background characteristics and occupational status attainment involve the effect of father's occupational status, father's and mother's education and rural origin on current job. Three studies show a significant expected effect of father's occupational status on current job for both sexes. In the Sewell et al. (1980) research, father's occupational status is only significant for men. For first job, Treas and Tyree (1979) find significant expected effects of father's job for both sexes. Sewell et al. (1980) only find such an effect for men. Research evidence consistently shows no significant relationship for either father's education or mother's education on the current job of either sex. The two studies with data on first job show inconsistent significant relationships of father's education on first job for both males and females. Only the Sewell et al. (1980) study includes data on the relationship of mother's education to first job. Mother's education is not significant for either sex. Significant negative effects of farm origin on the current job of both sexes are consistently reported by two studies. Sewell et al. (1980) have comparable data for first job. The findings for first job vary by sex with rural origin significantly affecting the first job of men but not women.

The influence of number of siblings is contradictory: Featherman and Hauser (1976a) find significant negative effects for both men and women whereas McClendon (1976) only finds such effects for women. On the other hand, Sewell et al. (1980) finds that, for men, coming from a large family exerts a positive significant effect on the occupational status of current job but has no effect for women. For first job, however, the latter study finds sibling size negatively related to the occupational status of first job for both sexes. Only the Sewell et al. (1980) study includes the employment status of mother. Although mother's employment status has no influence on the current occupational status of either sex or on the first job of women, it exerts a significant positive effect on the first job of men.

The two most important and consistent variables affecting the occupational status attainment of both men and women are education and status of first job. Three studies of occupational status of current job show significant sex interactions

with education. Only the McClendon (1976) findings disagree.
Both studies with additional information on first job also
show significant sex interactions of education with first job
and significant sex interactions of first job with current
job. While the weight of evidence for these two variables
clearly suggests important differences in the process of
occupational attainment between men and women, the direction
of the interaction effects is contradictory. Featherman and
Hauser (1976a) and Sewell et al. (1980) find that education
has a stronger positive effect on current job status for females than males, while Treas and Tyree (1979) find the education effect is greater for males. Moreover, findings with
respect to the sex interaction effects of both education on
first job and first job on current job are contradictory between the two studies with this information. Sewell et al.
(1980) show a greater education effect on first job and a
greater first job effect on current job for men. In contrast,
Treas and Tyree (1979) show a greater education effect on
first job and a greater first job effect on current job for
women. While additional research is needed on these two
variables, the widely accepted statement that the occupational status attainment of women and men is similar seems premature.

    Although the impact of family background characteristics
on occupational attainment is largely mediated through the
respondent's education, three of the studies find significant
interaction effects of father's occupational status on current
job. Father's occupational status shows a significantly more
positive effect on the current job of sons than daughters.
Only McClendon (1976) disagrees. Moreover, this effect is
apparent for first job and is consistently supported by both
studies. Three studies also show significant interaction
effects of sibling size on current job. The pattern of effect differs among the studies. Featherman and Hauser's data
show a significantly more negative impact of sibling size on
current job for women than men. Sewell et al. (1980) find
that the sex interaction with sibling size on current job has
a positive effect for men, but no effect for women. On the
other hand, the sex interaction with sibling size in
McClendon's research shows a negative effect on current job
for women, but no effect for men. Evidence on the two remaining significant sex interactions -- mother's employment
and rural origin on first job -- is limited to a single study.
Sewell et al. show that the employment status of mother has
a significant positive effect on the first job of sons but
no effect for daughters, and rural origin has a significant
negative effect on the first jobs of men but no effect for
women. In summary, family background variables show more important and more consistent interactions with sex for the

educational than for the occupational process. For occupational attainment the most important interaction effects are
associated with education and first job.

Although these four major studies all utilize the male-
based SEI scores, the evidence presented challenges earlier
reports concluding that the process linking family background
characteristics to education and to occupational status is
similar for men and women. While our research will contribute additional evidence, our major objective is to ascertain
whether substantive conclusions comparing the level and process of occupational attainment for men and women are affected by the socioeconomic measure used. Does a socioeconomic
measure that incorporates the increasing participation of
women in the labor force and the impact of that participation
on the socioeconomic status of occupations more sensitively
reflect differentes in the level and process of occupational
attainment for men and women than a measure that excludes
women? The answer to this question has important implications
for earlier research efforts comparing the occupational attainments of men and women.

Data

The data used in this study are drawn from the samples of
young men and women in the National Longitudinal Surveys of
Labor Market Experience, conducted by the Bureau of the Census and the Ohio State University under separate contracts
with the U.S. Department of Labor. These are representative
samples of the non-institutionalized civilian population of
men aged 14 to 24 years old in 1966, and women aged 14 to 24
in 1968. The analysis for this research is based on men and
women who were employed during the survey week conducted
seven years after the initial interview, in 1973 for men and
in 1975 for women. By the latter survey date, a much larger
proportion of this young age group had completed their education and entered the work force.

Two additional restrictions imposed on the sample are race
and parental household structure. Because race is an
important characteristic interacting with family background
variables to affect occupational status, the sample is limited to whites. In addition the samples consist only of white
men and women who lived with both parents when they were 14
years old, in order to facilitate the availability of complete information on family background. With these restrictions the sample of men consists of 2155 individuals and the
sample of women of 1210 individuals. This sample of young
men and women allows us to take a careful look at the occupational attainment process in their early careers. Because

over half of our sample were enrolled in school at the initial survey, their current jobs essentially should reflect similar processes to those studies with information on first job.

The measurement of occupational status plays a central role in this research. Thus, information on each of the two scoring procedures is summarized below. Duncan's Socioeconomic Index (SEI) is calculated for detailed occupations by combining the weighted male education component -- that is, the percent of males in each occupation who are high school graduates --, with the weighted male income component -- that is, the percent of males in each occupation reporting income in excess of $3500 a year. The weights for male education and income were derived from a regression analysis of 1947 NORC prestige scores for 45 occupations (Duncan, 1961). The original Duncan SEI scores were based on the detailed 1950 census occupational codes, but later updated to agree with the 1960 occupational codes without any alteration of the original cutoffs. Documentation for the SEI scores was provided along with the data tapes from the National Longitudinal Survey.

The original occupational status score derived by Nam and associates was also based on males. The scores for detailed occupations were calculated by arraying occupations separately by the median male education level and the median male income level and then determining the cumulative number of males ranked below a given occupation in each of the two arrays. For each occupation, the education and income components consist of one-half the sum of all men in that occupation plus all men in occupations ranked lower on the array. Averaging these components and dividing by the experienced male civilian labor force results in an occupational status score. This occupational status score represents the percent of males in the labor force who are in occupations having lower combined median levels of education and income. These original male scores developed with the 1960 census occupational categories correlated .97 with Duncan's SEI in 1960 (Nam et al., 1963; Nam and Powers, 1968).

Although occupational status scores based on total incumbents were subsequently derived using the 1970 detailed occupational codes (Nam et al., 1975; Powers and Holmberg, 1978), these total status scores (hereafter referred to as TSS) were not available for the 1960 occupational codes used in the NLS data set. Using the one in a thousand public use sample tape from the 1960 census, the procedures described by Nam and associates were used to calculate the total status scores used in this study. Both sets of occupational status

scores are shown for detailed occupation categories in the
Appendix table. It is important to note that all the
occupational variables within a single equation are coded to
the same socioeconomic measure. Thus, when the focus of
analysis is on the SEI socioeconomic measure, all the occupational variables in that equation, including mother's and
father's occupation are coded to that measure.

   Our initial concern in selecting family background variables to include in our research models was to maximize comparability with the earlier studies on sex and the occupational
status attainment process. It is important, however, to real-
ize that the focus on sex differences in occupational attainment is a relatively recent development in the status attainment literature which for over a decade had focused solely on
males. In light of this, it is not surprising that research
comparing the occupational status of men and women has been
slanted toward characteristics of the father. For example,
in Featherman and Hauser's (1976a) research, the only parental
characteristic is father's occupation; in Treas and Tyree's
(1979) study, the only two family background variables are
father's occupation and father's education; in McClendon's
(1976) work, the three parental characteristics are father's
occupation, father's education, and mother's education.

   It is only in Sewell et al.'s (1980) recent article that
the work and education characteristics of both parents are
included: father's occupation, father's education, mother's
employment status, and mother's education. Without denying
the importance of developing comparable models, we agree with
Sewell et al.'s (1980) strategy that it is necessary to incorporate the work and education characteristics of both
parents, especially when the comparative analysis of men
and women is the focus of research interest. We have, however, extended the dichotomous variable of mother's employment status (i.e., working versus nonworking) to include
distinctions of occupational status among the working mothers.
This variable, called the mother's occupational status,
includes four categories: mothers not working, mothers employed in low status jobs, mothers employed in middle status
jobs, and mothers employed in high status jobs. Thus, the
work characteristics of mothers more closely parallel the
father's occupational status variable. In addition to father's and mother's education and father's and mother's occupational status, the other two family background characteristics included in our research are rural origin and number
of siblings.

   Variables used in the models are operationalized as
follows:

Father's Education. The number of years of school completed by the respondent's father when respondent was 14.

Mother's Education. The number of years of school completed by the respondent's mother when respondent was 14.

Father's Occupational Status. The status of father's job when the respondent was 14.

Mother's Occupational Status. For women, mother's occupation was available at age 14. However, for males it was only available in 1966, the initial year of their survey. Occupational Status Scores were operationalized using three dummy variables for the following categories: 0-33.99, 34.00-66.99, and 67.00-99.99. Those mothers who were not in the labor force serve as the reference group.

Residence of Origin. A dummy variable was created to represent residence in rural areas. The reference group consists of those respondents raised in urban areas.

Siblings. The number of siblings reported at the initial survey date.

Education. The total number of years of school completed by the respondent, measured at the final interview date.

Respondent's Occupation. Respondent's job during survey week of the interview.

To test for interactions, a simple t-test of differences between coefficients, illustrated by Chiswick and Chiswick (1975:213) is used. Eight different interaction tests are done in this study. Briefly summarized these interactions are: 1) for males, interactions between the two socioeconomic measures are tested separately for the educational and occupational attainment process; 2) for females, interactions between the two socioeconomic measures are tested separately for the educational and occupational attainment process; 3) for the educational attainment process, sex interactions are tested separately using the SEI and the TSS and 4) for the occupational status attainment process, sex interactions are tested separately using the SEI and the TSS. With a single exception, one-tailed significance tests are used for both interaction effects and independent variable effects based on the pattern of significant effects from the earlier studies. These earlier studies, however, show contradictory findings for both current and first job on the direction of the sex interaction with education. Thus, for this test we utilize a two-tailed procedure.

Table 2. Descriptive Statistics on Family Background, Education and Occupational Status.

Variables	MALES (N=2155)	FEMALES (N=1210)
Father's Education		
$\overline{X}$	10.5	11.0
SD	3.4	3.4
Father's Occupational Status (TSS)		
$\overline{X}$	55.3	56.7
SD	24.6	23.8
Father's Occupational Status (SEI)		
$\overline{X}$	37.0	37.5
SD	22.7	23.2
Mother's Education		
$\overline{X}$	10.8	11.3
SD	2.9	2.7
Mother's Occupational Status (TSS)		
Not in the Labor Force	51.3	49.4
Low Status Jobs	13.8	12.3
Middle Status Jobs	26.1	27.9
High Status Jobs	8.8	10.4
	100.0%	100.0%
Mother's Occupational Status (SEI)		
Not in the Labor Force	51.3	49.4
Low Status Jobs	21.3	19.4
Middle Status Jobs	23.5	26.1
High Status Jobs	3.9	5.1
	100.0%	100.0%
Residence of Origin		
Rural	28.4	22.8
Urban	71.6	77.2
	100.0%	100.0%
Number of Siblings		
$\overline{X}$	2.8	2.8
SD	2.2	2.0
Education		
$\overline{X}$	13.3	13.2
SD	2.5	2.1
Occupational Status (TSS)		
$\overline{X}$	61.5	59.5
SD	24.1	20.3
Occupational Status (SEI)		
$\overline{X}$	41.3	48.4
SD	24.6	19.5

Findings

The descriptive statistics on family background variables
and respondent characteristics to be used in the analysis are
presented in Table 2. Although the young white women come
from more urban families than men, the overall pattern of family background characteristics is very similar. Consistent
with the status attainment literature reviewed earlier (with
the exception of Sewell et al. (1980) whose sampling design
included educational criteria), we find that the mean educational achievements of men and women are very similar and
that the variability in educational achievements is less among
women than men. For occupational status, regardless of the
socioeconomic measure used, variation is less for women than
men. This finding is also consistent with earlier research.

Because of the young age of our sample, we expected that
their early career occupational attainment would most closely
parallel earlier findings on first job. Consistent with the
earlier findings for first job based on the SEI measure, we
find that women have higher status jobs than men. The socioeconomic measure based on total incumbents in an occupation,
however, leads to substantively different conclusions. These
different conclusions occur in spite of the high correlation
between SEI and TSS for males (r=.91) and females (r=.88).
Based on the TSS, the early career achievements of men and
women are more similar, with men in slightly higher status
jobs.

Table 3 shows the distribution of these young men and
women over the broad occupational groups and presents data
on the mean SEI and TSS scores for each occupational group.
Because the overall means for the two socioeconomic measures
vary, it is difficult to make absolute comparisons without
standardizing. Therefore, appropriate Z scores are presented
along with the original means. Although the means differ,
the variance in the two socioeconomic measures is similar.

Professional and managerial occupational groups are ranked
at comparably high levels with both TSS and SEI, while private
household service workers as well as non-farm laborers are
ranked at comparably low levels. The greatest discrepancies
between the two measures are for the two farm categories -
farm laborers/foremen and farm managers. These occupational
groups are much lower on the TSS measure than on the SEI.
Because only 3.5 percent of the young men and none of the
young women are employed in these farming groups, this discrepancy between the two measures cannot be used to explain
the substantively different conclusions on the level of
occupational attainment.

Table 3. Distribution and Mean Occupational Status Scores by Major Occupational Groups.

Occupational Groups	Both Sexes					Males					Females				
	Distri-bution	TSS x̄	TSS z score	SEI x̄	SEI z score	Distri-bution	TSS x̄	TSS z score	SEI x̄	SEI z score	Distri-bution	TSS x̄	TSS z score	SEI x̄	SEI z score
Professional/ Technical	20.1	84.3	1.04	69.3	1.12	17.2	88.7	1.24	73.2	1.29	25.3	78.8	.80	64.4	.91
Managerial/ Administrators	11.3	82.7	.97	66.1	.98	14.5	82.6	.97	65.6	.96	5.5	83.5	1.01	68.4	1.08
Clerical	19.7	60.2	-.01	50.2	.29	6.9	62.4	.09	44.4	.04	43.5	59.5	-.04	51.9	.37
Sales Workers	5.2	62.7	.10	51.0	.33	5.9	68.6	.36	53.9	.45	3.9	46.2	-.62	42.7	-.03
Craftmen	15.3	57.9	-.11	31.2	-.53	22.8	57.8	-.11	31.1	-.53	1.3[a]	∶	-	-	-
Operatives	15.3	44.0	-.72	19.7	-1.03	19.5	45.8	-.64	20.2	-1.00	7.5	35.1	-1.03	17.3	1.13
Private Household Service Workers	7.4	37.3	-.99	21.0	-.97	4.4	48.3	-.53	25.5	-.77	13.0	30.3	-1.31	18.1	-1.10
Farm Laborers/ Foremen	0.8	5.7	-2.39	7.5	-1.55	1.3	5.7	-2.39	7.5	-1.55	0.0	-	-	-	-
Laborers except Farm Mine	3.5	23.9	-1.59	7.7	-1.54	5.4	23.9	-1.59	7.7	-1.54	0.0	-	-	-	-
Farmers/ Farm Managers	1.4	16.4	-1.92	15.1	-1.23	2.2	16.4	-.19	15.1	-1.23	0.0	-	-	-	-
	100.0%					100.1%					100.0%				
Overall x̄		60.4		43.4											
Overall SD		22.9		23.1											

a) N is fewer than 25 cases.

As noted by Powers and Holmberg (1978), an important difference between occupational status scores based on males with scores based on total incumbents is the relative ranking of clerical and crafts occupational groups in 1970. Even though the statistics on occupational groups in our table is represented only by the young people employed in these categories, we find important discrepancies between the TSS and SEI measures for clerical and craft jobs. On the TSS measure, clerical and crafts occupational groups have very similar status (60.2 versus 57.9), while on the SEI measure the differences are dramatic (50.2 versus 31.2). White collar - blue collar distinctions are highlighted on the SEI measure. Clerical workers have status noticeably above average (Z= .29) and crafts workers have status noticeably below average (Z=-.53). On the TSS measure, the status of clerical and crafts occupational groups are not only more similar, but closer to the average (Z=-.01 and -.11, respectively). The relative ranking in these occupational groups is important in understanding the different conclusions resulting from these socioeconomic measures because the greatest number of young men are concentrated in crafts, while the greatest number of young women are concentrated in clerical jobs. For males, the considerably lower status attributed to operative workers by the SEI relative to the TSS is also important.

Occupational status scores of men and women can also be compared within the broad occupational categories. The TSS and SEI measures both agree that the types of jobs women hold within the professional, sales, and service occupational groups are notably lower in status than the jobs men hold. There are too few women in crafts jobs to allow any comparisons. The greatest discrepancies between the TSS and SEI measures are for clerical and operative jobs which we have just identified as important in understanding the different conclusions resulting from the use of the two measures. For clerical workers, the TSS measure shows that men are in slightly higher status clerical jobs than women (62.4 versus 59.5). The SEI measure shows just the opposite with women concentrated in clerical jobs with noticeably higher status (51.9 versus 44.4). For operative workers, the TSS measure suggests that men have noticeably higher status operative jobs than women (45.8 versus 35.1) and the SEI shows that men are in only slightly higher status operative jobs than women (20.2 versus 17.3).

The distribution of occupational status scores by deciles, shown in Table 4, agrees with earlier research based on the SEI that women are less likely than men to be in either the highest or lowest status jobs. The distribution for TSS is

Table 4. Distribution of Occupational Status Scores by Deciles.

Occupational Status (Deciles)	MALES		FEMALES	
	TSS	SEI	TSS	SEI
0–9	1.6	6.8	.5	1.9
10–19	6.6	22.8	4.1	13.5
20–29	2.5	10.8	4.7	3.7
30–39	7.2	11.3	11.5	6.9
40–49	12.9	12.6	6.2	24.9
50–59	17.1	6.1	16.0	9.0
60–69	10.4	11.3	29.1	24.1
70–79	11.5	10.5	6.7	13.1
80–89	15.6	6.2	15.4	2.7
90–99	14.5	1.5	5.8	.3
TOTAL	99.9%	99.9%	100.0%	100.1%

consistent with this statement. While these comparisons are useful, they focus on the extremes of the SEI distribution where very few cases are found. This is also true for the TSS with the exception that a considerably higher proportion of men are employed in the highest status jobs than with the SEI. In fact, the greatest differences in distribution between the two socioeconomic measures are evident for males. On the SEI, the largest number of men are concentrated at the low end with almost 23 percent employed in jobs with status scores of 10 to 19. Only 7 percent of males on the TSS fall in this decile. The female distribution is also shifted upward by the TSS, but not as far as among men.

Before turning our attention to the occupational status attainment process, we will examine the impact of family background variables on the educational achievements of these young white men and women. As noted earlier, education is a major factor not only directly affecting occupational attainment but also mediating the influence of family background characteristics. There are four equations shown in Table 5, one for each sex using the TSS socioeconomic measure and one for each sex using the SEI socioeconomic measure. Both standardized and unstandardized regression coefficients are presented. After we discuss the process separately for men and women, we examine the way in which the process differs by sex.

Both the TSS and SEI measure show significant expected effects for father's education, father's occupational status, mother's education, mother's employment in high status jobs, rural origin, and number of siblings on the educational achievement of young men. Using SEI, sons whose mothers were employed in middle status jobs have significantly higher educational achievement than sons whose mothers were not in the labor force or who were employed in low status jobs. Although the direction using TSS is similar for mothers employed in middle status jobs, the effect is not significant. Even though the significance for this variable differs between the two socioeconomic measures, our tests for interaction were all negative. In other words, for the educational attainment of young men the impact of family background variables is substantively similar and does not vary significantly between the two measures.

Turning now to the educational attainment of young women, we find that both the TSS and SEI measure show significant expected effects for father's education, mother's education, mother's employment in low and high status jobs and number of siblings on their educational attainment. Using SEI, father's

Table 5. Partial Regression Coefficients of Education on Family Background.

Variables	MALES				FEMALES			
	TSS		SEI		TSS		SEI	
	b (SE)	B	b (SE)	B	b (SE)	B	b (SE)	B
Father's Education	.162* (.019)	.210	.151* (.019)	.196	.126* (.021)	.195	.114* (.022)	.176
Father's Occupational Status	.010* (.002)	.100	.012* (.003)	.108	.004 (.003)	.049	.008* (.003)	.087
Mother's Education	.171* (.021)	.192	.153* (.021)	.172	.195* (.125)	.247	.185* (.025)	.235
Mother's Occupational Status								
Low Status Jobs	-.013 (.139)	-.002	-.173 (.119)	-.029	-.652* (.181)	-.092	-.511* (.151)	-.089
Middle Status Jobs	.076 (.116)	.013	.300* (.123)	.050	-.025 (.132)	-.005	.209 (.142)	.039
High Status Jobs	.336* (.180)	.038	.798* (.261)	.061	.793* (.231)	.090	.862* (.301)	.075
Rural Origin	-.192* (.116)	-.035	-.224* (.110)	-.041	.032 (.133)	.006	.067 (.128)	.014
Number of Siblings	-.173* (.023)	-.150	-.175* (.023)	-.151	-.124* (.027)	-.119	-.124* (.027)	-.119
R^2	24.9		25.6		25.7		25.9	

* $p < .05$

occupational status, is also significant. Although the direction of the effect using TSS is similar, it is not significant. In spite of differences in significance for father's occupational status, tests for interaction between the two measures were all negative. Thus, within each sex, we find that the influence of family background variables on education is similar regardless of which socioeconomic measure is used.

Using the SEI, we then tested for sex interactions of family background variables with education. Two significant interactions emerged with this measure. Rural origin had a depressing effect on the educational achievements of men, but no effect on the educational achievements of women. Relative to both nonworking mothers and mothers employed in middle and high status jobs, mothers working in low status jobs had a negative effect on their daughter's educational attainment but no effect on their son's educational attainment. Using the TSS, we ran similar sex interaction tests. We found the same significant sex interaction with mother's employment in low status jobs. Although the TSS model does not show the sex interaction with rural origin, it does show a significant sex interaction with father's occupational status. Father's occupational status had a positive effect on the son's educational attainment, but no effect on the daughter's educational attainment. In contrast to the within-sex comparisons where measurement interactions were nonexistent, we found that sex interaction effects do vary. SEI identifies interaction with rural origin while TSS identifies interaction with father's occupational status.

In Table 6, both the TSS and SEI measures show significant expected effects for father's occupational status, rural origin, mother's employment in high status jobs and education on the occupational status attainment of young men. Using TSS, number of siblings has a significant negative effect. While the direction is similar, significance is not reflected with the SEI measure. In addition, the TSS model shows that sons whose mothers were employed in low status jobs have achieved significantly higher occupational status than sons with nonworking mothers or mothers employed in middle status jobs. Although the direction using SEI is similar for these two variables, the effects are not significant. Even though the significance for these two variables is different depending on the socioeconomic measure, our tests for measurement interactions on both number of siblings and mother's employment in low status jobs were negative. In fact, the only significant measurement interaction that occurred was related to the most important variable affecting occupational status in both the SEI and TSS models - education. The Duncan SEI measure shows significantly more positive occupational status returns to education for young men than does the TSS.

Table 6. Partial Regression Coefficients of Occupational Status on Family Background and Education.

Variables	MALES				FEMALES			
	TSS		SEI		TSS		SEI	
	b (SE)	B	b (SE)	B	b (SE)	B	b (SE)	B
Father's Education	-.334 (.181)	-.045	-.355 (.194)	-.047	.070 (.208)	.011	.060 (.204)	.010
Father's Occupational Status	.096* (.023)	.097	.068* (.023)	.062	-.017 (.026)	-.020	-.023 (.026)	-.027
Mother's Education	.064 (.205)	.007	-.059 (.197)	-.007	.573* (.248)	.075	.507* (.244)	.069
Mother's Occupational Status Low Status Jobs	2.627* (1.327)	.039	.629 (1.084)	.011	-2.175 (1.762)	-.031	-2.402* (1.417)	-.045
Middle Status Jobs	-.530 (1.115)	-.009	.706 (1.122)	.012	-.716 (1.275)	-.015	-.607 (1.327)	-.012
High Status Jobs	3.409* (1.726)	.040	6.539* (2.387)	.051	-1.122 (2.240)	-.013	-.397 (2.824)	-.009
Rural Origin	-3.916* (1.107)	-.074	-2.744* (1.004)	-.051	-2.525* (1.280)	-.054	-2.117* (1.200)	-.047
Number of Siblings	-.606* (.223)	-.054	-.337 (.211)	-.030	-.235 (.264)	-.023	-.342 (.256)	-.035
Education	4.333* (.207)	.447	5.573* (.197)	.567	4.486* (.278)	.462	4.212* (.270)	.451
R^2	26.8		36.1		26.7		25.5	

*$p < .05$

Turning to the occupational status attainment of young women, we find that both the TSS and SEI identify significant expected effects for mother's education, rural origin and education on the occupational status attainment of women. Using SEI, daughters whose mothers were employed in low status jobs had significantly lower occupational status scores than daughters with nonworking mothers. Although the direction using TSS is similar, the effect is not significant. Tests for interaction between the two measures were all negative. Thus, within each sex, we find that the relationship of education to occupational status attainment varies between the two measures only for men.

Within the TSS and SEI analyses, we then tested for sex interactions of family background variables and respondent's education on occupational status. Two significant sex interactions that emerged with both measures were related to father's occupational status, and mother's employment in low status jobs. Father's occupational status has a positive effect on son's occupational status but no effect on the daughter's occupational status. Compared to nonworking mothers, mother's employment in low status jobs has a positive effect on the occupational status attainment of their sons and a negative effect on the occupational status attainment of their daughters. While three additional sex interactions were identified with the SEI model, no additional interactions were identified with the TSS model. The SEI models shows that the employment of mothers in high status jobs has a positive effect on the occupational achievement of sons, but no effect on the occupational achievement of daughters. Mother's education has a positive effect on the occupational attainment of daughters, but no effect on the occupational attainment of sons. Finally, although education has a significant positive relationship with occupational status for both sexes, the SEI shows significantly more positive returns to education for men than for women. In summary, while the within-sex comparisons reveal only one measurement interaction with education for males, we find that not only do sex interactions with education vary between the SEI and TSS models, but also that sex interaction effects with mother's employment in high status jobs and mother's education vary depending on the measurement model used.

Summary and Conclusions

Recent evaluations of prestige scales and socioeconomic status scores have argued, on both theoretical and methodological grounds, that the socioeconomic dimension of occupation is more central than prestige to research focusing on the relationship of family background characteristics to occupational attainment. Four major studies comparing the occupational status attainment of men and women utilize the Duncan Socio-economic Index (SEI) as their socioeconomic measure. The construction of the SEI is based on male incumbents in an occupation. Nam and Powers have constructed an alternative socioeconomic measure that is based on total incumbents (both male and female) in an occupation. It has already been shown that these total status scores (TSS) importantly affect the ranking of middle range occupational groups. The major objective of our research is to ascertain whether a socioeconomic measure that incorporates the increasing participation of women in the labor force as opposed to a socioeconomic measure that excludes women, affects substantive conclusions on the level and process of occupational attainment of women compared to men. Using both the TSS and SEI socioeconomic measures, this research examines the educational and occupational status attainment of young white men and women from the National Longitudinal Survey of Labor Market Experience.

Although based on the SEI, the evidence from these earlier studies challenge the widely accepted conclusion that the process linking family background characteristics to education and to occupational status is similar for men and women. With the exception of Sewell et al.'s (1980) work, family background variables in earlier models have placed more emphasis on the characteristics of the father than on the characteristics of the mother. Our research model includes the educational and occupational characteristics of both parents. In summarizing our findings, we begin by comparing our results on sex differences in the educational and occupational status attainment with earlier research. Since the earlier literature is based on the SEI measure, these comparisons are restricted to findings from the SEI analyses. Subsequently, we will discuss the implications of using an alternative socioeconomic measure.

For educational attainment, earlier research shows the most consistent sex differences with father's occupation (3 out of 4 studies), father's education (2 out of 3 studies), and number of siblings (2 out of 3 studies). Father's occupation and father's education have a greater positive effect on the educational attainment of their sons than their daughters. Number of siblings has a greater negative effect on the education of men than women. These three family background variables, along with mother's education, are among the four relatively most important variables affecting the educational achievements of the young white men and women in our study. While our pattern of findings is consistent with earlier research on these three variables, none of these sex interaction effects is significant. Two sex interactions that are significant relate to rural origin and mother's employment in low status jobs. Rural origin has a negative effect on the education of men, but no effect on women. Compared to nonworking mothers, mothers who were employed in low status jobs had a negative effect on the education of their daughters, but no effect on the education of their sons.

For occupational status attainment, earlier research shows the most consistent sex interactions with education (3 out of 4 studies) and father's occupation (3 out of 4 studies). Two studies include additional information on first job. For first job, sex interactions with education and father's occupation are consistently reported. As in previous studies, education is the major factor affecting occupational attainment of both men and women in our study. Significant sex interactions with both education and father's occupation are identified. Father's occupational status has a more positive effect on the occupational attainment of their sons than of their daughters. The direction of the sex interaction with education on first job, which most closely approximates the early career attainment of our young cohort, is contradictory in earlier research. Sewell et al. (1980) show greater positive returns for men, while Treas and Tyree (1979) show greater positive returns for women. Our findings agree with the former study, that is, men experience greater occupational status returns to education than women.

While earlier studies on sex and occupational attainment process have predominantly ignored the education and occupational characteristics of the mother, we find significant sex interactions with both of these variables. Mother's education has a positive effect on the occupational status of their daughters, but no effect on their sons. Compared to nonworking mothers, mothers who were employed in low status jobs had a negative effect on the occupational status of their daughters, but no effect on their sons, while mothers who were employed in high status jobs had a positive effect on the occupational status of their sons, but no effect on their daughters. Although the sex interactions associated with father's occupation and mother's education are consistent with like-sexed parent role modeling effects, the sex interaction with mother's occupational status is more complex. In summary, our findings based on the SEI measure reflect important sex differences in the process of occupational attainment, not only for education, the major factor affecting occupational achievement, but also for father's occupation, mother's education and mother's occupation.

Does a socioeconomic measure based on total incumbents in an occupation lead to substantively different conclusions

regarding the level and process of occupational status attainment than the male-based SEI measure used in earlier studies?
When the focus of analysis is on identifying variables affecting the educational and occupational attainment separately for
men and women, the two socioeconomic measures lead to similar
conclusions with a single exception. For males, there is a
measurement interaction associated with the effect of education on occupational status. The SEI model shows significantly greater occupational status returns to education than
does the TSS model.

When the focus of analysis becomes comparative whether
one is comparing the level of occupational status of women
relative to men or comparing differences in variable effects
between men and women, the socioeconomic measure does affect
the conclusions. Thus, the SEI measure shows that women have
higher occupational status than men in their first job, while
the TSS measure shows that the occupational status of first
jobs is similar for men and women. In our study, the most
important sex interaction on which the two socioeconomic
measures differ is the effect of education on occupation
attained early in the life cycle. The SEI measure suggests
that the occupational status returns to education are greater
for men than women, while the TSS measure suggests that occupational status returns to education are similar for men
and women.

Since the socioeconomic measure does affect the comparative analysis of occupational status attainment between men
and women, researchers must carefully consider whether the
SEI or TSS more accurately reflect the "socioeconomic" dimension of the occupational structure. An important difference
between the two measures, as we discussed earlier, is that
the SEI highlights the blue collar/white collar distinction
while the TSS reflects a greater similarity between skilled
blue collar workers and lower level white collar workers.
This distinction is readily apparent in the relative ranking
of clerical and craft jobs. Another important difference
between the measures is that the socioeconomic dimension of
the SEI is confounded with the prestige dimension since the
education and income weights of occupations are calibrated
based on occupational prestige. The TSS measure is not confounded with other dimensions of the occupational structure.
The former issue dealing with blue collar/white collar distinctions is inherently complex and will not be addressed in
this paper. On the latter issue, we find the TSS measure
preferable. In addition the TSS comparison of the level of
occupational status of women relative to men is more consistent than the SEI level comparisons with the general literature on sexual inequality in the labor force, where patterns

of both earnings inequality and sex segregation are less
noticeable among the younger ages and tend to increase over
the life cycle. While we agree with earlier criticisms of
the status attainment literature that aggregating all ages
in the labor force may mask important sex differences in
career development over the life cycle, we believe it is
equally important to recognize that male-based SEI scores
lead to substantively different conclusions regarding the
comparative level and process of occupational attainment
for women relative to men.

Appendix A

Table A-1. SEI and TSS Occupational Status Scores for the Detailed 1960 Census Occupational Codes.

	SEI	TSS
Professional, Technical and Kindred Workers		
Accountants and Auditors	78	91.6
Actors	60	78.2
Airplane Pilots and Navigators	79	91.9
Architects	90	95.2
Artists and Art Teachers	67	83.6
Athletes	52	78.2
Authors	76	91.6
Chiropractors	75	94.8
Clergymen	52	79.6
College Presidents, Professors and Instructors n.e.c.	84	96.2
Dancers and Dancing Teachers	45	73.2
Dentists	96	99.5
Designers	73	92.0
Dieticians and Nutritionists	39	57.6
Draftmen	67	88.2
Editors and Reporters	82	91.3
Engineers, Technical		
Aeronautical	87	96.0
Chemical	90	98.5
Civil	84	95.1
Electrical	84	96.5
Industrial	86	94.0
Mechanical	82	96.3
Metallurgical	82	93.6
Mining	85	93.6
Sales	87	97.4
n.e.c.	87	95.2
Entertainers, n.e.c.	31	78.2
Farm and Home Management Advisors	83	90.8
Foresters and Conservationists	48	79.4
Funeral Directors and Embalmers	59	88.8
Lawyers and Judges	93	99.3
Librarians	60	80.9
Musicians and Music Teachers	52	59.2
Natural Scientists, n.e.c.	80	97.5
Chemists	79	95.8
Other Natural Scientists	80	97.5
Nurses, Professional	46	63.0
Nurses, Student Professional	51	44.6
Optometrists	79	94.8
Osteopaths	96	94.8
Personnel and Labor Relations Workers	84	92.8
Pharmacists	82	95.0
Photographers	50	78.6
Physicians and Surgeons	92	99.8
Public Relations Men and Publicity Writers	82	91.4
Radio Operators	69	84.7
Recreation and Group Workers	67	48.4
Religious Workers	56	49.2
Social and Welfare Workers, Except Group	64	85.0
Social Scientists	81	96.3
Sports Instructors and Officials	64	81.8

Table A-1, continued

	SEI	TSS
Surveyors	48	62.1
Teachers, Elementary Schools	72	80.9
Teachers, Secondary Schools	72	87.8
Teachers, n.e.c.	72	73.2
Technicians, Medical and Dental	48	72.0
Technicians, Electronic and Electrical	62	85.1
Technicians, Other Engineering and Phy	62	84.0
Technicians, n.e.c.	62	73.0
Therapists and Healers, n.e.c.	58	80.9
Veterinarians	78	94.8
Professional, Technical and Kindred Workers	65	90.8
Farmers and Farm Managers		
Farmers, Owners and Tenants	14	15.5
Farm Managers	36	33.7
Managers, Officials and Proprietors, Except Farm		
Buyers and Department Heads, Store	72	85.6
Buyers and Shippers, Farm Products	33	79.1
Conductors, Railroad	58	61.1
Credit Men	74	84.1
Floormen and Floor Managers, Store	50	79.1
Inspectors, Public Administration	63	79.5
Federal Public Administration and Postal Service	72	85.8
State Public Administration	54	75.6
Local Public Administration	56	75.6
Managers and Superintendents, Building	32	29.7
Officers, Pilots, Pursers, and Engineers, Ship	54	63.8
Officials and Administrators, n.e.c., Public		
Administration	66	84.2
Federal Public Administration and Postal Service	84	92.0
State Public Administration	66	89.3
Local Public Administration	54	76.8
Officials, Lodge, Society, Union, etc.	58	81.2
Postmasters	60	81.4
Purchasing Agents and Buyers, n.e.c.	77	92.8
Managers, Officials and Proprietors, n.e.c., Salaried	61	79.1
Construction	62	81.0
Manufacturing	79	92.1
Transportation	71	87.1
Communications, Utilities and Sanitary Services	76	89.0
Wholesale Trade	70	88.1
Retail Trade	70	88.1
Food and Dairy Products Stores	50	75.8
Eating and Drinking Places	39	61.6
General Merchandise and Limited Price Variety	68	81.8
Apparel and Accessories	69	79.4
Furniture, Housefurnishings and Equipment Stores	68	88.0
Motor Vehicles and Accessories, Retailing	65	83.1
Gasoline Service Stations	31	66.0
Hardware, Farm Equipment and Building Material	64	81.7
Other Retail Trade	59	81.1

Table A-1, continued

	SEI	TSS
Banking and Other Finance	85	91.9
Insurance and Real Estate	84	92.5
Business Services	80	92.6
Auto Repair Services and Garages	47	67.2
Miscellaneous Repair Services	53	68.4
Personal Services	50	62.2
All Other Industries, Inc. n.r.	62	78.0
Managers, Officials and Proprietors, n.e.c. Self-Employed		
Construction	49	76.4
Manufacturing	61	80.6
Transportation	43	65.1
Communications, and Utilities and Sanitary Services	44	89.0
Wholesale Trade	59	80.0
Retail Trade		
Food and Dairy Products Stores	33	43.6
Eating and Drinking Places	37	50.6
General Merchandise and Limited Price Variety	47	61.4
Apparel and Accessories Stores	65	72.7
Furniture, Housefurnishings and Equipment Stores	59	81.8
Motor Vehicles and Accessories, Retail	70	72.3
Gasoline Service Stations	33	62.2
Hardware, Farm Equipment and Building Material, Retail	61	78.4
Other Retail Trade	49	73.1
Banking and Other Finance	85	91.9
Insurance and Real Estate	76	83.7
Business Services	67	94.2
Auto Repair Services and Garages	36	65.4
Miscellaneous Repair Services	34	68.4
Personal Services	41	61.3
All Other Industries, Inc. n.r.	49	73.0
Clerical and Kindred Workers		
Agents, n.e.c.	68	85.6
Attendants and Assistants, Library	44	47.8
Attendants, Physician's and Dentist's Office	38	43.2
Baggagemen, Transportation	25	54.4
Bank Tellers	52	68.3
Bookkeepers	51	58.3
Cashiers	44	37.2
Collectors, Bill and Account	39	77.6
Dispatchers and Starters, Vehicle	40	71.1
Express Messengers and Railway Mail Clerks	67	78.3
File Clerks	44	46.4
Insurance Adjusters, Examiners and Investigators	62	88.6
Mail Carriers	53	78.3
Messengers and Office Boys	28	32.2
Office Machine Operators	45	56.2
Payroll and Timekeeping Clerks	44	72.6
Postal Clerks	44	78.6
Receptionists	44	50.2
Secretaries	61	64.8
Shipping and Receiving Clerks	22	54.4
Stenographers	61	64.7
Stock Clerks and Storekeepers	44	54.9
Telegraph Messengers	22	51.3
Telegraph Operators	47	51.3

Table A-1, continued

	SEI	TSS
Telephone Operators	45	51.3
Ticket, Station and Express Agents	60	78.3
Typists	61	55.5
Clerical and Kindred Workers, n.e.c.	44	61.6
Sales Workers		
Advertising Agents and Salesmen	66	82.0
Auctioneers	40	33.5
Demonstrators	35	33.5
Hucksters and Peddlers	08	20.4
Insurance Agents, Brokers and Underwriters	66	86.2
Newsboys	27	9.6
Real Estate Agents and Brokers	62	84.3
Stock and Bond Salesmen	73	87.7
Salesmen and Sales Clerks, n.e.c.	47	51.1
Manufacturing	65	89.0
Wholesale Trade	61	82.7
Retail Trade	39	37.4
Other Industries, Inc. n.r.	50	78.4
Craftsmen, Foremen and Kindred Workers		
Bakers	22	47.7
Blacksmiths	16	44.8
Boilermakers	33	65.9
Bookbinders	39	44.7
Brickmasons, Stonemasons and Tile Setters	27	52.1
Cabinetmakers	23	39.4
Carpenters	19	40.8
Cement and Concrete Finishers	19	36.0
Compositors and Typesetters	52	73.0
Cranemen, Derrickmen and Hoistmen	21	47.7
Decorators and Window Dressers	40	48.6
Electricians	44	71.9
Electrotypers and Stereotypers	55	79.6
Engravers, Except Photoengravers	47	79.6
Excavating, Grading and Road Machinery Operators	24	49.2
Foremen, n.e.c.	49	69.4
Construction	40	59.1
Manufacturing		
Metal Industries	54	77.0
Machinery, Except Electrical	60	80.3
Electrical Machinery, Equipment and Supplies	60	80.3
Transportation Equipment	66	81.7
Other Durable Goods	41	65.4
Textiles, Textile Products and Apparel	39	56.5
Other Nondurable Goods, Inc. Not Specified		
Manufacturing	53	73.8
Railroads and Railway Express Service	36	54.8
Transportation, Except Railroad	45	63.0
Communications and Utilities and Sanitary Services	56	79.8
Other Industries, Inc. n.r.	44	72.0
Forgemen and Hammerman	23	44.8
Furriers	39	61.4
Glaziers	26	61.4
Heal Treaters, Annealers and Temperers	22	61.4
Inspectors, Scalers and Graders, Log and Lumber	23	65.8

Table A-1, continued

	SEI	TSS
Inspectors, n.e.c	41	65.8
Construction	46	68.4
Railroads and REA's	41	57.6
Transportation, Except Railroad, Communication and Other Public Utilities	45	68.4
Other Industries, Inc. n.r.	38	68.4
Jewelers, Watchmakers, Gold and Silversmiths	36	53.8
Job Setters, Metal	28	51.9
Linemen and Servicemen, Telephone, Telegraph and Power	49	76.3
Locomotive Engineers	58	57.1
Locomotive Firemen	45	67.7
Loom Fixers	10	36.1
Machinists	33	68.6
Mechanics and Repairmen		
Air Conditioning, Heating, Refrigeration	27	88.3
Airplane	48	78.2
Automobile	19	51.8
Office Machine	36	75.5
Radio and Television	36	68.1
Railroad and Car Shop	23	52.6
n.e.c.	27	55.3
Millers, Grain, Flour, Feed, etc.	19	58.4
Millwrights	31	58.4
Molders, Metal	12	44.8
Motion Picture Projectionists	43	61.4
Opticians, Lens Grinders and Polishers	39	61.4
Painters, Construction and Maintenance	16	30.5
Paperhangers	10	36.1
Pattern and Model Makers, Except Paper	44	73.1
Photoengravers and Lithographers	64	78.2
Piano and Organ Tuners and Repairmen	38	55.3
Plasterers	25	45.8
Plumbers and Pipe Fitters	34	57.4
Pressmen and Plate Printers, Printing	49	69.7
Rollers and Roll Hands, Metal	22	58.5
Roofers and Slaters	15	38.7
Shoemakers and Repairers, Except Factory	12	9.1
Stationary Engineers	47	78.9
Stone Cutters and Stone Carvers	25	61.4
Structural Metal Workers	34	60.3
Tailors	23	30.2
Tinsmiths, Coppersmiths and Sheet Metal Workers	33	63.4
Toolmakers, Die Makers and Setters	50	73.8
Upholsterers	22	45.1
Craftsmen and Kindred Workers, n.e.c.	32	61.4
Former Members of the Armed Forces	18	43.5
Operatives and Kindred Workers		
Apprentices		
Auto Mechanics	25	53.7
Bricklayers and Masons	32	53.7
Carpenters	31	53.7
Electricians	37	53.7
Machinists and Toolmakers	41	53.7
Mechanics, Except Auto	34	53.7
Plumbers and Pipe Fitters	33	53.7

Table A-1, continued

	SEI	TSS
Building Trades, n.e.c.	29	53.7
Metalworking Trades, n.e.c.	33	53.7
Printing Trades	40	53.7
Other Specified Trades	31	53.7
Trade Not Specified	39	53.7
Asbestos and Insulation Workers	32	49.3
Assemblers	17	44.6
Attendants, Auto Service and Parking	19	34.9
Blasters and Powdermen	11	40.9
Boatmen, Canalmen and Lock Keepers	24	40.9
Brakemen, Railroad	42	64.0
Bus Drivers	24	54.0
Chainmen, Rod and Axmen, Surveying	25	40.9
Checkers, Examiners and Inspectors, Manufacturing	17	54.0
Conductors, Bus and Street Railway	30	61.1
Deliverymen and Routemen	32	61.1
Dressmakers and Seamstresses, Except Factory	23	20.0
Dyers	12	40.9
Filers, Grinders and Polishers, Metal	22	52.2
Fruit, Nut, and Vegetable Graders and Packers, Except	10	5.8
Furnacemen, Smelters and Pourers	18	49.7
Graders and Sorters, Manufacturing	17	22.1
Heaters, Metal	29	49.7
Knitters, Loopers and Toppers, Textile	21	26.0
Laundry and Dry Cleaning Operatives	15	14.3
Meat Cutters, Except Slaughter and Packinghouse	29	58.7
Milliners	46	40.9
Mine Operatives and Laborers, n.e.c.	10	39.2
Coal Mining	02	28.0
Crude Petroleum and Natural Gas Extraction	38	53.1
Mining and Quarrying, Except Fuel	12	38.7
Motormen, Mine, Factory, Logging Camp, etc.	03	42.5
Motormen, Street, Subway, and Elevated Railroad	34	61.1
Oilers and Greasers, Except Auto	15	40.4
Packers and Wrappers, n.e.c.	18	28.4
Painters, Except Construction and Maintenance	18	42.9
Photographic Process Workers	42	50.9
Power Station Operators	50	76.3
Sailors and Deck Hands	16	44.0
Sawyers	05	14.6
Sewers and Stitchers, Manufacturing	17	18.4
Spinners, Textile	05	14.5
Stationary Firemen	17	46.6
Switchmen, Railroad	44	62.4
Taxicab Drivers and Chauffeurs	10	34.1
Truck and Tractor Drivers	15	43.8
Weavers, Textile	06	35.5
Welders and Flame-Cutters	24	53.7
Operatives and Kindred Workers, n.e.c.	18	40.9
Manufacturing		
Durable Goods		
Sawmills, Planing Mills, etc.		
Sawmills, Planing Mills and Mill Work	07	19.7
Miscellaneous Wood Products	09	16.7
Furniture and Fixtures	09	19.5
Stone, Clay and Glass Products		
Glass and Glass Products	23	50.2

Table A-1, continued

	SEI	TSS
Cement and Concrete, Bypsum and Plaster Products	10	26.0
Structural Clay Products	10	22.3
Pottery and Related Products	21	26.6
Miscellaneous Nonmetallic Mineral and Stone Products	15	54.1
Metal Industries		
Primary Metal Industries		
Blast Furnaces, Steel Works, and Rolling and Finishing Mills	17	53.1
Other Primary Iron and Steel Industries	12	46.4
Primary Nonferrous Metal Industries	15	27.1
Fabricated Metal Industries, Inc. Not Specified Metal		
Cutlery, Hand Tools, etc.	16	40.9
Fabricated Structural Metal Products	16	44.7
Miscellaneous Fabricaded Metal Products	15	44.4
Not Specified Metal Industries	14	40.9
Machinery, Except Electrical		
Farm Machine and Equipment	21	50.8
Office, Computing and Accounting Machines	31	58.0
Miscellaneous Machinery	22	55.3
Machinery, lectrical Equipment, etc.	26	50.0
Transportation Equipment		
Motor Vehicles and Equipment	21	52.9
Aircraft and Parts	34	68.4
Ship and Boat Building and Repair	16	27.1
Railroad and Miscellaneous Transportation Equipment	23	27.1
Professional and Photographic Equipment and Watches		
Professional Equipment and Supplies	23	43.2
Photographic Equipment and Supplies	40	27.1
Watches, Clocks and Devices	28	27.1
Miscellaneous Manufacturing Industries	16	27.1
Nondurable Goods		
Food and Kindred Products		
Meat Products	16	32.4
Dairy Products	22	52.5
Canning and Preserving Fruits, Vegetables, etc.	09	11.7
Grain-Mill Products	14	26.3
Bakery Products	15	33.9
Confectionery and Related Products	12	26.3
Beverage Industries	19	45.9
Miscellaneous Food Preparations and Related Products	11	31.2
Not Specified Food Products	19	22.3
Tobacco Manufacturers	02	18.2
Textile Mill Products		
Knitting Mills	21	27.3
Dyeing and Finishing Textile, Except Wool	08	34.8
Floor Covering, Except Hard Surface	14	28.2
Yarn, Thread and Fabric Mills	02	21.2
Miscellaneous Textile Mill Products	10	28.2
Apparel and Other Fabricated Textile Products		
Apparel and Accesories	22	22.0
Miscellaneous Fabricated Textile Products	17	17.7
Paper and Allied Products		
Pulp, Paper and Paperboard Mills	19	61.0
Paperboard Containers and Boxes	17	44.3
Miscellaneous Paper and Pulp Products	19	42.7

Table A-1, continued

	SEI	TSS
Printing, Publishing and Allied Industries	31	49.7
Chemicals and Allied Products		
Synthetic Fibers	09	51.0
Drugs and Medicines	26	51.0
Paints, Varnishes and Related Products	15	51.0
Miscellaneous Chemical and Allied Products	23	59.9
Petroleum and Coal Products		
Petroleum Refining	56	76.7
Miscellaneous Petroleum and Coat Products	14	76.7
Rubber and Miscellaneous Plastic Products		
Rubber Products	22	40.9
Miscellaneous Plastic Products	22	51.6
Leather and Leather Products		
Leather, Tanned, Curried and Finished	10	22.2
Footwear, Except Rubber	09	20.7
Leather Products, Except Footwear	14	22.2
Not Specified Manufacturing Industries	16	22.3
Nonmanufacturing Industries, Inc. n.r.		
Construction	18	37.3
Railroads and REA	15	39.4
Transportation, Except Railroad	23	56.8
Communications, Utilities and Sanitary Services	21	56.3
Wholesale and Retail Trade	17	25.5
Business and Repair Services	19	47.6
Personal Services	11	25.5
Public Administration	17	56.6
All Other Industries, Inc. n.r.	20	22.3
Private Household Workers		
Baby Sitters, Private Household	07	14.3
Housekeepers, Private Household	19	7.1
Laundresses, Private Household	12	.3
Private Household Workers, n.e.c.	07	3.1
Service Workers, Except Private Household		
Attendants, Hospital and Other Institutions	13	30.0
Attendants, Professional and Personal Service, n.e.c.	26	31.6
Attendants, Recreation and Amusement	19	17.0
Barbers	17	40.8
Bartenders	19	44.7
Boarding and Lodging Housekeepers	30	32.7
Bootblacks	08	24.2
Chambermaids and Maids	11	12.2
Charwomen and Cleaners	10	11.8
Cooks	15	16.9
Counter and Fountain Workers	17	24.0
Elevator Operators	10	26.6
Hairdressers and Cosmetologists	17	43.2
Housekeepers and Stewards	31	32.7
Janitors and Sextons	09	19.2
Kitchen Workers, n.e.c.	11	12.5
Midwives	37	24.2
Porters	04	20.0
Practical Nurses	22	33.7
Protective Service Workers		
Firemen, Fire Protection	37	72.4
Guards, Watchmen and Doorkeepers	18	43.0
Marshals and Constables	21	62.5

Table A-1, continued

	SEI	TSS
Policemen and Detectives		
Public	39	74.7
Private	40	74.7
Sheriffs and Bailiffs	36	74.7
Watchmen (Crossing) and Bridge Tenders	34	62.5
Ushers, Recreation and Amusement	17	62.5
Waiters	25	31.6
Service Workers, n.e.c.	16	28.9
	11	24.2
Laborers, Except Farm and Mine		
Carpenter's Helpers	07	9.1
Fishermen and Oystermen	10	17.6
Garage Laborers, and Car Washers and Greasers	08	19.5
Gardeners	11	13.8
Longshoremen and Stevedores	11	44.3
Lumbermen, Raftsmen and Wood Choppers	04	6.4
Teamsters	08	5.3
Truck Drivers' Helpers	09	16.9
Warehousemen, n.e.c.	08	57.5
Laborers, n.e.c.	17	25.9
Manufacturing		
Durable Goods		
Sawmills, Planing Mills and Miscellaneous Wood Products		
Sawmills, Planing Mills and Mill Work	03	14.7
Miscellaneous Wood Products	02	18.2
Furniture and Fixtures	05	18.2
Stone, Clay and Glass Products		
Glass and Glass Products	14	36.7
Cement, and Concrete, Gypsum and Plaster Products	05	36.7
Structural Clay Products	05	33.0
Pottery and Related Products	07	36.7
Miscellaneous Nonmetallic Mineral and Stone Products	05	36.7
Metal Industries		
Primary Metal Industries		
Blast Furnaces, Steel Works, Rolling and Finishing Mills	09	44.8
Other Primary Iron and Steel Industries	04	31.9
Primary Nonferrous Industries	06	25.9
Fabricated Metal Industries, Inc. Not Specified Metals		
Cutlery, Hand Tools and Other Hardware	07	42.4
Fabricated Structural Metal Products	07	42.4
Miscellaneous Fabricated Metal Products	10	35.3
Not Specified Metal Industries	09	37.6
Machinery, Except Electrical		
Farm Machinery and Equipment	14	34.6
Office, Computing and Accounting Machines	17	34.6
Miscellaneous Machinery	10	34.6
Electrical Machinery, Equipment and Supplies	14	48.1
Transportation Equipment		
Motor Vehicles and Motor Vehicle Equipment	13	49.6
Aircraft and Parts	15	40.1
Ship and Boat Building and Repairing	02	40.1
Railroad and Miscellaneous Transportation Equipment	08	40.1
Professional and Photographic Equipment and Supplies and Watches		

Table A-1, continued

	SEI	TSS
Professional Equipment and Supplies	10	25.9
Photographic Equipment and Supplies	16	25.9
Watches, Clocks, Clock Works and Optical Devices	11	25.9
Miscellaneous Manufacturing Industries	12	35.3
Nondurable Goods		
Food and Kindred Products		
Meat Products	08	48.4
Dairy Products	13	16.4
Canning and Preserving Fruits, Vegetables, Seafood	06	16.4
Grain-Mill Products	06	16.4
Bakery Products	10	16.4
Confectionery and Related Products	10	16.4
Beverage Industries	16	16.4
Miscellaneous Food Preparations and Kindred Products	05	16.4
Not Specified Food Industries	14	16.4
Tobacco Manufacturers	00	35.3
Textile Mill Products	01	10.5
Yarn, Thread and Fabric Mills		
Other Textile Mill Products	07	13.7
Apparel and Other Fabricated Textile Products	11	35.3
Paper and Allied Products		
Pulp, Paper and Paperboard Mills	06	44.7
Paperboard Containers and Boxes	10	35.3
Miscellaneous Paper and Pulp Products	08	35.3
Printing, Publishing and Allied Industries	23	35.3
Chemicals and Allied Products		
Synthetic Fibers	04	30.7
Drugs and Medicines	22	30.7
Paints, Varnishes and Related Products	08	30.7
Miscellaneous Chemicals and Allied Products	08	30.7
Petroleum and Coal Products		
Petroleum Refining	26	35.3
Miscellaneous Petroleum and Coal Products	03	35.3
Rubber and Miscellaneous Plastic Products	12	35.3
Leather: Tanned, Carried, Finished	02	10.5
Footwear Except Rubber	10	10.5
Leather Products Except Footwear	12	10.5
Not Specified Manufacturing Industries	08	35.3
Nonmanufacturing Industries, Inc. n.r.		
Construction	07	19.0
Railroad and REA	03	35.0
Transportation, Except Railroad	09	32.8
Communications, and Utilities and Sanitary Services	06	32.6
Wholesale and Retail Trade	12	23.6
Business and Repair Services	09	27.8
Personal Services	05	5.0
Public Administration	07	41.6
All Other Industries, Inc. n.r.	06	10.5
Farm Laborers and Foremen		
Farm Foremen	20	32.9
Farm Laborers, Wage Workers	06	2.7
Farm Laborers, Unpaid Family Workers	17	18.1
Farm Service Workers, Self-Employed	22	32.9
Occupation Not Reported	19	43.6

References

Acker, Joan R.
    1980 "Women and stratification: a review of recent
          literature." Contemporary Sociology 9:25-39.

Chiswick, Barry R. and Stephan J. Chiswick
    1975 Statistics and Econometrics. Baltimore: University
          Press.

Cooney, Rosemary Santana, Alice S. Clague, Joseph J. Salvo
    1980 "Multiple dimensions of sexual inequality in the
          labor force." Public Data Use 8:279-293.

Duncan, Otis D.
    1961 "A socioeconomic index for all occupations." Pp.
          115-124 in Albert Reiss, O.D. Duncan, P.K. Hatt
          and C.C. North (eds.), Occupations and Social
          Status. New York: The Free Press of Glencoe.

Featherman, David and Robert Hauser
    1976a "Sexual inequalities and socioeconomic achievement
          in the U.S., 1962-1973." American Sociological
          Review 41:462-483.

    1976b "Prestige or socioeconomic scales in the studies
          of occupational achievement?" Sociological Methods
          and Research 4:402-422.

McClendon, McKee J.
    1976 "The occupational status attainment process of
          males and females." American Sociological Review
          41:52-64.

Nam, Charles B., Howard G. Brunsman, Paul C. Glick, and
    1963 Edward G. Stockwell. "Methodology and scores of
          socioeconomic status." U.S. Bureau of the Census,
          Working Paper No. 15. Washington, D.C.: Government
          Printing Office.

Nam, Charles B. and Mary G. Powers
    1968 "Changes in the relative status level of workers
          in the United States, 1950-1960." Social Forces
          47:158-170.

Nam, Charles B., John La Rocque, Mary G. Powers and Joan
    1975 Holmberg. "Occupational status scores: stability
          and change.: Pp. 570-575 in Proceedings of the
          Social Statistics Section of the American

Statistical Association. Washington, D.C. American
Statistical Association.

Powers, Mary G. and Joan J. Holmberg
1978 "Occupational status scores: changes introduced
by the inclusion of women." Demography 15:183-204.

Sewell, William H., Robert M. Hauser and Wendy C. Wolf
1980 "Sex, schooling, and occupational status." American
Journal of Sociology 86:551-583.

Treas, Judith and Andrea Tyree
1979 "Prestige versus socioeconomic status in the attainment process of American men and women." Social
Science Research 8:201-221.

Treiman, Donald J.
1977 Occupational Prestige in Comparative Perspective.
New York: Academic Press.

Treiman, Donald J. and Kermit Terrell
1975 "Sex and the process of status attainment: a comparison of working women and men." American Sociological Review 40:174-200.

Wolf, Wendy C. and Raechel A. Rosenfeld
1978 "Sex structure of occupations and job mobility."
Social Forces 56:823-844.

Index

Acker, Joan R., 15, 65, 133, 134, 138, 139, 141, 143, 161
Anderson, W. A., 3

Bemis, Stephen E., 57
Bills, David B., 133, 134
Blau, Peter M., 33, 85, 148
Blishen, Bernard R., 2, 6, 7, 17, 20, 21, 32, 45, 46, 47, 48, 49, 50-52, 130, 133, 136, 140-153 *passim*
Blishen-Carroll Index, 140-141, 143, 149, 151, 153
Blishen-McRoberts Index, 141, 148, 149, 151, 153
Blishen scale, 46, 48, 49, 51-52, 133
Bose, Christine E., 47, 59, 133, 135, 137, 138, 139
Boyd, Monica, 15, 20, 21, 131, 134, 135, 148, 149
Bradley, D., 137
Broman, Sarah H., 36
Bureau of the Census. *See* Census, Bureau of the

Cain, Pamela S., 12
Canada, 45, 51
   census in, 48, 50
   mobility study, 48, 51, 148
   SES scales, 44, 45

Canadian Classification and Dictionary of Occupations, 48
Canadian Mobility Study, 48, 51, 148
Carroll, William K., 6, 20, 21, 46, 47, 50-51, 133, 140-153 *passim*
Census, Bureau of the, 7, 10, 11, 12, 33, 35, 36, 56, 59, 63, 85, 140
Chiricos, Theodore G., 36
Chiswick, Barry R., 165, 173
Chiswick, Stephan J., 165, 173
Clague, Alice S., 14, 21, 143
class, 1, 29, 33, 36, 43-44, 64-65
class intervals, 52
Commerce, Department of, 12
Cooney, Rosemary S., 14, 21, 143, 161, 163
Coser, Lewis, 133
Counts, George S., 3, 31
Coxon, Anthony, 98
Crowder, N. David, 133

Darroch, A. Gordon, 49-50
Davies, A. F., 5
DeCesare, Constance B., 57
DeJong, Peter Y., 65
Dictionary of Occupational Titles, 12
Duncan, Beverly, 33

Duncan, Otis D., 2, 4, 7, 9,
    17, 18, 19, 20, 21, 32,
    33, 35, 56, 66, 83-97
    passim, 130, 136, 138,
    148, 149, 152, 154, 162,
    163, 181, 184
Duncan Socioeconomic Index,
    8, 10, 87, 91, 95, 98,
    99, 109, 133, 171
Dworkin, Rosalind J., 133

earnings, 85. *See also*
    income
education, 44, 45, 46, 51,
    85, 164, 169
  occupational status and,
    183
  women's income and, 107
educational attainment
  family background and, 179
  process of, 170
  sex interaction and, 181,
    184
Edwards, Alba M., 10-12,
    34
Eichler, Margit, 133, 137
England, Paula, 137, 138,
    151
ethnicity, 44-45, 49, 50

family background, 169, 172
  educational attainment and,
    179
  measurement of, 168, 172
  See also occupational
    status, family back-
    ground and
Featherman, David L., 2, 10,
    13, 15, 18, 19, 20, 33,
    56, 66, 83, 84, 85, 87,
    95, 97, 102, 107, 109,
    130-148 *passim*, 161-172
    passim
Fligstein, Neil D., 135
French, K. S., 36

Garfinkel, Stuart H., 57
Gerth, H. H., 29
Glick, Paul C., 7, 14, 33,
    59, 140

Goldthorpe, John, 33, 97,
    131
Gottfredson, Linda S., 12
Gray, John, 135, 137, 139
Guppy, L. N., 47, 137, 138

Haller, Archibald O., 133,
    134
Hartman, G. W., 3
Hatt, Paul K., 2, 3, 4, 5,
    8, 31, 32, 56
Haug, Marie, 2, 7, 32, 43,
    44, 45, 46, 65, 66, 136
Hauser, Robert M., 2, 13,
    15, 20, 33, 56, 66, 83,
    84, 85, 87, 95, 97, 102,
    103, 107, 130, 131, 134,
    148, 149, 161-172 *passim*
Hedges, Janice M., 57
Heyns, Barbara, 135, 137,
    139
Hodge, Robert W., 6, 31, 51,
    56, 84, 86, 95
Hollingshead, August B., 14,
    33
Holmberg, Joan J., 14, 15,
    16, 17, 20, 40, 140, 143,
    163, 171, 177
Hope, Keith, 33, 97, 131
Horan, Patrick, 15, 133
Huber, Joan, 131, 133, 143
Humphreys, Elizabeth, 135
Hunt, William C., 10, 34

immigrants, 45, 49, 50
immigration, 49-50
income, 43, 44, 45, 46, 51,
    85

Jacobs, Jerry, 137, 140,
    142, 145
Jones, Charles, 83, 95, 98
Jones, Frank E., 48, 131,
    134
judgmental approach, 30

Kennedy, Wallace A., 36
Kiser, Clyde V., 14

Labor, Department of, 12

labor force
  educational upgrading of,
    89
  female, 46, 51, 55-57, 84,
    90, 110
  male, 45, 46, 51, 84, 90,
    106, 107
  total, 90, 106, 110
LaRocque, John, 14

Marini, Margaret Mooney, 131,
  134
Marx, Karl, 43
McClendon, McKee J., 57, 66,
  102, 131, 161-172
  passim
McRoberts, Hugh A., 15, 17,
  20, 21, 46, 47, 48, 130,
  136, 140-153 *passim*
men. *See* labor force, male;
  occupational status,
  sex interaction and; occupational status scale,
  of men; prestige, dif-
  ferences between male-
  and female-dominated
  occupations; sex differences; socioeconomic
  scales, male-based
methodology, 51-52
metric indexes, differences
  among, 102
Mills, C. Wright, 29
Mills, Donald L., 52
mobility, 51, 108, 134
mobility study, Canadian,
  48, 51, 148
multidimensional measure,
  12, 14-15
Myrianthopoulos, N. C., 36

Nam, Charles B., 2, 7, 11,
  12, 13-17, 21-22, 33-40
  passim, 56, 59, 140,
  162, 163, 171, 184
National Longitudinal Survey,
  163, 170
Nichols, Paul L., 36
Nietz, J. A., 3
Nilson, Linda B., 133, 137

NORC study, 3-5, 6, 7, 9,
  10, 19, 20
  prestige score, 84-85, 95
  replication of study, 86
North, C. C., 2, 3, 4, 31, 32

occupation, 30, 31, 39, 44,
  45, 46
  characteristics of, 90, 98
  classification of, 85, 87,
    93
  sex segregation in, 149,
    151
occupational attainment, 83,
  97, 106, 108. *See also*
  sex differences, in oc-
  cupational status at-
  tainment
occupational hierarchy, 44,
  60-61
occupational mobility, intergenerational, 51
occupational prestige. *See*
  occupational status
occupational status, 2-3,
  5-8, 10-15, 20-22, 55-
  57, 61, 66, 89, 93, 97,
  99, 102, 103, 109
  throughout career, 162,
    168, 170-171
  deciles, 177
  education and, 164
  family background and,
    165, 169, 181, 185
  indicators of, 93
  measurement of, 34-35
  sex interaction and, 165,
    168-169, 172, 183, 185
occupational status scale,
  of men, 103
occupational status scores,
  55, 56-57, 59, 61, 64,
  177
occupational structure, 109,
  110, 186
Olsen, Janice, A., 133, 137
Oppenheimer, Valerie K.,
  56, 57

party (power), 29

Pineo, Peter C., 6, 45, 46,
    48, 51–52, 130, 136, 138
Porter, John, 6, 45, 46, 48,
    49, 51–52, 130, 136, 138
Powell, Brian, 137
Powers, Mary G., 2, 7, 13–40
    passim, 59, 140, 143,
    162, 163, 171, 177, 184
prestige, 2–4, 6, 8, 9, 13,
    16, 17, 19, 20, 22, 31–
    33, 44, 45, 56, 97
  differences between male-
    and female-dominated
    occupations, 48
  socioeconomic indexes and,
    84, 99, 102, 108
prestige index, 84, 108
prestige metric, 107
prestige rankings, 130, 136–
    138, 152
prestige ratings, 86
prestige scale, 45, 51–52,
    83, 99, 183. *See also*
    Siegel Prestige Scale
prestige scores, 86, 101

Redlich, Frederick C., 33
regression equation, 6, 45,
    51–52
regression, multiple, 46
Reiss, Albert, Jr., 4, 13,
    44, 56, 83, 87, 130,
    131, 136
reputational approach, 30
Rosenfeld, Raechel A., 162
Rossi, Peter H., 6, 31, 51,
    56, 84, 86, 95

Salvo, Joseph J., 14, 21,
    143
sample
  age of, 175
  comparability of, 163
scales. *See* socioeconomic
    scales
Sewell, William H., 20, 102,
    103, 107, 131, 134, 149,
    162–185 *passim*
sex-comparative analyses,
    108

sex differences
  in occupational or
    socioeconomic hier-
    archies, 137, 151,
    153–154
  in occupational status
    attainment, 102–103,
    106–108, 131, 143,
    145, 148, 149, 163,
    170
  segregation in occupations,
    47, 149, 151
  in socioeconomic status,
    143, 153
sex interaction, 168–169,
    173. *See also* educa-
    tional attainment, sex
    interaction and; occu-
    pational status, sex
    interaction and
sex-specific scale, 108.
    See also socioeconomic
    indexes, sex-specific
Siegel, Paul M., 2, 6, 9,
    19, 20, 31, 32, 51, 56,
    83, 84–99 *passim*, 136,
    138
Siegel Prestige Scale, 89,
    91, 93
Siltanen, J. L., 47, 137,
    138
situs, 5–6
social class. *See* class
socioeconomic indexes, 8, 9,
    18–19, 21–22, 83, 93,
    97, 99, 102, 106–109,
    133, 134, 135, 152
  construction of, 130, 131,
    133
  criticism of, 131, 133
  ordinal properties of, 99
  reference population of,
    139
  revised, 99
  sex-specific, 140–142, 151,
    152. *See also* sex-
    specific scale
  total labor force, 140, 153
  See also prestige, socio-
    economic indexes and

Socioeconomic Index of
    Occupations, 32
socioeconomic measures, 45
    multiple-item, 35-38
socioeconomic metric, 107
socioeconomic scales, 45,
    50-51, 97
    Blishen, 46, 48, 49, 51-
        52, 133
    Canadian, 44, 45
    construction of, 51-52
    criticism of, 46-47, 48
    female-based, 47-48, 50-
        51, 52
    male-based, 46-47, 48, 52,
        108
    use of, 49-51, 52
socioeconomic scores, 85, 86,
    101, 110
socioeconomic status, 1, 2,
    7, 10, 12, 13, 15-16,
    19-23, 29, 31, 33-38,
    39, 40, 43-45, 50, 64,
    97. *See also* status
    attainment
socioeconomic system, 43
Spenner, Kenneth I., 97
status attainment, 15, 19,
    20, 21-23, 56, 64, 65,
    97, 110. *See also*
    socioeconomic status
Stevens, Gillian, 10, 18,
    19, 109, 137, 140, 142,
    143
stratification, 1, 2, 9, 12,
    17, 43-46, 51, 64
Sussman, Marvin R., 136
Svalastoga, Kaare, 5, 9
Sweet, James A., 56

Terrell, Kermit, 20, 47, 56,
    57, 59, 66, 131, 166
Terrie, E. Walter, 14, 16,
    40

Treas, Judith, 13, 20, 33,
    56, 84, 95, 97, 103,
    131, 154, 162-169
    passim, 172, 185
Treiman, Donald J., 1, 2,
    12, 20, 44, 47, 56, 57,
    59, 66, 97, 131, 133,
    161, 162
Tuckman, Jacob, 45
Tyree, Andrea, 13, 20, 33,
    56, 84, 95, 97, 103,
    131, 154, 162-172 *passim*,
    185

Vanneman, Reeve, 65
vertical mosaic, 46, 49, 52

Waite, Linda, 56
Waldo, Gordon P., 36
Walker, C., 137
Warner, W. Lloyd, 14
Weber, Max, 1, 17, 29
    concept of class, 43-44
Weisshoff, Francine B., 57
Whelpton, P. K., 14
Wolf, Wendy C., 20, 102,
    131, 134, 135, 149,
    162, 166
women. *See* education,
    women's income and;
    labor force, female;
    educational attainment,
    sex interaction and;
    occupational status,
    sex interaction and;
    prestige, differences
    between male- and
    female-dominated oc-
    cupations; sex differ-
    ences; socioeconomic
    indexes, sex-specific;
    socioeconomic scales,
    female-based
Wright, Erik O., 65